DEEP ENVIRONMENTAL POLITICS

DEEP ENVIRONMENTAL POLITICS

The Role of Radical Environmentalism in Crafting American Environmental Policy

PHILLIP F. CRAMER

PRAEGER

Westport, Connecticut
London

Library of Congress Cataloging-in-Publication Data

Cramer, Phillip F., 1975–
    Deep environmental politics : the role of radical environmentalism
in crafting American environmental policy / Phillip F. Cramer.
        p.   cm.
    Includes bibliographical references and index.
    ISBN 0–275–96051–X (alk. paper)
    1. Environmental policy—United States. 2. Deep ecology—United
States. 3. Green movement—United States. I. Title.
    HC110.E5C73   1998
    333.7'0973—dc21   97–34749

British Library Cataloguing in Publication Data is available.

Library of Congress Catalog Card Number: 97–34749
ISBN: 0–275–96051–X

First published in 1998

Praeger Publishers, 88 Post Road West, Westport, CT 06881
An imprint of Greenwood Publishing Group, Inc.

Printed in the United States of America

The paper used in this book complies with the
Permanent Paper Standard issued by the National
Information Standards Organization (Z39.48–1984).

10 9 8 7 6 5 4 3 2 1

To my loving parents

Contents

Illustrations

Preface

Environmental problems have increasingly surfaced in newspaper headlines, community meetings, congressional hearings, and international conferences. Politicians on all levels have expressed concern over the harmful effects of environmental degradation. As policy makers learn from scientists, they are discovering that the threat is real. As local policy makers learn from other local policy makers, they are realizing that local environmental problems may not be local after all. The purpose of this book, however, is not to answer every critic or address every environmental harm. The thousands of books, articles, and films produced before this book and the many that will undoubtedly be produced after it attest to the fact that humans are drastically altering the land, water, and air.[1]

Currently, humans depend on the environment to feed their mouths, pad their pocketbooks, and even fuel their wars. But now it is the environment that has become the nemesis, rather than the source, for the never ending human appetite for resources. A pending environmental crisis may very well be the next source of international conflict. By the same token, however, the environment may serve as a great peacemaker by bringing together people from around the world. Regardless of which road human civilization decides to travel, the far-reaching consequences of environmental degradation (both direct and indirect) must not be ignored by scholars or researchers. This book examines the political consequences of environmentalism, and in particular, of radical environmentalism.

The political process is one characterized by both paradox and plurality, and complexity and contradiction. Though the primary focus of this book is to ascertain the effects of deep ecology on American environmental politics, it sheds significant

---

[1]For those who choose a more optimistic outlook of affairs, I would ask them to at least agree that the perception that humans are degrading the environment is quite common in American society.

light onto the political process in general. This process applies to both inter- and intra-group differences. The study explores the relationship between the philosophical views of society and the actions of its policy makers. It attempts to bridge the gap between theory and practice of modern-day political problems. This book is a case study of the political process. It provides a window into the world of politics through an exploration of legislation, congressional testimony, court decisions, and media reporting. The problem explored in this book concerns environmental degradation and the policy approaches designed to address it.

In many recent books pertaining to deep ecology, one critical aspect has been excluded: a measure of the effects of deep ecology on environmental politics. This book is intended to assuage the lack of quantitative and qualitative research on the effect of deep ecology and radical environmentalism on environmental politics. As deep ecology grows and its focus grows to include national and even international policy, so too does the need for research in this area. This book fills this gap of research and paves the way for future research not only on the effects of deep ecology at the local and national level, but also at the international level.

Much has been written about deep ecological beliefs, ideals, and tactics. But what effect has deep ecology had on environmental politics in this country and in others? How has it influenced policy agendas? What effect has it had on environmental political discourse? What tangible results, measured in public policy, has this philosophy achieved? How has deep ecology influenced the courts? What are the prospects for natural objects gaining legal rights? What trends exist in media coverage of deep ecology? Does the media show bias when reporting on deep ecology? These and other questions are addressed by my comprehensive study of this most interesting environmental movement we call deep ecology. The book combines the aspects of theory development with policy analysis. It is a practical tool for both students and professionals.

Part I of the book provides the reader with an introduction to deep ecology. Chapter 1 examines deep ecology and other environmental perspectives. It is written so that anyone can quickly grasp the main ideas of deep ecology. Chapter 2 takes a brief look at the roots of deep ecology and a more expansive view of four American environmentalists who not only were pioneers in the field of deep ecology but who also had involvement in environmental politics.

Chapter 3 examines the rhetoric of deep ecology and its relationship with politics in the United States. Drawing from one of the primary sources of deep ecological rhetoric, the *Earth First! Journal*,[2] this chapter not only attempts to illustrate the link between deep ecological activism and environmental politics, but it also exemplifies how deep ecologists view politics, politicians, and policies. The *Earth First! Journal* as well as a few of the more popular books written about deep ecology show how deep

---

[2]This is not to say that all articles in the *Earth First! Journal* are by deep ecologists. But perhaps more than any other source, the *Journal* does provide a vast array of articles that illustrate the practical applications of deep ecology beliefs.

ecologists attempt to influence politics by simultaneously shunning and embracing government action.

Part II, Deep Ecology and Politics, looks at both past legislation and current congressional testimony to measure the degree of influence that deep ecological principles have had on environmental politics. It also examines the relationship between deep ecology and the court system. Little has been written on the relationship between deep ecology and politics. The first instance of deep ecological principles becoming involved in politics in the West occurred in 1587 when the village of Saint-Julien brought suit against a colony of weevils that were attacking their vineyards. The court decided against the villagers and the judge declared that "the insects, being creatures of God, possessed the same rights as people to live in the place."[3] While the verdict was based on religious principles, it is the first example of politics and laws conforming to the intrinsic worth of species, an idea at the very center of deep ecology.

Such anecdotal stories are easy to pick out and explain how deep ecological principles have had an influence. But when measuring this influence on a grander scale, in terms of the laws and legislation of the United States, it becomes more complicated. Chapter 5 examines major environmental legislation to trace the influence of deep ecological philosophies. Using a comprehensive understanding of the ecophilosophy, every section, paragraph, and sentence of selected environmental legislation is scrutinized. Even the title and the section of the legal code in which the particular law is found are examined to search for both deep and shallow ecological principles. The legislation reviewed has been selected based on its overall impact on environmental politics and its frequency of reference in deep ecological literature.

Chapter 6 attempts to decipher the language of legislative rhetoric, much as Chapter 3 examined the rhetoric of deep ecologists. Because testimony and rhetoric play such an important role in the political process, congressional testimony between 1993 and 1996 was examined to note how those who mentioned terms associated with deep ecology viewed the philosophy as a whole. Chapter 7 takes a more scientific approach by categorizing all testimony in the last three years in which the term "environment" was uttered. Each piece of testimony is graded in five different deep ecological subjects on a scale from one to five, ranging from shallow to very deep ecology. Finally, Chapter 8 examines the relationship between deep ecological principles and the American legal system. Case law is surveyed to trace the influence of deep ecological ideas on the application of environmental law. Additionally, legal scholarship on environmental ethics is explored to surmise the prospects, both theoretically and practically, of legal rights for natural objects.

Because the media plays such an important role in the political process, Part III examines the relationship between deep ecology and both the mainstream and alternative medias in the United States and abroad. The media has played (and will continue to play in the foreseeable future) an important role in framing issues for public policy discourse. The media both influences policy makers and educates the

[3]Donald Worster, "The Rights of Nature; Has Deep Ecology Gone Too Far?" *Foreign Affairs* (November/December, 1995): 111.

mass public. Thus the manner in which deep ecology is treated by the media is an important indicator of the effects of this ecophilosophy on the political process.

With the term "deep ecology" occurring in over two hundred different news media publications, there can be no doubt that the philosophy has been the subject of at least occasional coverage in the past years. The ecophilosophy has found its way into national and regional newspapers, scientific and popular magazines, foreign papers and international news wires, and television and radio broadcasts. Chapter 10 takes a look at the rhetoric of the media and its treatment of deep ecology with the goal of orienting the reader to the varying perspectives in the news media.

While Chapter 10 provides an overview of media coverage of deep ecology, it does not provide quantified data to help answer the central question of this book: what effect has deep ecology had on environmental politics? Chapter 11 examines trends in all media coverage through a detailed and comprehensive measurement of deep ecology and the media. The chapter attempts to identify the treatment of deep ecological issues by various forms of news media by isolating certain trends in coverage and reporting. Additionally, the chapter discusses the relationship between the media and politics as studied in this work.

The book serves as a case study for those interested in both environmental politics and the political process in general. It attempts to comprehensively study a subject that is frequently plagued with bias. The final chapter draws this study of both politics and environmental philosophy to a close. It attempts to discern the overall impact of deep ecology and radical environmentalism on the Congress, courts, and media. It explores the prospects for deep ecology as a guiding philosophy for individuals, society, and politics.

Before the reader begins, he or she should be reminded of two things. First, this book should be read for both its specific findings and its general application to all aspects of the political process. It offers insight into how government responds to interest groups and how the dominant social paradigm of society changes through the evolution of ideas and ethics.

Second, this author has attempted to make this study as nonbiased as possible. I undertook this research with the aim of producing a methodically sound, critical, and analytical study of deep ecology. Though I sympathize with the deep ecology movement, this book is written neither in support nor in opposition of the movement.

Acknowledgments

I would like to thank the many individuals to whom I am indebted. My research was a culmination of years of intellectual curiosity with radical environmentalism and the political process. There are many people to whom I owe tremendous gratitude. Without their support, help, and encouragement, this book would not be before you today. First and foremost, my family, and especially my parents, to whom this book is dedicated, deserve special recognition for their help through the years. They never stopped believing in me. More than anyone else, I am indebted to them.

One individual to whom I would like to extend a very special thank you is Dr. John Outland of the political science department at the University of Richmond. His help and support really made this book a reality. He was there for me from the very beginning of this project and even undertook the painful task of reviewing the first draft of the manuscript. He has been both a wise mentor and a trusted friend throughout the entire process.

Another person who deserves special mention is Anna Johnson. She has given so much of her time and effort to help me refine and revise this book. Anna has been by my side since the first day of my research, and her support and encouragement have meant a lot. She also has the unique ability to be painfully honest and still help me through difficult times.

The University of Richmond Undergraduate Research Committee provided me with the initial support for my research. Their help, under the guidance of David Evans, deserves a lot of credit for encouraging and supporting original research. A special group very worthy of mention is the "Ecosquad." These individuals, Brian Cavanaugh, Dr. Richard Couto, Meredith Fallon, and Anna Johnson, helped me formulate and refine the ideas in this book. The long discussions we shared every week gave me the opportunity to air out many of the ideas and test some of my theories.

My trusted friend, Mike Abelow, was a great help in the revision process of the manuscript and has served as a springboard of ideas for many years. Others I would like to mention include Scott Berger and Jean Lenville, for always being interested in what I was doing; Dean Richard Mateer, Dr. David Thomas, and Dr. Al Dawson, for their years of encouragement and guidance; Dr. Nicholas Brown, for providing me with an opportunity to discuss my work; Lisa Heller, for her help in initiating my research; Nicholas Zeppos, for his help and encouragement; and Wendi Schnaufer and the rest of the great folks at Praeger Publishers, for everything they did to help bring this project to fruition.

Finally, I would like to thank Les U. Knight who graciously allowed me to republish his "Eco-Depth Gauge," which originally appeared in the first issue of the *These EXIT Times* (January 1991). There are many more people, too numerous to mention, to whom I am also indebted. Hopefully, they know who they are and will accept my sincere thanks.

I

Background on Deep Ecology

Urban-industrial society is a dinosaur causing immense destruction in its death throes. New intellectual-social paradigms for postindustrial society are emerging. The paradigm that embodies contemporary ecological consciousness is called the "deep ecology movement."

—George Sessions

The deep ecology movement touches every major contemporary, personal, economic, and philosophical problem.

—Arne Naess

1

Tenets of Deep Ecology

Environmental issues have received increasing attention as our knowledge about the natural world expands. Many individuals, organizations, and groups have taken up the cause to preserve our environment and to stop future environmental degradation. Economics motivates some, while others are stimulated by a moral commitment, and some people just feel that it is the right thing to do. However, there is one group that subscribes to a unique set of values. They reject traditional anthropocentric beliefs in favor of a biocentric outlook. Their aim is to create a worldwide environmental ethic. We call such individuals deep ecologists.

Deep ecology was first described by Norwegian ecophilospher Arne Naess, who coined the term "deep ecology" in a 1973 article.[1] Naess "argues for a 'Deep Ecology (or Environmental) Movement.' He considers 'Deep Ecology' a value priority philosophy advocating environmental harmony and systemic equilibrium."[2] To differentiate the deep ecologist from the shallow ecologist, Naess states that "combating pollution and resource depletion would be but a small part of the deep ecologist's concern. Deep ecology views humans as just one species among many others. Humans have no special right to dominate or destroy the environment, including other life-forms."[3]

George Sessions, who has written extensively about deep ecology, stated that the "urban-industrial society is a dinosaur causing immense destruction in its death throes. New intellectual-social paradigms for postindustrial society are emerging.

---

[1]Arne Naess, "The Shallow and the Deep, Long-Range Ecology Movements: A Summary," *Inquiry* 16 (Oslo, 1973): 95–100. Although Naess was the first to use the term, he in no way was the first individual to describe a deep ecological environmental perspective.

[2]Daniel H. Henning and William R. Magnum, *Managing the Environmental Crisis* (Durham, NC: Duke University Press, 1989): 25.

[3]Ibid.

The paradigm that embodies contemporary ecological consciousness is called the 'deep ecology movement.'"[4] Nevertheless, deep ecology is more of an intellectual movement than a paradigm, in the Kuhnian sense of the term. Deep ecology is a collection of ideas that combine to form this movement described by Sesssions. One reason that we describe the ecophilosophy as a collection of diverse and different ideas instead of a steadfast and permanent ideological perspective is explained by Warwick Fox. He stated that when "we perceive boundaries, we fall short of deep ecological consciousness."[5] Thus the deep ecology movement incorporates both the flexibility and the evolution of ideas while maintaining a firm sense of what it means to be a deep ecologist.

For some, deep ecology is a path for personal growth, whereas for others it is a compass for daily action. At this level, deep ecology takes on a personal meaning; a meaning that largely depends on the individual and her own perspective.[6] Nevertheless, it is a philosophy based on the inherent worth of all life (and many would include all that is nonliving as well) and is a local and international movement for social change with deep ecologists sprinkled on both sides of the Atlantic and the Pacific. To those involved in the movement, deep ecology is about transforming the human way of life. It encourages a fundamental shift in the way people experience nature while changing how individuals, localities, and states respond to the environmental crisis. Caused by the anthropocentric nature of human life on this planet, this environmental crisis is imminent, according to the deep ecologists. They seek the healing of alienation from self, community, and the Earth that shallow ecology has caused. These environmentalists do not see problems such as oil availability as a problem of shortage; rather, they see it as a problem of consumption. Deep ecologists look to the root causes of society's degradation of nature and the subsequent degradation of peoples throughout the world.

One of the most immediate goals of deep ecologists is the preservation of species and the minimization of humanity's destructive interference with the rest of the natural world. The deep ecological vision is an empowering one; which is one reason why many who subscribe to the movement are also activists. Deep ecology is not just concerned with the preservation of all that is natural but also with the nourishment of the human spirit through a newfound relation with nature. Michael Zimmerman notes that "Naess regards deep ecology not only as a campaign to save wilderness and to protect biodiversity, but also as a movement to liberate humanity from enslaving attitudes and practices."[7]

---

[4]George Sessions quoted in Max Oeslchlaeger, *The Idea of Wilderness: From Prehistory to the Age of Ecology* (New Haven, CT: Yale University Press, 1991): 301.

[5]Warwick Fox quoted in Max Oeslchlaeger, *The Idea of Wilderness: From Prehistory to the Age of Ecology* (New Haven, CT: Yale University Press, 1991): 301.

[6]Arne Naess and David Rothenberg, *Ecology, Community and Lifestyle: Outline of an Ecosophy* (New York: Cambridge University Press, 1989): 12.

[7]Michael E. Zimmerman, *Contesting Earth's Future: Radical Ecology and Post Modernity* (Berkeley: University of California Press, 1994): 38.

One example of how the deep ecologists would change current thinking is that of species loss. Currently, the calls from international as well as from local institutions for species preservation are based on the extrinsic worth of species, or what species can provide humans. Such an approach discusses how species should be preserved because they are critical to the invention of new medicines or play an integral role in the survival of humans. While this approach protects biodiversity, it views species as a resource. Deep ecologists, on the other hand, wish to change this perspective. They feel species should have an intrinsic worth and should be preserved because they have an inherent worth separate from whatever values humans assign to them. Since some endangered species, such as the California condor, are already given inherent as opposed to extrinsic worth, deep ecologists want humans to take the next step: intrinsic worth for all living beings. Under such a mindset, people would then feel obligated to do whatever they could to preserve all species.[8]

BASIC PRINCIPLES

Though deep ecology is a collection of ideas, certain norms have become the staple of deep ecological belief. Deep ecologists argue for an ecological consciousness. This consciousness comprises two main values or norms. These two "ultimate norms," which Naess believes will lead to the deep ecology perspective, are self-realization and biocentric equality. Self-realization states that all life, which includes both human and nonhuman forms, has value itself. This value is independent of human purposes such as for resources or for medicine. Additionally, self-realization states that humans have no right to reduce the richness and diversity of the natural world except for vital human needs.[9] Bill Devall and George Sessions explain that "self-realization is the realization of the potentialities of life."[10] As the diversity of life increases, so too does the self-realization. Thus any decrease in diversity limits self-realization because the lack of diversity restricts the number of ways in which individuals, societies, and even species and life forms can realize themselves. "Most people in deep ecology have had the feeling . . . that they are connected with something greater than their ego, greater than their name, their family, their special attributes as an individual . . . without that identification, one is not easily drawn to become involved in deep ecology."[11]

---

[8]Merrit P. Drucker, "The Military Commander's Responsibility for the Environment," *Environmental Ethics* 11, no. 2 (Summer, 1989): 138.

[9]Kirkpatrick Sale, "Deep Ecology and Its Critics," *The Nation* 246, no. 19 (May 14, 1988): 671.

[10]Bill Devall and George Sessions, *Deep Ecology: Living as If Nature Mattered* (Salt Lake City, UT: Gibbs Smith Publisher, 1985). Available from www.envirolink.org/elib/enviroethics/deepsum.html; INTERNET.

[11]Ibid.

Figure 1.1
Deep Ecology's Basic Principles

Deep Ecology's Basic Principles
Arne Naess and George Sessions, April, 1984
Death Valley, California

1. The well-being and flourishing of human and non-human life on Earth have a value in themselves. These values are independent of the usefulness of the non-human world for human purposes.

2. The richness and diversity of life forms contribute to the realization of these values and are also values in themselves.

3. Humans have no right to reduce this richness and diversity except to satisfy vital needs.

4. The flourishing of human life and cultures is compatible with a substantial decrease of the human population. The flourishing of nonhuman life requires such a decrease.

5. Present human interference with the nonhuman world is excessive and the situation is rapidly worsening.

6. Policies must therefore be changed. These policies affect basic economic, technological, and ideological structures, the resulting state of affairs will be deeply different from the present.

7. The ideological change is mainly that of appreciating life quality (dwelling in situations of inherent value) rather than adhereing to an increasing higher standard of living. There will be a profound difference between big and great.

8. Those who subscribe to the foregoing points have an obligation directly or indirectly to try to implement the necessary changes.

Think Like A Mountain

Source: Arne Naess and George Sessions, "Deep Ecology's Basic Principles," Death Valley, California (April, 1984). Available from www.envirolink.org/elib/enviroethics/deepeco.html; INTERNET.

The second norm is that of biocentric equality. All species are equal. Humans should not, and must not, place themselves above other species on their value hierarchy. The deep ecologists believe in the primacy of wilderness. They reject industrial society as well as the idea that humans are stewards of the Earth. They challenge whether society fulfills basic human needs such as love, security, and access to nature. Thus, deep ecology questions our society's underlying assumptions.[12] These assumptions include faith in the capitalistic and market-based economy, materialism, shallow environmentalism, and even democracy as we know it today.

In addition to the two norms, Devall and Sessions, in their book *Deep Ecology: Living as If Nature Mattered*, provide the deep ecology platform. Sessions and Naess in 1984 originally formed this platform and Arne Naess has periodically updated and revised it ever since. Figure 1.1 is the original deep ecology platform. The first three statements lay forth the value foundation for this environmental perspective. The next five are extrapolations from the first three and serve as a guide for deep ecological action. Table 1.1, which provides an outline of the tenets of deep ecology, contrasts the dominant world view with the deep ecology platform.

TENETS OF DEEP ECOLOGY

While deep ecology is a collection of ideas and perspectives, there are eight basic tenets that most deep ecologists accept.[13] These most basic beliefs provide the ecophilosophy's foundation. The following principles are a synthesis of many different writings on the subject of deep ecology.

1. Harmony with nature. The deep ecologists believe that the current relationship between humans and the natural world is destructive because of its human-centered orientation. They call for a rejection of the human-in-environment image in favor of the relational, total-field image. Shallow ecologists believe that humans can preserve the richness and diversity of life by continuing more of the same, but only with greater care. Deep ecologists see the problem as inherent to humankind's relations to the natural world, which presently endanger the richness and diversity of life.

2. Intrinsic worth of all species. Besides changing the relationship with nature is the affirmation that the well-being and flourishing of human and nonhuman life have value in themselves. These values are independent of the usefulness of the nonhuman world for human purposes. The deep ecologists argue that the richness and diversity of life forms contribute to the realization of these values and also possess value themselves. This belief has been termed "intrinsic worth" or "biospherical egalitarianism." A tree or owl has the same worth as a cactus or frog, which all have the same worth as a bacterium or human. This is equivalent to the biospecies equality mentioned above, which serves as one of the two ultimate norms of deep ecology.

3. Vital needs. Deep ecology states that humans have no right to reduce the richness and diversity of the natural world except to satisfy vital needs. Though deep ecologists rarely precisely define the term "vital needs," it does call for elegantly simple material needs. Some of the more popular rhetoric includes: "Complexity,

---

[12]Devall and Sessions, *Deep Ecology: Living as If Nature Mattered*.

[13]These tenets were derived from a diverse group of writings about deep ecology that includes Naess, Devall, Sessions, Oeschlaeger, Zimmerman, Nash, Martell, and Sale.

not complication" and "Simple in means, rich in ends."[14] Human life is privileged only to the extent of satisfying vital needs that maintain the richness and diversity of life.

Table 1.1
Dominant World View vs. Deep Ecology

Dominant World View	Deep Ecology
Dominance over Nature	Harmony with Nature
Natural Environment as Resource for Humans	All Nature Has Intrinsic Worth/ Biospecies Equality
Material/Economic Growth for Growing Human Population	Elegantly Simple Material Needs (Material Goals Serving the Larger Goal of Self-realization
Belief in Ample Resource Reserves	Earth "Supplies" Are Limited
Advanced Technological Progress and Solutions	Appropriate Technology and Non-dominating Science
Consumerism	Doing with Enough (Re-using/Recycling)
Centralized/National Community	Bioregionalism (Minority Tradition)

Source: Adapted from Bill Devall and George Sessions, *Deep Ecology: Living as If Nature Mattered* (Layton: Peregrine Smith Books, 1985): 69.

    4. Limited "supplies" means decreased human population. Not only is there an ethical obligation on the part of humans to satisfy only their vital needs, but it is also a necessity, according to the deep ecologists; for the Earth's "supplies" are limited. To help preserve the natural world, the deep ecologists mandate a decrease in human population. They believe that the flourishing of human life and cultures is compatible (and even possible) only with a substantially smaller human population. Arne Naess has called for a reduction of the human population to no more than 100 million people. Such a population would sustain a variety of cultures as well as a diverse flora and fauna.[15] The fight against resource depletion and over consumption is central to the deep ecology movement.
    5. Appropriate technology. Recognizing that humans are part of nature and thus harvest the limited supplies of natural resources, deep ecologists promote

---

[14]Arne Naess, "Deep Ecology and Ultimate Premises," *The Ecologist* 18, nos. 4/5 (1988): 130.
    [15]Devall and Sessions, *Deep Ecology: Living as If Nature Mattered.* See also Naess and Rothenberg, *Ecology, Community and Lifestyle: Outline of an Ecosophy*, p. 141.

appropriate technology and nondominating science. Deep ecologists fight against pollution and for the preservation of the natural wilderness. Some members of the movement go further, arguing for the demise of all technology and a return to the hunter and gather life-style while other deep ecologists find a place for technology as long as it helps fulfill the goals of deep ecology (for example, deep ecology has become a permanent fixture on the Internet and activists use the Internet to network and alert other interested individuals). One technology that many deep ecologists supported long before it gained mainstream acceptance was recycling. Recycling helps humans live with "just enough" to survive while "harvesting" earth's limited "supplies" as little as possible.

6. Quality versus quantity. The deep ecologists want an increase in the quality of life. They differentiate this from the standard of living. Deep ecologists do not measure the quality of life in terms of material belongings or per capita income, but rather they utilize such terms as beauty and self-realization. Standard of living, by contrast, is associated with the quantity of life or how much a person has in monetary terms.

7. Societal changes. The deep ecology movement incorporates many changes for society and also for nature. It has a deep contempt for "civilization" as defined by the shallow ecologists. Included among these beliefs are an anti-class posture and a promotion of changes affecting basic economic, technological, and ideological culture components. These changes, however, must be consistent with cultural diversity. The deep ecologists aim to keep with the minority tradition. They wish to identify with primal people and find a sense of place through spirituality. Thus, deep ecology contrasts with the dominant social paradigm. It breaks from the technocratic-industrial worldview which views humans as

isolated and fundamentally separate from the rest of nature, as superior to, and in charge of, the rest of creation. But the view of humans as separate and superior to the rest of Nature is only part of larger cultural patterns. For thousands of years, Western culture has become increasingly obsessed with the idea of dominance: with dominance of humans over nonhuman Nature, masculine over the feminine, wealthy and powerful over the poor, with the dominance of the West over non-Western cultures. Deep ecological consciousness allows us to see through these erroneous and dangerous illusions.[16]

8. Local autonomy and decentralization. Deep ecology shuns centralized and national control of all policies (though this is not always true, as seen later in the book). Currently, those who are nearest the land and the wilderness are taken out of the political process, while those who are the most detached from the land end up making policy. Bioregionalism, a deep ecological way of living that incorporates governance with the land, allows better protection of the land and the wilderness because those who have developed respect for land are allowed to make policy.

Through these eight basic tenets, deep ecology is able to go "beyond a limited piecemeal shallow approach to environmental problems and attitudes to articulate

---

[16]Ibid.

a comprehensive religious and philosophical worldview."[17] Deep ecology is in many ways a religion for those who adopt its ways (more will be written about this later). But being a deep ecologist is not just about holding these beliefs; individuals subscribing to these fundamentals of deep ecology are obligated to promote sociocultural change.[18] Many deep ecologists have formed loose associations, the largest one being Earth First! They have become disenchanted with the current pace and progress of environmental policy as guided by many mainstream (and shallow ecological) environmental groups. As David Foreman, a co-founder of the group Earth First!, stated:

Too many environmentalists have grown to resemble bureaucrats—pale from too much indoor light; weak from sitting too long behind desks; co-opted by too many politicians. . . . By playing a "professional" role in the economic rational game, we, too, acquiesce in the destruction of the Earth. Instead, we must redefine the battle. We must stop playing the games of political compromise the industrial power brokers have designed for us. . . . The time has come to translate the non-violent methods of Gandhi and Martin Luther King to the environmental movement. We must place our bodies between the bulldozers and the rain-forest; stand as part of the wilderness in defense of herself; clog the gears of the polluting machine, and with courage, oppose the destruction of life.[19]

Deep ecology gains its strength through grass-roots activism. One would perhaps expect such a characteristic from an environmental perspective that embraces decentralization and personal environmental responsibility.

SHALLOW ECOLOGY AND ANTHROPOCENTRISM

The basic tenets of deep ecology distinguish it from shallow ecology. Whereas shallow ecologists perpetuate anthropocentric solutions and relations with nature, deep ecologists question such underlying assumptions. Shallow ecologists see humans as stewards of the earth who have been given a mandate to ensure a plentiful supply of natural resources while protecting diversity as best they can without making any true changes in life-style. Their central objective is the health and affluence of people in developed countries. They are concerned with such matters as clean water and air, not for other species per se, but primarily for humans. Shallow ecologists see the value of diversity and species richness but for anthropocentric reasons such as tourism, medicines, and even beauty. Deep ecologists, on the other hand, subscribe to biospecies equality and an eco-centric outlook on life.

[17]George Sessions and Bill Devall, "Deep Ecology," in *American Environmentalism: Readings in Conservation History*, ed. Roderick Nash (New York: McGraw-Hill, 1990): 314.

[18]Max Oeslchlaeger, *The Idea of Wilderness: From Prehistory to the Age of Ecology* (New Haven, CT: Yale University Press, 1991): 303.

[19]David Foreman, "It's Time to Return to Our Wilderness Roots," *Environmental Action* 15, no. 5 (December–January, 1984). Available from www.envirolink.org/elib/enviroethics/deepsum.html; INTERNET.

Figure 1.2
Eco Depth Gauge

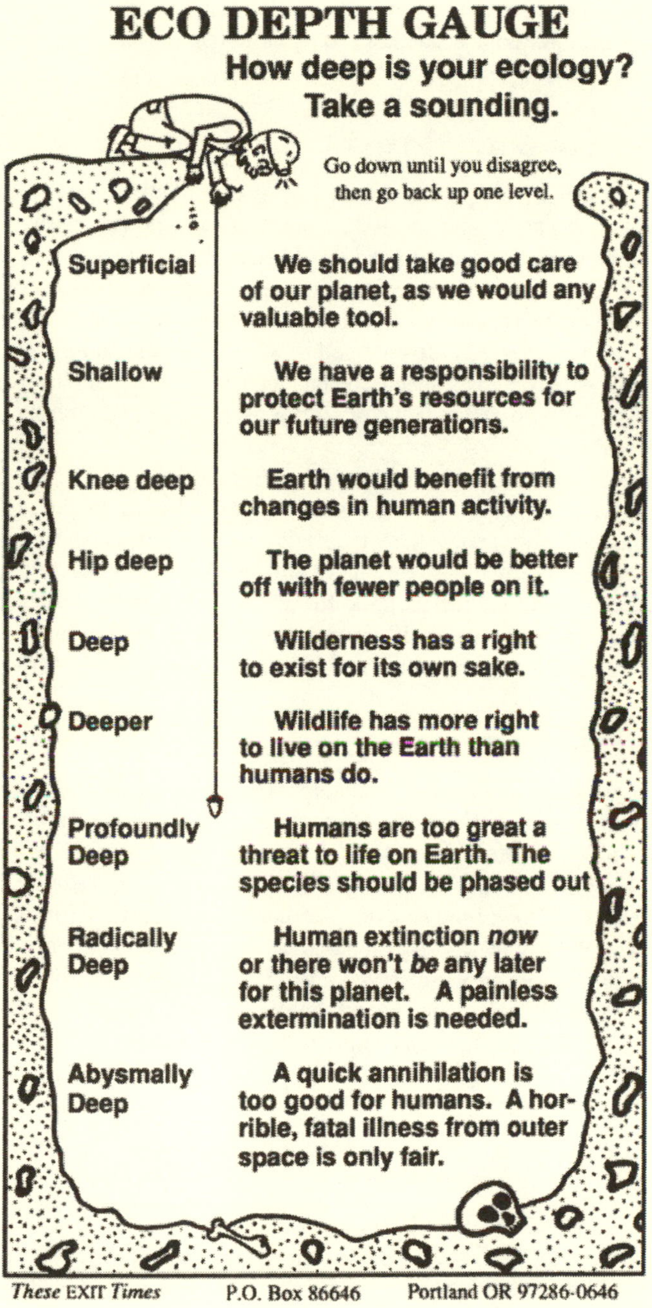

ECO DEPTH GAUGE
How deep is your ecology?
Take a sounding.

Go down until you disagree,
then go back up one level.

Superficial	We should take good care of our planet, as we would any valuable tool.
Shallow	We have a responsibility to protect Earth's resources for our future generations.
Knee deep	Earth would benefit from changes in human activity.
Hip deep	The planet would be better off with fewer people on it.
Deep	Wilderness has a right to exist for its own sake.
Deeper	Wildlife has more right to live on the Earth than humans do.
Profoundly Deep	Humans are too great a threat to life on Earth. The species should be phased out
Radically Deep	Human extinction *now* or there won't *be* any later for this planet. A painless extermination is needed.
Abysmally Deep	A quick annihilation is too good for humans. A horrible, fatal illness from outer space is only fair.

These EXIT *Times*   P.O. Box 86646   Portland OR 97286-0646

This is not to say that the distinction between the polar ideologies is always clear. Figure 1.2 provides a humorous scale of the varying degrees of deepness. There are varying degrees of shallow and deep ecology. Just as there are many shades of gray in the political spectrum, so too are there many such shades in the environmental arena. Two of the more popular shallow ecological beliefs are resource conservationism and preservationism.

RESOURCE CONSERVATIONISTS

Whereas deep ecologists believe in the holistic quality of nature, resource conservationists view natural systems as no more than collections of parts. Ecosystems consist of different species and parts and should be evaluated as such. Resource conservationists see humans as a separate entity from the rest of the environment. Furthermore they believe that the environment, which they refer to as an ecomachine, can be engineered to produce desired outcomes and prevent undesired consequences. Unlike the intrinsic worth given to all species by the deep ecologists, the resource conservationists measure the worth and value of all things, cultural and natural, through the use of the market.

Resource conservationists measure societal well-being by the national and per capita income. For them, quantity of life is a direct parallel to the quality of life. Finally, resource conservationists reject the vital needs concept of the deep ecologists as well as their shunning of technology, for this group determines progress according to the utilitarian formula of the greatest good for the greatest number.[20] Needless to say, resource conservationism has influenced a great deal of non-environmental public policy and most of the environmental public policy prior to the 1960s.

PRESERVATIONISTS

Preservationism has perhaps had more influence on public policy than any other environmental perspective in the last thirty years. Yet in no way is preservationism a new philosophy. It dates to the late 1800s and can be found in the writings of John Muir and Henry David Thoreau (though, as will be seen later, these two writers are also credited with some of the first deep ecological writings). This environmental perspective or philosophy calls for nature to be enjoyed and experienced by humans. Although similar to resource conservationism in this respect, preservationism states that is the duty of all humans to protect the wilderness for the enjoyment of future generations. Because it still views nature in a human context, it is also very anthropocentric.[21]

---

[20]Oeslchlaeger, *The Idea of Wilderness: From Prehistory to the Age of Ecology*, p. 287.

[21]Josh Knauer, "Environmental Ethical Theory Applied in the Modern Environmental Movement" (1996). Available from www.envirolink.org/elib/enviroethics/essay.html; INTERNET.

Preservationists believe that natural systems are self-creating, evolutionary wholes with synergistic characteristics that preclude complete reduction and analysis. This is one step past resource conservationists but short of deep ecology. Max Oeslchlaeger writes:

In spite of its evident dissimilarities with resourcism, preservationism has sometimes been equated with shallow ecology, little more than an instrument to sustain the economic development of Western civilization while forestalling such environmental disasters as the greenhouse effect. Deep ecologists argue that the preservationists' agenda remains committed to the domination of nature through an ostensibly "value-free" science and technology. So viewed, ecology is simply a sophisticated tool that, in conjunction with such other Modernist techniques as cost-benefit analysis, will ensure that a full measure of value is gained from wild nature.[22]

Preservationists think, like the deep ecologists, that *Homo sapiens* are related internally to the environment as are all other species internally related to one another. Because they believe that human actions can impair the ability of natural systems to maintain themselves or to evolve further, they see humans as responsible stewards of the land. This is an important point of disagreement between the preservationists and the deep ecologists, even though they agree that human values must go beyond those measured by the national income accounts to include the preservation of wild lands and life.[23] This is a far departure, in both respects, from resourcism, but still falls short of completely abondoning the quantity-of-life mindset.

Table 1.2
Environmental Ethics: Reasons for Caring about the Environment

Types of environmentalism	Reasons for caring
Deep ecologists (eco-centric)	Intrinsic value of all environmental entities
Sentient ecologists (sentient-centric)	Intrinsic value of sentient beings Extrinsic value of non-sentient things
Shallow ecologists (anthropo-centric)	Intrinsic value of humans Extrinsic value of non-humans

Source: Adapted from Luke Martell, *Ecology and Society: An Introduction* (Amherst: UMASS Press, 1994): 162.

SENTIENT ECOLOGISTS

The primary difference between deep ecology and both resourcism and preservationism is its adoption of an eco-centric outlook that puts the total environment at

---

[22]Oeslchlaeger, *The Idea of Wilderness: From Prehistory to the Age of Ecology*, p. 292.
[23]Ibid., p. 289.

the center, unlike the two former eco-philosophies, which remain anthropocentric
in nature. One relatively new grouping of environmental philosophies is sentience.
It includes those who have departed from anthropocentrism (which is found in both
resourcism and preservationism) but who have not gone as far as putting the entire
living and nonliving world at the center of their value system. It could be argued
that some people who call themselves deep ecologists would fit into this category,
though most would probably classify themselves as eco-centric. Luke Martell described
sentience as a philosophy that "argues we should take special care to protect and respect
all creatures who have the capacity to enjoy life and should also protect parts of the
environment which have value for such creatures."[24] Table 1.2 illustrates one way
of classifying environmental ethics based on a shallow, sentient, and deep ecology
scale.

ECOCENTRISM

Anthropocentrism originated with the rise of agriculture when humans realized
that they could dominate their environment and control it to provide for a bulging
human population. Anthropocentrism is still the dominant environmental outlook
of those who call themselves environmentalists. Biocentrism, which is very similar
to sentient ecology, puts life at the center of the value system. It got its start with
the beginning of the nineteenth century with Charles Darwin. The latest strain of this
value evolution is ecocentrism, which gained its popularity after World War II with
Aldo Leopold (who will be discussed in further detail in Chapter 2). Ecocentrism
puts natural systems at the center of the value hierarchy. It calls for the protection
not just of species but of entire ecosystems and environments.[25]

Many still question whether preservationism would thus at least partly qualify
as biocentric because of its extension of values to include the natural world. Nevertheless, "from an ecocentric or biocentric perspective, preservationism remains anthropocentric, since human interests are the utlimate arbiters of value. In other words,
biocentrism and ecocentrism go beyond strict preservationism by questioning speciesism:
the idea that humankind is somehow superior to and therefore entitled to impose its
values on nature."[26] Ecocentrism, which embodies much of deep ecology's environmental tenets, holds that natural systems are the basis of all organic existence and
therefore possess intrinsic value. Ecocentrism also agrees that humankind is an element
within, rather than the reason to be of, natural systems, and is hence dependent upon
this intrinsic value. Furthermore, ethical human actions (actions that promote the
good life for humankind) necessarily promote all life on Earth (preserves such intrinsic
values as diversity, stability, and beauty).[27] As shallow ecology is almost synonymous

---

[24]Luke Martell, *Ecology and Society: An Introduction* (Amherst: UMASS Press, 1994):
161–162.
[25]Oeslchlaeger, *The Idea of Wilderness: From Prehistory to the Age of Ecology*, p. 293.
[26]Ibid., p. 292.
[27]Ibid., p. 294.

with anthropocentrism, so too is deep ecology almost synonymous with ecocentrism. Yet there are some disagreements over such a classification. Within the eco-centric sphere are left biocentrists who have many important differences with the deep ecologists. They have a type of critical support for the ecophilosophy. Their criticism is much like that from the social ecologists who want to incorporate a greater social element into their environmental activism. "Left biocentrists agree that industrial capitalism has to go—both industrialism and capitalism. The nature of its replacement is the subject of continuing thinking and discussions."[28] Such a split and bifurcation of environmental perspectives make it increasingly difficult to isolate the influence of deep ecology on environmental politics. At the same time, these "fine line" distinctions are important to the study at hand.

ENVIRONMENTAL ORGANIZATIONS

Deep ecology has penetrated many environmental organizations. "Deep ecology's main philosophies can be seen in many environmental organizations today. The most famous, if not notorious, is Earth First!"[29] Earth First! is not a traditional organization, but rather a loose association of deep ecologists who keep in touch with one another through their newsletter and Earth First! activities. Their activities include tree sitting, road blockades, taking over federal buildings, and educational programs.

Another organization that has its roots in deep ecology is the Sea Shepherd Conservation Society started by Paul Watson. Using such actions as documentation, sinking whaling boats, and the ramming of illegal driftnetters, the Sea Shepherds actively defend marine mammals and all marine life from illegal exploitation by humans. Many of their actions are considered extreme, but that label is often associated with deep ecology.[30]

Deep ecological organizations have a love/hate relationship with many mainstream organizations. If one were to judge this relationship by rhetoric found in deep ecological literature or on local television, it would appear this relationship is more one of hate, than love. But that would be wrong. Brock Evans, while the vice president of the Audubon Society, said of Earth First!: "I honor Earth First for having the guts to do the things they do. It is not for me, but I understand why they do what they do. And, ultimately, we all help each other."[31] There are even crossovers between the deep ecological organizations and the more mainstream environmental groups. For example, the Sierra Club and Wilderness Society regional representatives frequently attend Earth First! events. As Dave Foreman stated, "We all work very well together.

---

[28]David Orton, "The Wild Path Forward: Left Biocentrism, First Nations, Park Issues and Forestry; Canadian View," *Green Web Bulletin #44* (This article was later published in the Fall 1995 issue of the *Wild Earth* magazine).

[29]Knauer, "Environmental Ethical Theory Applied in the Modern Environmental Movement."

[30]Ibid.

[31]Brock Evans, quoted in the *Los Angeles Times*, 15 Apr. 1990, sec. Mag., p. 10.

Dale Turner, who is the assistant editor of the *Earth First! Journal*, was conservation chair of the Sierra Club in Arizona at the same time. I'm a member of the Sierra Club, the Wilderness Society and the Nature Conservancy."[32] Foreman is now on the board of directors of the Sierra Club after helping found the group Earth First!

RELIGION AND DEEP ECOLOGY

Deep ecology borrows from many Eastern religions in its thoughts and outlooks. However, deep ecology itself can be classified as a religious belief in the land and of the environment. For many, this ecophilosophy provides the morals and norms to lead life while for others it gives them a sense of purpose and place. Bill Devall and George Sessions write that "if we seek only personal redemption we could become solitary ecological saints among the masses of those we might classify as 'sinners' who continue to pollute."[33] Using religious rhetoric to describe their beliefs is nothing new to deep ecology. Many deep ecologists think that more science and dominating technology will not be sufficient to stop the ecological crisis (as many shallow ecologists believe) until we find a new religion,[34] with that religion being deep ecology.

Deep ecology has a religious component. It borrows heavily from religion and those who practice the philosophy possess religious feelings about their mission to make others realize their destructive ways and to teach them how to better live in their natural surroundings.[35] But the ecophilosophy does not borrow from all religions equally; for many commentators argue that deep ecology is a rejection of Judeo-Christian religion.[36] They contend that Christianity promotes humans as the supreme form of life on the Earth and furthers the notion that all other forms of life are there to meet humankind's needs. Consider the often-quoted passage from the Bible "Let us make man in our image, after our likeness; and let them have dominion over the fish of the sea, and over the birds of the air, and over the cattle, and over all the earth, and over every creeping thing that creeps upon the earth."[37] Similar shallow ecological themes can be found in Islam. Muhammed "emphasized the human responsibility for nature with the following words: 'The world is green and beautiful and God has appointed you His stewards over it. He sees how you acquit yourselves.'"[38] Deep ecology rejects such concepts as human stewardship regardless of how holy the concept

---

[32]Dave Foreman, Earth First! founder, in an interview in *E Magazine* (September/October, 1993).

[33]Devall and Sessions, *Deep Ecology: Living as If Nature Mattered*, p. 14.

[34]Lynn White, Jr., "The Historical Roots of Our Ecological Crisis," *Science* (March 10, 1967): 1206.

[35]Devall and Sessions, *Deep Ecology: Living as If Nature Mattered*.

[36]James Drozdowski, "Saving an Endangered Act: The Case for a Biodiversity Approach to ESA Conservation Efforts," *Case Western Reserve Law Review* 45 (1995): 553.

[37]Gen. 1:26.

[38]Kelly Nolen, "Residents at Risk: Wildlife and the Bureau of Land Management's Planning Process," *Environmental Law* 26 (Fall, 1996): 771.

may be. These notions of stewardship most closely parallel the environmental perspective of resourcism.[39]

This is not to say that deep ecology rejects religion, for deep ecology mirrors Eastern religions and philosophies. The deep ecological belief in holism and the complex interconnectedness that make up the living and nonliving Earth is very similar to the reverence for the living planet found in various religious movements, such as "Buddhism, Taoism, Transcendentalism, and the spirituality systems of Native Americans, among others. The ecological recognition of interconnection, and denial of Cartesian subject/object models of the world, is a direct link to Buddhist/Taoist tenets."[40]

Deep ecology also mirrors ancient Eastern philosophy. At the very core of anthropocentrism is the value of selfishness. It is selfishness at the entire species level.[41] The deep ecologists reject such selfishness, as did the Chinese philosopher Chuang Tzu. For Tzu "only the selfless person can live up to the standards of nature because your body is just one temporary form in nature's constantly changing process. Selfishness is trying to hang onto what you have."[42] The roots of deep ecology will be discussed more in Chapter 2 but these examples of the linkages between deep ecology and Eastern religion give the reader a basis for why deep ecology has evolved into a religion unto itself.

Deep Ecology and Odinism

Odinism, a Germanic pagan religion, named after the principal god of the pagan Scandinavia, Odin, often associated with warfare and magically acquired knowledge, has embraced deep ecological principles. In a talk by C. G. Oswin, the apparent links between deep ecology and Odinism were made very clear:

Perhaps true religious feeling begins here and only here. . . . We don't want a kind of Green future which envisages a World Collective Farm (a kind of grand kibbutz, administered by the U.N., built upon the horrific concept of the world-citizen). No! Authentic peoples, following their equally authentic "own religions," must take the stage again if there is to be any hope for the future. The Earth is the mightiest deity of all! . . . Deep Ecology is Odinism! Odinism is Deep Ecology! Hail the Awakening that saves both people and land![43]

---

[39]Oeslchlaeger, *The Idea of Wilderness: From Prehistory to the Age of Ecology*, p. 287.

[40]Steve Hackett, "Some Thoughts on a Deep Ecology Economy" (n.p., n.d.). Available from SH2@axe.humboldt.edu; INTERNET.

[41]Phillip Cramer, "Toward an Environmentally Ethical International Society" (Unpublished paper, 1995).

[42]Zhuangzi, *Zhuangzi Speaks: The Music of Nature,* adapted and ill., Tsai Chih Chung (Princeton, NJ: Princeton University Press, 1992): 54.

[43]C. G. Oswin, "Deep Ecology and Odinism," a talk given at the National Moot of the Odinic Rite (London, Heroes Day 11th November 1995 ce). Available from www.luna.co.uk/~heathen/ecology.html; INTERNET.

Followers of Odinism believe that they are here by the grace of nature and not by
"some abstract Hebrew conception of God." They have adopted the human-in-nature
relationship rather than a stewardship role. Odinists can trace this belief back to their
native ancestors, who had a special and meaningful relationship with the land and
the animals.

DEEP ECOLOGY AND THE GOVERNMENT

It is very difficult to lay forth or even predict a picture of a deep ecological
government. Some envision a bioregional model of politics in which people are organized by environmental, as opposed to political or ethnic, criteria. Such a model
would help individuals live in harmony with the land. The people would be the primary
purveyors of policy making and all laws and legislation would be formed in concert
with the land. Other visions of a deep ecological governance system range from a
plethora of communes throughout the world to one central world government. In
any of the cases, the government or lack thereof, would behave according to deep
ecological principles, reminding individuals of their own ecological roots and responsibilities.

Some interesting parrellels between deep ecology and current political thought
have been made by environmental theorists. Arne Naess thinks that supporters of
the deep ecology movement "seem to move more in the direction of nonviolent anarch-
ism than towards communism."[44] Another interesting comparison links deep ecology
with libertarianism. James Buchanan, a founder of the "public choice" school of
economics and the 1986 winner of the Nobel Prize in economics, is a prominent
libertarian who expresses antipathy to scientific management. He sees the American
welfare state orginating in the teachings and doctrines of American progressivism.
Such teachings, according to Buchanan, have instilled a social engineering mentality
on the welfare state. Both Buchanan and deep ecologists agree, to a large degree,
on a desirable direction for the future of society: "a sharp decentralization of governing
responsibilities in the United States."[45] Such parrellels and paradoxes, whereby radical
environmentalism and reactionary conservatism overlap, serve only to wet the appetite
of the political theorist.

DEEP ECOLOGY AND THE ECONOMY

One of the challenges set before deep ecologists is the description of what a
deep ecological world would look like. The deep ecologists describe a world made
up of environmentally conscious human inhabitants (anywhere from 20 to 2 percent

---

[44]Naess and Rothenberg, *Ecology, Community and Lifestyle: Outline of an Ecosophy*,
p. 156.

[45]Robert H. Nelson, "'A New Era for the Western Public Lands': Government as Theater:
Toward a New Paradigm for the Public Lands," *University of Colorado Law Review* 65 (Spring,
1994): 335.

of the current number of inhabitants) living in harmony with the land. Government would be decentralized. With respect to the economy, Steve Hackett is one individual who has examined this problem. He argues that it can only be generated from the bottom up, not imposed top-down (this is assuming that all of the society holds deep ecology values).[46] Hackett describes the question of the deep ecology economy by relating it to the question of what an Islamic or Christian economy would be like. In such cases, a normative value system creates the motivational basis for human conduct and choice in an environment of scarce resources. According to Hackett:

Owners of firms would have the profit motive, but it would be constrained by an overarching environmental ethic. Low cost, heavily polluting processes would not be used. This would be similar to technology-forcing regulation (e.g., no DDT, no child-labor sweatshops, etc.), but would be grounded in a community value system; such "rules" would actually be informal institutions that would be reinforced (and cheating sanctioned) by social relations. As a consequence market prices would tend to be higher for all goods (at least until R&D efforts operate to lower the cost of "clean" technology), as price would reflect the full cost (private costs + costs of being clean) of production rather than simply the firms' private costs.[47]

In such an economy, products would be produced having the least effect on the environment, while being extremely durable so as to not need frequent replacement. The products would also be easily disassembled, either for recycling or for reuse in other products. But such products would cost a lot more, especially when they include the price for the toll they take on the environment. In a deep ecology value system, people would be doing with less, only fulfilling vital needs, so the amount of products that a consumer would purchase would probably be substantially decreased. Furthermore, there would be pressure from consumers for environmentally sound products that would provide additional incentive to manufacturers to produce less wasteful products.

The Elmwood Institute has attempted to examine and review a company's operations from the perspective of deep ecology. Under the guise of an "eco-audit," the Elmwood plan would minimize a company's environmental impact and make all of its operations ecologically sound not only by adopting a system of production as outlined by Hackett, but also by moving away from the corporate culture of domination. While the Elmwood guide for action does not provide a detailed direction on how to undertake an "eco-audit," it does describe "the corporate culture required to produce such an eco-audit, and it argues that only an audit of this 'deep ecological' nature will really reduce the environmental impact of a company's operations."[48]

Both Hackett and the Elmwood Institute refuse to place a dollar value on environmental degradation. This approach is echoed by Paul Hofseth, an expert on energy problems and a firm supporter of the deep ecological movement. Arne Naess provides

---

[46]Hackett, "Some Thoughts on a Deep Ecology Economy."

[47]Ibid.

[48]Fritjof Capra, "Biodiversity and Ecological Management: Ecologically Conscious Management," *Environmental Law* 22 (Winter, 1992): 535.

a summary of Hofseth's normative arguments against pricing nature: "If somebody A asks a person B what he or she will pay in order that A does not break B's arm, the amount suggested by B cannot, says Hofseth, be taken as a measure of the price or value of the arm. B has a right to his arm. It is not permitted to break human arms. Analogously, access to free nature is a right."[49] The idea of a "right to nature" will be examined in more detail later.

The largest problem in a deep ecology economy is its disproportionate toll on lower income people, not even to mention those in less-developed countries. Thus, many believe that a deep ecology economy could only occur after some type of re-distribution of funds. Some pure deep ecologists would claim that this is irrelevant, for in a deep ecological world, there would be no such thing as an economy, at least in the sense of the term as now used. For in a deep ecology world, there would not be any civilization and many humans would return to the hunter-and-gatherer life-style. But even the most idealistic deep ecologists realize that such change cannot occur overnight (or even over-century).

Arne Naess provides particularly insightful advice to those supporters of the movement who want to change the current economic structure. Naess argues that "we need in society *even as it is now operating* people who are competent to take part in economic decision making and take part in informing the public about the consequences of different decisions."[50] The deep ecology movement must have supporters who are well acquainted with economics and who can stand up to opponents. The lesson Naess attempts to preach is that even deep ecologists, who detest economic growth, need to be able to discuss it because those attempting to degrade the environment often refer to the necessity and desireableness of economic growth to support themselves.

DEEP ECOLOGY AND NAZISM

To talk of nazism almost instantly conjures images of inhumane force and brutality. Thus any discussion of deep ecology and the laws of Nazi Germany is certainly to be tainted, but one in need of illumination. Hitler was a vegetarian; Himmler recognized the rights of animals. But even more significant, Nazi ideology represented an attempt to view humans as a part of nature, rather than over or above it.[51] Consider the advice of a Nazi scientist:

A new National Socialist science cannot create, as if by sorcery, arbitrary and amateurish world systems and conceptions—only infinite damage could come of this. Rather, it must reverentially immerse itself in nature itself, and in the great Nordic discoverers and interpreters of nature,

---

[49]Naess and Rothenberg, *Ecology, Community and Lifestyle: Outline of an Ecosophy*, p. 124.

[50]Ibid., p. 106.

[51]Elizabeth Mensch and Alan Freeman, "The Politics of Virtue: Animals, Theology and Abortion," *Georgia Law Review* 25 (Spring, 1991): 923.

to find there the essence of German being in glorious abundance. . . . "Natural science is not a root, but a blossom. Let us take care of the roots. The blossom will appear by itself."[52]

This ideology was embodied with the laws of Nazi Germany. A 1933 law on the protection of animals set forth the principle that animals should be protected for their own sake. The law was extremely detailed and ran to almost 180 pages. The idea of instrinsic worth was repeated throughout the German law.[53] It is one of the few examples in the Western world of such an explicit statement of deep ecological ideals. Opponents of deep ecology have not hesitated to invoke Nazi imagery in their criticisms of the movement, which is where attention is now turned.

CRITICS AND CRITICISM

Deep ecology has its critics. These critics fall into three areas. First, there are those who describe deep ecologists as promoters of genocide. They think that deep ecologists believe in massive human diebacks in order to preserve the environment. The next group of critics question the very ability of the deep ecology movement to meet its goals. They criticize the notion of thinking globally, yet acting locally. Finally, there are those critics who see deep ecology as a mask for totalitarianism with the possibility of creating dangerous divisions in the world. They see eco-fundamentalism as a rival of religious fundamentalism with the ability to draw new fault lines between the West and the Rest.

The first group of critics accuse deep ecologists of promoting eco-fascism to the point where deep ecologists demand the genocide of 90 percent of the entire world's population.

The critics of Deep Ecology and radical environmentalism have been anything but restrained. They have accused radical ecologists of being fascists and Marxists, terrorists and mystics, people with axes to grind and hucksters in pursuit of wine, women, and song, destroyers of local economies, purveyors of distrust, obscurantists, atheists, misogynists and misanthropes.[54]

Murray Bookchin, a social ecologist, has described deep ecologists as racist, survivalist, macho Daniel Boones who feed on the human disasters and the suffering of humankind.[55] Critics point to an infamous quotation in the *Earth First! Journal* that stated, "If radical environmentalists were to invent a disease to bring human populations back to sanity, it would probably be something like AIDS. It [AIDS] has the potential to end industrialism, which is the main force behind the environmental crises."[56]

---

[52]Ibid.

[53]Luc Ferry, *UNESCO Courier* (April, 1993): 4.

[54]Christopher Manes, *Green Rage: Radical Environmentalism and the Unmaking of Civilization* (Boston: Little, Brown and Company, 1990): 151.

[55]Sale, "Deep Ecology and Its Critics," p. 670.

[56]*Earth First! Journal.*

The deep ecologists respond to such criticism. They claim that deep ecology is not genocide, but rather acknowledges that the current rate of growth is not sustainable. It is true that deep ecologists have argued that AIDS is Earth's mechanism to fight back against unprecedented human growth and strain on the Earth. Yet this remark is not callous, it is merely descriptive. The Earth is a living ecosystem that includes viruses that help protect it in times of crisis.[57] Deep ecologists claim that we are in such a time of crisis. No species can attempt to control nature; to do so would lead to a worse fate than any natural earthly virus could ever cause.

The second group of critics argue that deep ecology is not a true philosophy but rather more of a secular religion based on irrationality than a legitimate philosophy. These same critics consider deep ecology more a mystical than a scientific discipline by pointing to the contradictions and discrepancies within the so-called philosophies. Murray Bookchin, one of deep ecology's foremost critics, argues that

the entire conceptual framework of deep ecology is entirely a product of human agency—a fact that imparts to the human species a unique status in the natural world. All ethical systems (including those that can be grounded in biotic evolution) are formulated by human beings in distinctly cultural situations. Remove human agency from the scene, and there is not the least evidence that animals exhibit behaviour that can be regarded as discursive, meaningful, or moral.[58]

The notion of intrinsic worth is a human invention, designed to place human values on other species. Thus, as Bookchin argues above, there must be something unique and worth admiring about the ability for humans, and only humans, to formulate such concepts and ideals. He labels the works of Arne Naess as intellectual poverty. Bookchin states that "deep ecology, eco-theology, and air-headed spiritualists have found more 'secret harmonies' between humanity and nonhuman nature than I know what to do with."[59]

Other critics argue that deep ecology, though a legitimate ideal, would be impossible to put into practice, calling their program for social reform hopeless utopianism.[60] Wendell Berry, a leading agrarian writer, claims that the civil rights movement has not meant better communities, that the women's movements have not given us better marriages, and that the environmental movement "has not changed our parasitic relationship to nature."[61]

Deep ecologists would counter that Berry fails to recognize the different types of environmental movements. Deep ecology goes beyond anthropocentric means

---

[57]Sale, "Deep Ecology and Its Critics," pp. 674–675.

[58]Murray Bookchin, "Deep Ecology, Anarchosyndicalism and the Future of Anarchist Thought," 11 June 1992. Available from www.lglobal.com/TAO/Freedom/book2.html; INTERNET.

[59]Ibid.

[60]Oeslchlaeger, *The Idea of Wilderness: From Prehistory to the Age of Ecology*, p. 304.

[61]Jeremiah Creedon, "The Power of Global Thinking?" *Utne Reader* no. 56 (March/April, 1995): 22.

to solve the impending environmental crisis. It advocates an entirely new way of thinking, one that might even be able to fulfill the goals of other movements, such as the civil rights' and women's movements, because of deep ecology's ability to unite and globalize. In response to Bookchin, they would argue that they have no choice but to use human values because that is all with which we have to work. They too, are uncomfortable with this part of the philosophy, but realize there is no other choice. Furthermore, deep ecology, as described in this first chapter, is coherent and logical, using the religious links to illustrate how this philosophy can not only gain widespread support but also serve as a moral compass for its followers.

When it comes to environmental activism at the global level, critics feel that humans are not smart enough to act on the global scale. They see "a paralyzing contradiction that distracts people from the small but crucial problems they could actually solve."[62] Additionally, the critics question the idea of putting the burden on the individual to change his or her practices, rather than changing the entire system. They claim that we must be wary of claims that rely too much on the individual and too little on changing the treadmill or system. Foster uses the analogy of a giant squirrel cage. It is the treadmill that is responsible for environmental degradation, not the individual.[63] The deep ecologists have two answers. First, "we must find a way of putting people first *in order to protect the environment*. There are many ways of reducing the economic stakes in environmental destruction on the part of those who have little direct stake in the treadmill itself."[64] Second, deep ecology will be able to change this global treadmill that Foster describes. A change at the individual level will inevitably lead to a change at the international level. Each of the ecological changes humanity takes to preserve the environment will add stress on the social and governmental structure. "Environmentalists are, therefore, social activists, with varying degrees of commitment toward affecting change consistent with such (spaceship earth) ecological and social goals."[65] A type of global Maori people will not only be able to change the individuals' relationship to nature, but also be able to change the ethics of the entire international system.

The last group of critics are perhaps the most vehement. They view the deep ecology movement with fear. Deep ecology has been attacked as "wrongheaded and dangerous" and a threat to a "reasonable, right-minded form of ecological truth."[66] They point to Germany in 1930 when the Green Revolution reached its full flower. They illustrate how ecologists can successfully lobby in the political sphere for antivivisection laws, implementation of organic farming, and the redistribution of large land holdings to the German peasants. This was called the back-to-the-land movement, which has many parallels to the current deep ecology movement. Critics then make

---

[62]Ibid.

[63]Johm Bellamy Foster, "Global Ecology and the Common Good," *Monthly Review* 46, no. 9 (February, 1995): 2–5.

[64]Ibid., p. 9.

[65]Byran, quoted in Henning and Mangum, *Managing the Environmental Crisis*, p. 25.

[66]Sale, "Deep Ecology and Its Critics," p. 670.

the link between these laws and public policies and the National Socialist Party led by Adolf Hitler, implying a direct link between deep ecology and fascism.

Other critics who have fear and distrust for the movement claim it will unravel the current state-centric international order; "this unraveling of the Westphalian system and partial reversion to the world of the middle ages poses, in my view, the real threat of eco-imperialism, modeled less on the model of the nineteenth century scramble for Africa than on that of the Crusades."[67] The "Rest" will not give in to the demands of the West for this transformation. They want the same technology and growth that the West currently possesses. Lal likens the environmental movement to current fundamentalist movements of religious flavor, describing both as "undermining humanity's traditional relationship with God or Nature." A radical environmental mindset will be the major fault line between the West and Rest.[68] Lal concludes his assault on deep ecology by stating that "eco-fundamentalism is the inevitable mutant, which will continue to cause the world a good deal of grief for some time to come."[69]

The basis for Lal's entire argument is that those in lesser developed states reject environmentalism and especially deep ecology. Deep ecologists counter by citing a recent study by Brechin and Kempton that noted a large increase in local environmental action and concern in recent decades. They have found more than 100 million members of grass-roots movements and organizations in the rural areas of lesser developed states.[70] The comprehensive study done by Brechin and Kempton revealed that environmentalism is a global phenomenon, found in both rich and poor states. "Arguing from two types of new evidence—widespread grass roots environmental activism and two cross-national opinion surveys—[Brechin and Kempton] conclude that public environmental concern exists globally; it is not restricted only to advanced industrialized countries."[71] This point, however, remains a source of contention between proponents and opponents of deep ecology.

CONCLUSION

Though merely a collection of ideas, deep ecology has appealed to an increasing number of environmental activists. Because most of these activists attempt to influence public policy and environmental politics, deep ecology may best be explained as a holistic understanding. The basics of deep ecology are illustrated when "Naess argues for bringing holistic deep ecology and its associated values along with its scientific aspects into policy and prescriptive areas for change."[72] There has been much written about deep ecology. Its tenets and basic principles have been recorded, debated,

---

[67]Deepak Lal, "Eco-Fundamentalism," *International Affairs* 71, no. 3 (July, 1995): 526.

[68]Ibid., pp. 521–528.

[69]Ibid., p. 528.

[70]Michael Brechin, *Crises in World Politics: Theory and Reality* (New York: Pergamon Press, 1993): 247.

[71]Ibid., p. 265.

[72]Henning and Mangum, *Managing the Environmental Crisis*, p. 25.

and criticized. Today's environmental movement is made up of individuals whose interests range from resourcism to deep ecology. The former is represented by such groups as the U.S. Forest Service whereas the latter is represented by such groups as Earth First! and the Sea Shepherd Society.[73]

As deep ecology is the relative newcomer to the environment movement, there is still a question as to what effect it has really had on environmental politics. This book attempts to answer that question. Hopefully, the overview given in this chapter, along with roots of the movement found in the next chapter, will provide the reader with a good idea of this most interesting environmental perspective.

---

[73]Knauer, "Environmental Ethical Theory Applied in the Modern Environmental Movement."

2

Roots of Deep Ecology

This chapter takes a brief look at the roots of deep ecology and a more expansive view of three American environmentalists who were not only pioneers in the field of deep ecology but who also had involvement in environmental politics. Throughout the history of the United States, environmental and wilderness concerns have been subject to much debate. The Puritans, who arrived in New England during the colonization of America, regarded their surrounding forest areas as places of darkness, mystery, and evil.

In the later writings of the transcendentalists, Ralph Waldo Emerson and Henry David Thoreau one finds a spiritual reverence for the natural world, with wilderness being an essential part of healthy human life. Following Emerson and Thoreau were naturalists such as John Muir and John Burroughs who popularized the wilderness while becoming involved in the political atmosphere of the time. Theodore Roosevelt was one of the first to give wilderness a political voice, but his, and that of his Director of the Forest Service, Gifford Pinchot, outlook of wilderness was decidedly resourcist, leading to the first major schism in environmental ideology in the United States. Pinchot's vision was rooted in utilitarianism and promoted the "wise use of the earth and its resources" for "the greatest good of the greatest number for the longest time."[1]

The Pinchot school of conservation would become the major opponent to the preservationism of John Muir and would serve as the contrasting ideology to the emerging philosophy of deep ecology. Aldo Leopold, who initially followed this management style of Pinchot's, eventually changed his way and contributed perhaps more than any other American to the foundation of deep ecology. In Leopold's writings, one finds an extension of ethics to the land, in what he called the Land Ethic. His philosophy

---

[1]Nathanael Dresser, "Cultivating Wilderness: The Place of Land in the Fiction of Ed Abbey and Wendell Berry," *Growth & Change* 26, no. 3 (Summer, 1995): 350.

would later serve as a basis for the writings of Arne Naess, who coined the term "deep ecology."

This condensed history of early American environmentalism is in no way complete, but should illustrate the roots of environmental thinking in America. The roots of deep ecology are not confined to just the United States of America; however, for it derives its philosophies from a potpourri of sources. As Devall and Sessions astutely point out:

> Deep ecology derives its essence from the following traditions and philosophies: . . . the perennial philosophy, the pastoral/naturalist literary tradition, the science of ecology, the "new physics," some Christian sources, feminism, the philosophies of primal (or native) peoples, and some Eastern spiritual traditions. The writings of Martin Heidegger, Gary Snyder, Robinson Jeffers, John Muir, and David Brower have also contributed greatly to the deep ecology perspective.[2]

The rich history of deep ecology is quite evident, for it borrows not only from a wide array of pioneering individuals but also from a diverse set of cultures and ideologies.

IDENTIFICATION WITH PRIMAL PEOPLES

The Native Americans held beliefs toward the land similar to deep ecology. Black Elk, a Sioux from the northern Great Plains, born in 1863, gave an interview to anthropologist John G. Neihardt in 1931. His words show a deep philosophical relationship to the earth. The Native American stated, "Is not the sky a father and the earth a mother, and are not all living things with feet or wings or roots their children?"[3] For him and other Native Americans, not only are humans a product of the environment, but they are related to all other inhabitants of the land. Viewing plants and animals as brothers and sisters, while anthropomorphic, does allow for an extension of ethics to them, and thus forms the basis for an ecocentric outlook, as found in today's deep ecologists.

Black Elk noted that everything of this world works in circles. Whether it was the sky, earth, or stars, all was round. To him, the life of the human was circular from childhood through death. The similarity between the life of a human and that of all other life helped further link humans to the land. Black Elk stated, "Birds make their nests in circles, for theirs is the same religion as ours."[4] As was seen in the previous chapter, deep ecology invokes religious-type feelings. For Native Americans, their religion largely incorporated the respect and admiration for the environment found in deep ecology. Native Americans, while holding many diverse viewpoints, have historically shown a respect for the interconnectedness of nature through ritual and

---

[2]Bill Devall and George Sessions, *Deep Ecology: Living as If Nature Mattered* (Salt Lake City, UT: Gibbs Smith Publisher, 1985): 80.

[3]Black Elk, "Native Americans Define the Natural Community," in *American Environmentalism: Readings in Conservation History*, ed. Roderick Frazier Nash (New York: McGraw-Hill, 1990):14.

[4]Ibid.

daily practice.[5] Many deep ecologists point to the way that Native Americans coexisted and lived with the land not only as support for their beliefs but also as an example of how society is possible within the deep ecological philosophy.[6]

Another group of natives that the deep ecologists gain inspiration from is the Maori people. The Maori people have no word for an environmental ethic, rather it is just the way they live. To them, living with the land is just part of their life-style and culture. This identification with primal people is one of the tenets of deep ecologists, who frequently use them as examples of cultures that embody many of the principles of deep ecology.

Though deep ecology and certain native worldviews can be described as sharing complementary outlooks, many of these worldviews are decidedly anthropocentric. Evidence of this human-centered outlook can be found in the anthropomorphic nature of animals displayed in many native stories as well as in their self-centered use of animals.[7] David Suzuki and Peter Knudtson, in their book *Wisdom of the Elders*, provide an examination of a number of aboriginal views. They write, "Aboriginal peoples' relationship with other life-forms comes from a deep respect that is ultimately self-interested."[8] So although this native worldview incorporates a sense of deep stewardship, it is ultimately human-centered.

Thus deep ecology builds upon, but extends beyond, traditional native thinking. David Orton described the relationship quite lucidly. He stated:

My own preliminary position is that deep ecology is a movement of indigenous attitudes to nature, which centre around human use, however respectfully carried out. One might characterize the best Native positions regarding relationships to the natural world as "deep stewardship"—a position that still remains human-centered. Although adequate for gathering and hunting societies with little technology and small numbers of people, it is not encompassing enough for the survival of the natural world in the 1990s.[9]

---

[5]Josh Knauer, "Environmental Ethical Theory Applied in the Modern Environmental Movement," 1996. Available from www.envirolink.org/elib/enviroethics/essay.html; INTERNET.

[6]Many deep ecologists quote a speech from Chief Seattle when he was forced into selling his land. The Native American remarked that the concept of land ownership and property was a foreign one, for how can land be owned by humans, when humans are "owned" by the land. The authenticity of this speech, however, has been discredited as a piece of fiction created by filmmakers.

[7]David Orton, "Native Americans and the Environment: Some Limitations of a Left Critique and Deep Dilemmas in Environmental-First Nations Relationships," *Green Web Bulletin #46*. Available from http://pantheon.cis.yale.edu/~lisamc/deep.html; INTERNET.

[8]David Orton, "The Wild Path Forward: Left Biocentrism, First Nations, Park Issues and Forestry; Canadian View," *Green Web Bulletin #44* (This article was later published in the Fall, 1995 issue of the *Wild Earth* magazine).

[9]Ibid.

Though deep ecologists have built upon the traditions and outlooks of many native peoples, the roots of modern-day deep ecologists can perhaps best be found in the writings and thoughts of early American environmentalists.

AMERICAN DREAMERS AND ECO-ADVENTURERS

Henry David Thoreau

Henry David Thoreau, known more for the mixture of transcendentalism and romanticism in his writing, has been adopted by many modern deep ecologists as one of the first in the modern era to live and write like a deep ecologist. When read casually, his writings seem to verify our simplistic notions about Thoreau's romanticism, but when read more thoroughly, some of his more memorable quotations, lines like "In wildness is the preservation of the world,"give us a limited understanding of his ideas.[10]

Thoreau wrote in his journal, dated March 23, 1856:

I seek acquaintance with nature, . . . to know her moods and manners. Primitive nature is the most interesting to me. I take infinite pains to know all the phenomena of spring, for instance, thinking that I have here the entire poem, and then, to my chagrin, I learn that it is but an imperfect copy that I possess and have read, that my ancestors have torn out many of the first leaves and grandest passages, and mutilated it in many places. I should not like to think that some demigod had come before me and picked out some of the best of the stars. I wish to know an entire heaven and an entire Earth.[11]

Clearly, Thoreau had become very close to his natural surroundings and had a large degree of contempt for society and the modern world, which had already stolen much of the natural world. In "Walking," Thoreau wrote: "I wish to speak a word for Nature, for absolute freedom and wildness, as contrasted with a freedom and culture merely civil—to regard man as an inhabitant, or a part and parcel of Nature, rather than a member of society."[12]

Thoreau's view of humans as part of nature, rather than as part of a society above nature, is extremely similar to the deep ecological beliefs in the relationship between people and the environment. Thoreau is still anthropocentric because nature is serving human ends, but his writings are a far departure from those of most other environmentalists, especially those who would come after him such as Gifford Pinchot, who subscribed to a utilitarian view of nature and natural resources.

---

[10]Tom Robotham, "America's Love Affair with Nature May Destroy It in the End," *The Virginian-Pilot* (Norfolk), 1 October 1995, sec. J, p. 1.

[11]David Brower, "Step Up the Battle on the Earth's Behalf," *San Francisco Chronicle,* 18 August 1993, sec. A, p. 15.

[12]Henry David Thoreau, "Walking," in *The Portable Thoreau*, ed. Carl Bode (New York: Viking Press, 1964): 592.

Many modern-day deep ecologists have contempt for civilization and the operations of society that greatly emphasizes progress. This belief can be found in Thoreau's writings such as "A Natural History of Massachusetts," in which he wrote, "In society you will not find health, but in nature. Unless our feet at least stood in the midst of nature, all our faces would be pale and livid. Society is always diseased, and the best is the most so."[13] Such thoughts are echoed in *Walden* in which Thoreau states, "Our village life would stagnate if it were not for unexplored forests and meadows which surround it." Many deep ecologists, while acknowledging Thoreau's reverence of wilderness, would have difficulty in his anthropocentric tone, which is increasingly evident as he continues, "We need the tonic of wildness,—to wade sometimes in marshes where the bittern and the meadow-hen lurk, and hear the booming of the snipe; to smell the whispering sedge where only some wilder and more solitary fowl builds her nest, and the mink crawls with its belly close to the ground. . . . We can never have enough of nature."[14]

Thoreau uses anthropocentric reasons for the goodness of nature, but to his credit (which is the reason why many deep ecologists have called him one of their own), Thoreau went much farther than any other of his contemporaries, which explains why his ideas were not even widely accepted until fifty years later. Thoreau took issue with earlier romantic writers, explaining in "Walking":

Ben Jonson exclaims,
  "How near to good is what is fair!"

So I would say,
  How near to good is what is *wild*!

Life consists with wildness. The most alive is the wildest. Not yet subdued to man, its presences refreshes him. . . . Hope and the future for me are not in lawns and cultivated fields, not in towns and cities, but in the impervious and quaking swamps.[15]

For deep ecologists, the future is also found in the wilderness, not in human-made civilization.

Thoreau seems to ask people to go beyond merely a leisure-time appreciation of nature and wilderness. Rather, Thoreau calls for a heightened and sustained appreciation and awareness of all that is natural. This same reverence toward the environment is embodied in the philosophies of deep ecology. Besides this heightened sense of awareness, Thoreau wanted people to develop their own relationship with the wilderness,

---

[13]Henry David Thoreau, "A Natural History of Massachusetts," in *The Portable Thoreau*, ed. Carl Bode (New York: Viking Press, 1964): 33. ("A Natural History of Massachusetts," originally published as a book review, unsigned, in Ralph Waldo Emerson's *Dial* for July, 1942.)

[14]Henry David Thoreau, *Walden and Other Writings of Henry David Thoreau*, ed. Brooks Atkinson (New York: Random House, 1950): 283.

[15]Thoreau, "Walking," p. 611.

instead of merely following him in his travels and experiences. Deep ecology also asks the same of its followers, not to take the platform for its own sake, but rather to develop their own relationship with the land.

Through this relationship, both Thoreau and modern-day deep ecologists thought that the human soul would be cleansed in a spiritual sense. Thoreau wrote in *Walden* of the effect that the natural environment had on humans:

The indescribable innocence and beneficence of Nature—of sun and wind and rain, of summer and winter,—such health, such cheer, they afford forever! and such sympathy have they ever with our race, that all Nature would be affected and the sun's brightness fade, and the winds would sigh humanely, and the clouds rain tears, and the woods shed their leaves and put on mourning in midsummer, if any man should ever for a just cause grieve. Shall I not have intelligence with the earth? Am I not partly leaves and vegetable mould myself?[16]

Contained within this language are the ideas, as expressed before, of humans being part of nature but also the ideas of nature elevating the human soul. This latter idea can be construed as anthropocentrism, putting humans first and using the environment for solely human purposes. Nevertheless, many deep ecologists interpret such rhetoric as a belief in the mystical qualities of nature that can help and heal the corrupted societies of today. As for the societies of today, both deep ecologists and Thoreau view them with contempt and distrust. He wrote that "most of the luxuries, and many of the so-called comforts of life, are not only not indispensable, but positive hindrances to the elevation of mankind."[17]

This elevation was only possible in the natural world, away from towns and cities. However, there is another side to Thoreau that some scholars have suggested runs counter to deep ecology. Though Thoreau says he "'loves the wild not less than the good,' he makes it clear that he was no primitivist, no simple-minded worshiper of the 'noble savage.' Indeed, contrary to popular belief, he did not entirely reject the concept of civilization."[18] Such scholars point to Thoreau's statement, "I left the woods for as good a reason as I went there. Perhaps it seemed to me that I had several more lives to live and could not spare any more time for that one."[19] But using such a statement to support this contention that Thoreau left Walden to adopt a more "contemporary" life-style, would be wrong. Thoreau continued to travel and give his due homage to the natural world. Leaving Walden was in no way a total departure from his deep ecological life-style.

Henry David Thoreau was not just one who revered the earth. Rather, he was an inspiration for public policy as well. He served as one of the most eloquent spokespersons for early deep ecological thought. Believing that nature should be admired for its own sake, not just for how useful it might be to people, he advocated "national preserves" that would be set aside for bears and panthers. He even said that some

---

[16]Thoreau, *Walden*, p. 125.
[17]Ibid., p. 13.
[18]Robotham, "America's Love Affair with Nature May Destroy It in the End," p. J1.
[19]Ibid.

of the hunter race may still exist, not for idle sport or food, but for inspiration and our own true recreation.[20]

Thoreau is interesting, for nature offered him not only personal inspiration but also the desire to search for a better political community. John Taylor, who has investigated the relationship between nature and politics in Thoreau's writings, concludes:

[Thoreau] found that nature provided him with the means to criticize American politics and society and to imagine a more just political order. In nature, he believed, a person experiences the independence and humility that are necessary for building and sustaining a moral, free, and democratic community. . . . Nature supplied Thoreau with the principles he needed to ground both his social criticism and his vision of a more equitable America. For this better nation to exist, people must listen to the lessons of nature rather than the clattering of commercial society.[21]

Thoreau wrote about politics as well about nature. He described politics as a narrow field that had a "still narrower highway" that led to it. He stated that "I sometimes direct the traveler thither. If you would go to the political world, follow the great road, follow that market-man, keep his dust in your eyes, and it will lead you straight to it; for it, too, has its place merely, and does not occupy all space."[22] His inspiration for activists would arrive with his essay "Civil Disobedience" in which he instructed the selective breaking of the law in order to press for the rights of all that is natural. Like Thoreau, "many of the activists influenced by Deep Ecology believe that this value should be defended when necessary by civil disobedience—selectively breaking the law."[23] This form of civil disobedience can be found in the daily operations of deep ecological groups such as Earth First! (EF!) and the Sea Shepherd Society.

John Muir

Like Thoreau, John Muir spent much of his life in the wilderness, writing about his experiences in his journal, which later served as the basis for his many books. Muir, however, went one step beyond Thoreau, not in his philosophical beliefs, but rather in his activism, attempting to influence such individuals as President Theodore Roosevelt and many local and national politicians. Muir could very well be the first

---

[20]Tricia Andryszewski, *The Environment and the Economy: Planting the Seeds for Tomorrow's Growth* (Brookfield, CT: The Millbrook Press, 1995): 22. (Quoting from Steward L. Udall, *The Quiet Crisis* [New York: Avon Books, 1963]: 63.)

[21]John Taylor, quoted in D. R. Jones, "Lost Legacies of Thoreau and Pinchot: A Review of Bob Pepperman Taylor's *Our Limits Trangressed: Environmental Political Thought in America,*" *Environmental Law* 23 (Spring, 1993):1027.

[22]Thoreau, "Walking," p. 599.

[23]Andryszewski, *The Environment and the Economy: Planting the Seeds for Tomorrow's Growth*, p. 84.

environmental activist who shared many of the philosophies of modern deep ecologists and was also able to influence public policy.

Muir has taken on almost mythical qualities, especially in environmental circles. Yet until recently, little was known about the actual man behind the writing and travels. During Muir's childhood and formative years, he was able to read Shakespeare, Plutarch, the romantic poets, Milton, and the works of other authors that neighbors lent to him. After gaining a job in a machine shop (they were impressed by many of the young Muir's inventions he made in the early hours of the morning), he went on to spend 2½ years at the University of Wisconsin, developing a solid knowledge of science.[24]

However, it was the wilderness that attracted and urged the young Muir to embark on his many travels. He later said that his real education began when he matriculated into the "university of the wilderness." Muir wrote in a letter to Emily Pelton, while living in the mountains, "I live alone, or, rather, with the rocks and flowers and snows and blessed storms; I live in blessed mountain *light*, and love nothing less pure. You'll find me rough as the rocks and about the same color—granite. But as for loss of pure-mindedness that you seem to fear, come and see my teachers; come, see my Mountain Mother, and you will be at rest on that point."[25]

Like Thoreau, Muir had contempt for society and forced civilization, as do the deep ecologists. Muir recognized the ability of nature and wilderness to awaken people from "the stupefying effects of the vice of over-industry and the deadly apathy of luxury."[26] Muir wrote, "Thousands of tired, nerve-shaken, over-civilized people are beginning to find out that going to the mountains is going home; that wildness is a necessity; and that mountain parks and reservations are useful not only as fountains of timber and irrigating rivers, but as fountains of life."[27] Muir described the mission of many present-day deep ecologists: awaken people from their anthropocentric and resourcist outlook of nature into something deeper and more meaningful. Muir describes how many, under the Pinchot school, did not see the intrinsic worth of the five hundred species of trees that compose the forests, rather they see the usefulness of these species to humans.[28]

Muir was distraught over this anthropocentric mindset and dismayed over the constant push for so-called progress. Writing in a sarcastic tone, Muir stated that:

I suppose we need not go mourning the buffaloes. In the nature of things they had to give place to better cattle, though the change might have been made without barbarous wickedness. Likewise many of nature's five hundred kinds of wild trees had to make way for orchards

---

[24]Bob Sipchen, "The Muir Mystique; After 150 Years, the Naturalist Has Become Patron Saint to All Environmental Factions, but His Legacy Is Still in Dispute," *Los Angeles Times*, 20 April 1988, p. 1, col. 2.

[25]John Muir, "A Letter to Emily Pelton, Yosemite Valley, April 2, 1872," in *The Life and Letters of John Muir,* vol. 1, ed. William Frederic Bade (New York: Houghton Mifflin, 1923): 323.

[26]John Muir, *Our National Parks* (1901; reprint, New York: AMS Press, 1970): 1.

[27]Ibid.

[28]Ibid, p. 332.

and cornfields. . . . Accordingly, with no eye to the future, these pious destroyers waged interminable forest wars. . . . the invading horde of destroyers called settlers made its fiery way over the broad Rocky Mountains, felling and burning more fiercely than ever. . . .[29]

Like Thoreau and deep ecologists of today, Muir believed that all of nature, not just people, had a God-given or intrinsic right to exist. Muir fiercely defended this right to exist: "If a war of races should occur between the wild beasts and Lord Man, I would be tempted to sympathize with the bears."[30] According to Michael P. Cohen, who authored a 1984 biography of Muir (entitled *The Pathless Way, John Muir and the American Wilderness*), such rhetoric has elevated Muir to the spiritual father of environmental activism with his writings serving the equivalent of a bible for the environmental movement. Still, deep ecologists are not the only ones who quote Muir and use his writings as guidance for their thoughts. Many preservationists also quote Muir. They note Muir's personal enjoyment and use of the land. This explains why those in both the mainstreams as well as on the so-called fringes of environmentalism liberally quote Muir.

In any case, Muir has been criticized by the same people who are critical of the deep ecologists for his injection of passion and emotion into what they consider a rational, scientific debate. Chase states that "he certainly was one of those who helped to turn environmentalism into a kind of secular religion. . . . His appeal is an emotional appeal. His language is emotional, very biblical language."[31] The similarity between such criticism of Muir and that of deep ecology is also a testament to the powerful rhetoric that accompanies the philosophical beliefs shared by those who preach deep ecological ideals. Dave Foreman credits Muir with outlining the philosophy that underlines the group EF!. The rhetoric of EF! is similar to Muir's, which can be illustrated by Foreman when describing the philosophy that EF! embraces: "Wilderness deserves to exist for its own sake; second, all things are connected; third, the true wisdom is out there in the wilderness, and not in books—you need direct experience with wilderness to become enlightened."[32]

Recently, EF! even celebrated Muir's birthday in the only way they could. Members climbed onto platforms in old-growth trees designated to be cut, while performing similar acts of civil disobedience to protest the very issue that Muir spent the last part of his life fighting: the utilitarian and economically motivated timber-cutting policies of the U.S. Forest Service.

Muir was not just a philosophical writer, but rather an environmental activist who was able to capture the ear of many influential public policy makers. Muir was asked in 1903 to be the personal guide through the Sierra Nevada of President Theodore

---

[29]Ibid., pp. 335–336.

[30]Andryszewski, *The Environment and the Economy: Planting the Seeds for Tomorrow's Growth*, p. 24.

[31]Sipchen, "The Muir Mystique; After 150 Years, the Naturalist Has Become Patron Saint to All Environmental Factions, But His Legacy Is Still in Dispute," p. 1.

[32]Ibid.

Roosevelt on a camping trip. Roosevelt, however, was more a conservationist, and while he fought to preserve America's publicly owned lands for public use, his style would become the antithesis of that of Muir.[33]

Though there is the image of Muir being a naïve man who spent his entire life detached from "society," that image is very far from the truth. That image, created by Muir and his editor, is the one most people think of today. However, Muir became very involved in lobbying and grassroots activism. Muir frequently criticized many acts of humanity but he was not a misanthrope, a term that is now used to describe deep ecologists. According to Cohen, the Muir who helped to save Yosemite and to create the national parks system "was not the mythical Muir [rather] he was the one who could meet men of prominence and power and persuade them. He was the one who understood the power of conservation politics. This later Muir made his compromises."[34]

For example, Muir befriended E. H. Harriman, a railroad magnate whom many deep ecologists would consider a large-scale exploiter of the wilderness. Though Muir would say that he was richer than his friend Harriman because Harriman could never satisfy his own material wants (something that Muir could easily do), Muir called upon his friend to help in his battle to save Yosemite. According to Michael McCloskey, a former Sierra Club chairperson, Muir, who founded the Sierra Club, provided the example for many other grassroots environmentalists of the Sierra Club to follow. "They fell in love with a place—in [Muir's] case Yosemite and the Sierra— saw it endangered, and learned that they had to work with others (to preserve it)."[35]

According to Foreman, "Muir epitomizes what's best about the grass-roots citizen activist," but as Muir aged, he realized that he needed to become a lobbyist and the result was the Sierra Club, of which Muir served as the first president. Today the Sierra Club is a major environmental organization on Capitol Hill but is frequently criticized by the deep ecologists for subscribing to shallow ecology and losing touch with the ideals and philosophies of its great founder. Muir spent considerable time persuading the public and Congress to preserve the wilderness.[36] He criticized Gifford Pinchot's and the Forest Service's policy of not allowing state woodlands to "lie idle." In his book *Our National Parks*, Muir compared U.S. forest policy with that of France, Switzerland, Russia, and Japan, pointing out the superior job those countries were undertaking to protect the woodlands.[37]

In 1912 John Muir entered the biggest battle of his life, a quest to save Hetch Hetchy Valley from being dammed to supply water to California as well as supplement

---

[33]Andryszewski, *The Environment and the Economy: Planting the Seeds for Tomorrow's Growth*, p. 26.

[34]Sipchen, "The Muir Mystique; After 150 Years, the Naturalist Has Become Patron Saint to All Environmental Factions, but His Legacy Is Still in Dispute," p. 1.

[35]Ibid.

[36]Phyllis M. Stanley, *American Environmental Heroes* (Springfield, NJ: Enslow Publishers, 1996): 32.

[37]Muir, *Our National Parks,* pp. 337–339.

electricity. Muir battled furiously to save the Valley. His one-time friend and ally Gifford Pinchot supported the construction of the dam and was able to convince President Roosevelt over the fierce objections of Muir. Not only did the Hetch Hetchy Valley disappear under water, but Pinchot and Muir became bitter enemies. The devastating result took a toll on the aging Muir. Muir argued that the entire future of the National Park system was at stake.[38] Muir's bitterness can be seen in *Yosemite*:

These temple destroyers, devotees of ravaging commercialism, seem to have a perfect contempt for Nature, and, instead of lifting their eyes to the God of the mountains, lift them to the Almighty Dollar. Dam Hetch Hetchy! As well dam for water-tanks the people's cathedrals and churches, for no holier temple has ever been consecrated by the heart of man.[39]

Muir's rhetoric is very similar to that of today's deep ecologists who see greed and economic motivations as the raison d'être of environmental destruction. The battle to save Hetch Hetchy is very similar to those that the deep ecology movement is currently waging. It is no coincidence then that it was the Glen Canyon Dam, which also erased pristine wilderness, that served as the original rally call of EF!.

Today, Muir would be disheartened by what his organization, the Sierra Club, and many other grassroots organizations of his day have become. He would probably be encouraged with such legislation as the 1964 Wilderness Act and the Endangered Species Act, but would probably side with many deep ecologists in their struggles to preserve more wilderness and overturn the utilitarian outlook of the U.S. Forest Service.

Muir, however, has not been forgotten. A poll by the California Historical Society ranked him the state's most important historical figure, above Junipero Serra, John Steinbeck, Walt Disney, and William Randolph Hearst.[40] There is an official Muir Day (his birthday) and there are glaciers (Muir Glacier in Alaska), lakes (Muir Lake in Wisconsin), and even schools (thirty in California alone) that bear his name. Although these places bear Muir's name, the deep ecologists would ask whether they bear his philosophies?

AMERICAN ENVIRONMENTAL SCIENTISTS

George P. Marsh

Before Muir wrote about his travels and captured many Americans' hearts and minds, George P. Marsh scientifically examined evidence of human destructiveness on the environment. Marsh published his findings first in 1864, in a book entitled *The Earth as Modified by Human Action*. Though he was not a philosopher, much

---

[38] Andryszewski, *The Environment and the Economy: Planting the Seeds for Tomorrow's Growth*, pp. 28–29.

[39] John Muir, *The Yosemite* (New York: The Century Company, 1912): 261–262.

[40] Sipchen, "The Muir Mystique; After 150 Years, the Naturalist Has Become Patron Saint to All Environmental Factions, but His Legacy Is Still in Dispute," p. 1.

of the rhetoric found in his breakthrough book can be interpreted as early deep ecological thought. Like today's deep ecologists, Marsh discussed the human relationship with nature. He described it as one needing harmony, arguing for the symbiotic relationship between the two. Marsh observed that trees were needed to prevent disease and that when humans cut down timber for their own consumption it disrupted the harmony. Though this could be described as anthropocentric, it was revolutionary for its time.

Marsh noted the high demand for lumber and the disastrous effect it had on the forests and the wilderness.[41] He scorned such human action as do many deep ecologists today. Marsh noted how forest fires and the damming of streams, which endangered wildlife, were both caused by the human felling of trees that also resulted in erosion.[42] Furthermore, Marsh observed the ecological destruction that accompanied the claiming of land from water by draining lakes. He stated, "Man has too long forgotten that the earth was given to him for usufruct alone, not for consumption, still less for profligate waste."[43]

Such rhetoric is deep ecological despite the traces of anthropocentrism in the idea that land is still a form of property. Today's deep ecologists shun attempts of humans to be stewards of the land. Marsh came to a similar conclusion, arguing that "the equation of animal and vegetable life is too complicated a problem for human intelligence to solve, and we never know how wide a circle of disturbance we produce in the harmonies of nature when we throw the smallest pebble into the ocean of organic life."[44] One thing was for sure, though: "man is everywhere a disturbing agent. Wherever he plants his foot, the harmonies of nature are to discords."[45]

Marsh has not received as much attention by environmentalists, for he was not an activist nor did he write for the masses. Rather, he was concerned with the scientific aspect of the relationship between humans and the environment. Nevertheless, his observations and subsequent conclusions do coincide with much deep ecological thought. Marsh noted what many deep ecologists now argue that "the action of man, indeed, is frequently followed by unforeseen and undesired results, yet it is never less guided by a self-conscious will aiming as often at secondary and remote as at immediate objects."[46] Because of the destructive nature of humans, Marsh argued that they were not part of Earth, a belief contrary to deep ecology. However, the basis and underlying assumptions are basically the same: that humans are destructive in their current cultural and societal formation.[47] The deep ecologists argue that a change

[41]George P. Marsh, *The Earth as Modified by Human Action: A Last Revision of "Man and Nature"* (New York: Charles Scribner's Sons, 1898): 345–349.

[42]Ibid., pp. 350–387.

[43]Ibid., p. 33.

[44]Max Oelschlaeger, *The Idea of Wilderness: From Prehistory to the Age of Ecology* (New Haven, CT: Yale University Press, 1991): 285.

[45]Marsh, *The Earth as Modified by Human Action: A Last Revision of "Man and Nature,"* p. 33.

[46]Ibid., p. 34.

[47]Ibid.

in society and cultural values is possible, and in fact necessary, to reverse their current destructive course. If Marsh were alive, he would probably agree with such a statement and support many of the tenets of deep ecology.

Aldo Leopold

Aldo Leopold is perhaps the grandfather of deep ecology (with Arne Naess being the father). Leopold, whose works were posthumously published,[48] argued for the extension of ethics to the land in what he called the land ethic. Leopold joined the U.S. Forest Service in 1909, serving as a Forest Assistant in New Mexico and Arizona, after being educated at Yale University. Later, Leopold moved to Madison, Wisconsin, and would found the profession of game management and become the chair of game management at the University of Wisconsin (it was created especially for him). Yet it was his book, *A Sand County Almanac,* in which he rejected the entire notion of game "management," that helped to create modern-day deep ecology.

Like deep ecologists, Leopold argued for the need for more wilderness for wildlife, but not for anthropocentric reasons. He assigned an intrinsic worth to the land, arguing for an extension of ethics to include the land. Basically, "the land ethic simply enlarges the boundaries of the community to include soils, waters, plants, and animals, or collectively: the land."[49] This extension of ethics would unpropertize land. Leopold traced the history of property to the time when women were the property of men and blacks were the property of whites. Consider the oft-quoted passage:

When God-like Odysseus returned from the wars in Troy, he hanged all on one rope a dozen slave-girls of his household whom he suspected of misbehavior during his absence. This hanging involved no question of propriety. The girls were property. The disposal of property was then, as now, a matter of expediency, not of right and wrong. Concepts of right and wrong were not lacking from Odysseus' Greece: witness the fidelity of his wife through the long years before at last his black-prowed galleys clove the wine-dark seas for home. The ethical structure of that day covered wives, but had not yet been extended to human chattels. During the three thousand years which have since elapsed, ethical criteria have been extended to many fields of conduct, with corresponding shrinkages in those judged by expediency only.[50]

Though the system of ethics has since been expanded to include all humans, the environment is still viewed as the property of humans. There is simply a lack of ethics for the land.

Leopold's land ethic is very similar to deep ecology in that it honors the intrinsic worth of all species and even nonliving parts of the environment. Nevertheless, the land ethic also changed the role of humans. "In short, a land ethic changes the role

---

[48]*A Sand County Almanac,* published two years after his death, was a collection of various journal entries and essays, some of which were previously published, but seldom read.

[49]Aldo Leopold, *A Sand County Almanac* (1949; reprint, New York: Ballantine Books, 1966): 239.

[50]Ibid., p. 237.

of Homo sapiens from conqueror of the land-community to plain member and citizen of it. It implies respect for his [*sic*] fellow-members, and also respect for the community as such."[51] Leopold explained, as do the deep ecologists, how the role of conqueror is self-defeating. Furthermore, the implication that the land ethic would lead to respect for fellow-members is also incorporated into deep ecology, for the deep ecologists feel that the current artificial alienation from the land is also responsible for much of the social conflict within today's society.

Just as deep ecologists identify with primal people, Leopold too looked into the past when humans and the land lived in biotic harmony. This pioneer of environmental ethics was also active in the political arena, especially in conservation policy. His approach of defining the value of the land in philosophical, and not economic, terms, put him at odds with most conservationists of his time, and perhaps most of those today. Leopold's love and admiration for the land led him to criticize the conservation policy of his time, a conservation policy that he was actively involved in during his time with the U.S. Forest Service. Leopold was disheartened by the economic self-interest that guided conservation policy that eliminated elements of the land community lacking commercial value at the time. In *A Sand County Almanac*, Leopold discussed the progress of conservation, arguing it was not only moving too slowly but was also fundamentally flawed. He urged the need for greater education (like many deep ecologists) but noted that the content of the education must change, for all the education in the world will not help the land unless a system of ethics is included within that education.

Leopold traces laws and government policy toward the land and finds that conservation is at a standstill. He wrote in his book:

Conservation is getting nowhere because it is incompatible with our Abrahamic concept of land. We abuse land because we regard it as a commodity belonging to us. When we see land as a community to which we belong, we may begin to use it with love and respect. There is no other way for land to survive the impact of mechanized man, nor for us to reap from it the esthetic harvest it is capable, under science, of contributing to culture. That land is a community is the basic concept of ecology, but that land is to be loved and respected is an extension of ethics. . . . This much is crystal-clear: our bigger-and-better society is now a hypochondriac, so obsessed with its own economic health as to have lost the capacity to remain healthy. The whole world is so greedy for more bathtubs that it has lost the stability necessary to build them, or even to turn off the tap. . . . Perhaps such a shift of values can be achieved by reappraising things unnatural, tame, and confined in terms of things natural, wild, and free.[52]

Such rhetoric can now be found in the pages of an EF! pamphlet or other deep ecology literature. Both the deep ecologists and Leopold blame the economic-driven ethics and values of society as being ultimately responsible for the misuse and destruction of the land.

---

[51]Ibid., p. 240.

[52]Aldo Leopold, foreword to *A Sand County Almanac*, by Aldo Leopold (New York: Ballantine Books, 1966). The foreword was written on March 4, 1948 in Madison, Wisconsin.

Leopold did not just criticize conservation policy overall, but rather found specific bureaus and governments to blame. One of his biggest fights was against the extermination of predators, specifically the wolf, an extermination that Leopold claimed would upset the balance. He recalls an encounter he had with a dying wolf while he was a game manager. Leopold watched the life drain from the eyes of this most remarkable creature. From that point on, he realized not only the intrinsic worth and beauty of the animal but also its sheer necessity in a healthy and fully functional ecosystem. Without wolves, the deer population would blossom beyond the earth's carrying capacity causing not only starvation but also a failure in the operation of the ecosystem to maintain other species. Leopold stated, "In the field the extermination of predators goes merrily on: witness the impending erasure of the timber wolf by fiat of Congress, the Conservation Bureaus, and many state legislatures."[53] His recognition of the holistic nature and interconnectedness of the environment, as well as the wrongheaded policies of the government, is very similar to the beliefs of many modern-day deep ecologists.

Leopold was both a lobbyist and teacher. "Like John Muir, Leopold urged Congress to preserve roadless wilderness which could only be reached by backpacking or canoeing. In his lectures he taught that without wild areas to serve as a basis for comparison, people may eventually lose sight of what healthy land is."[54] Aldo Leopold had even more in common with Muir. Leopold was one of the founders of the Wilderness Society, as Muir was the founder of the Sierra Club. Leopold added to Muir's spiritual foundation by building up the scientific, practical rationale for preserving wilderness. He emphasized the links and interconnection of all living things in an ecosystem. Before Leopold died in 1948, from fighting a brush fire on a neighbor's farm, he had laid the foundation for the 1964 Wilderness Act.[55]

CONCLUSION

Deep ecology is not a new philosophy, for it owes its roots and ideas to a diverse group of individuals and peoples. When the Norwegian philosopher Arne Naess coined the term in a 1973 article, "The Shallow and the Deep, Long-Range Ecology Movements," he was both summarizing hundreds of years of ecological thought and creating a new movement. This movement would receive a formalized platform in 1984 (appropriately on John Muir's birthday), when George Sessions and Naess wrote out the eight basic principles of deep ecology (see Chapter 1).

Naess has since become the modern-day father of deep ecology, subscribing to the deeper and more spiritual approach described by such Americans as Muir, Thoreau, and Leopold. However, today's deep ecologists go further than their predecessors. They challenge the underlying assumptions of society. Though ecology as a science does not ask what would be the best way to maintain a diverse and fully-

---

[53]Leopold, *A Sand County Almanac*, p. 247.

[54]Stanley, *American Environmental Heroes*, p. 63.

[55]Andryszewski, *The Environment and the Economy: Planting the Seeds for Tomorrow's Growth*, p. 31.

functioning ecosystem, deep ecology as a philosophy inherently involves our notions of ethics, politics, and our basic ideas of right and wrong.[56] The rest of the book is dedicated to answering such questions as: how do deep ecologists affect environmental politics; and what impact have they had in the political arena.

---

[56]Devall and Sessions, *Deep Ecology: Living as If Nature Mattered*, p. 65.

3

Rhetoric and Tactics of Deep Ecology

This chapter examines the rhetoric and tactics of deep ecology and its relationship with politics in the United States. Drawing from one of the primary sources of deep ecological rhetoric, the *Earth First! Journal*,[1] this chapter not only attempts to illustrate the link between deep ecological activism and environmental politics, but it also exemplifies how deep ecologists view politics, politicians, and policies. The *Earth First! Journal* as well as a few of the more popular books written about deep ecology show how deep ecologists attempt to influence politics by simultaneously shunning and embracing government action. The reader will quickly become aware that whereas Naess states that the central slogan of ecosophical lifestyle is "Simple in means, rich in ends,"[2] the means are not always so simple for supporters of the deep ecology movement.

THE ARNE NAESS APPROACH TO ACTIVISM

In his book *Ecology, Community and Lifestyle: Outline of an Ecosophy* (translated and edited by David Rothenberg), Arne Naess provides a practical guide to deep ecology activism. He discusses at length the role of politics in achieving deep ecological objectives, for according to Naess, "All our actions, and all our thoughts, even the most private, are politically relevant."[3] Political engagement, as well as a personal

---

[1]This is not to say that all articles in the *Earth First! Journal* are by deep ecologists. But perhaps more than any other source, the *Journal* does provide a vast array of articles that illustrate the practical applications of deep ecology beliefs.

[2]Arne Naess and David Rothenberg, *Ecology, Community and Lifestyle: Outline of an Ecosophy* (New York: Cambridge University Press, 1989): 88.

[3]Ibid., p. 130.

reduction in consumption, is a must for deep ecologists.[4] Naess discusses the importance of political tactics. The deep ecology movement must not turn against those supporters who are tactically minded even if it goes against their grain. For example, most deep ecologists hold contempt against industry and economic growth. Naess warns against writing and talking as if one is against industry in general. Rather, deep ecologists should be primarily concerned with big industry.[5]

From a practical point of view, Naess speaks in quite different words than many of those who will be examined in this chapter.[6] For example, Naess argues that green politics are dynamic and comparative, never absolute or idealistic. When confronted with an issue, deep ecologists should ask what would be a greener line of policy rather than asking what would be a deep green line of policy. They should then ask how can this greener line be realized in the current political arena.[7] Many view radical environmentalism, and in particular deep ecology, as striving toward nothing less than a revolution. Naess asks whether it will be reform or revolution:

I envisage a change of revolutionary depth and size by means of many smaller steps in a radically new direction. Does this essentially place me among the political reformists? Scarcely. *The direction is revolutionary, the steps are reformatory.* I can only say that I do not think that something resembling the revolutions we read about in history textbooks . . . would be of help in the industrial countries.[8]

Naess comprehensively defines these steps in a systematic account of the rules for Gandhian nonviolence in order to achieve political and social change. He calls for the maximal reduction of violence, warning deep ecologists never to resort to violence. Naess believes that members of the deep ecology movement should act as autonomous, fully responsible people. They should attempt to live together with those with whom they struggle and do constructive work with their opponents. Naess warns deep ecologists never to humiliate or provoke opponents. In fact, he thinks that they should seek personal contact with their opponents and trust them as they would trust themselves. Ultimately, these constructive norms for nonviolent action are aimed at turning the opponent into a believer in and supporter of deep ecology.

From these norms, Naess formulates two levels of hypotheses on the dynamics of the deep ecology movement. The philosopher states that the character of the means utilized in a group struggle determines the character of the result. Thus, even short-term violence contradicts the long-term reduction of violence. Naess believes that all humans

---

[4]Ibid., p. 92.

[5]Ibid., p. 155.

[6]Many of the deep ecologists examined in this chapter do, however, subscribe to Naess's advice that "for the worker within the ecological movement, it is important not to spread oneself too thin, but to make concentrated efforts at one or a very few tasks." Naess and Rothenberg, *Ecology, Community and Lifestyle: Outline of an Ecosophy*, p. 91.

[7]Naess and Rothenberg, *Ecology, Community and Lifestyle: Outline of an Ecosophy*, pp. 160–61.

[8]Ibid., p. 156.

have similar long-term interests; thus by living with opponents, deep ecologists can create a natural basis for trust and confidence in one another. Deep ecology can only win, according to Naess, when its members are able to turn their opponents into believers and supporters of the movement. Naess provides the deep ecological activist with a value and action framework for change.[9] But as the reader will quickly discover, Naess's advice is not always followed, especially if one considers some of Naess's key points for the success of a movement within the larger social sphere.

Naess warns against proclamations that claim one's movement is the most important. Additionally, Naess feels that deep ecologists must resist the tendency to search for weaknesses in other movements that have similar practical goals in mind. Deep ecologists, especially in their literature, tend to make an issue of the "stupidity" or "badness" of their opponents. Arne Naess states that such matters of contention are not issues at all. Two other important pieces of advice Naess offers include avoiding technical or academic language and avoiding spreading oneself too thin. In parting, Naess asks the supporter of the deep ecology movement to "always keep in mind how the goals of your movement relate to the *ultimate* values and goals of others."[10]

RHETORIC OF EARTH FIRST! AND DEEP ECOLOGY

Critics of deep ecology frequently use its own rhetoric against the movement. One quote that is found in almost all humanistic critiques of deep ecology was published in the *Earth First! Journal*. The article stated, "If radical environmentalists were to invent a disease to bring human populations back to sanity, it would probably be something like AIDS. It [AIDS] has the potential to end industrialism, which is the main force behind the environmental crises."[11] Likewise, critics who scorn deep ecology for its anti-capitalism outlook, cite statements such as Judi Bari's: "I think if we don't overthrow capitalism, we don't have a chance of saving the world ecologically. I think it is possible to have an ecological society under socialism. I don't think it's possible under capitalism."[12]

Unfortunately, remarks such as these are not entirely representative of deep ecological thought nor of radical environmental rhetoric. Many environmentalists use such extreme statements to attract attention to their cause; in fact, it could be said that many actions undertaken by radical environmentalists and deep ecologists are centered on gaining publicity for their cause. They do not feel that the American public is anti-environmental; on the contrary, they believe that the vast majority of Americans not only sympathize with the environmental movement, but also hold environmental concerns close to their hearts. Thus, publicity-gathering events are designed to alert this caring public to what is actually going on with respect to the destruction

---

[9]Ibid., pp. 145–150

[10]Ibid., pp. 148–150.

[11]This quote first appeared in an Earth First! newsletter and has been republished in various diatribes against the movement.

[12]Judi Bari, quoted in Walter Williams, *State Journal Register* (June 25, 1992).

of the environment. But even this explanation for the actions does not fully explain the motivations of individuals who subscribe to deep ecological thought. For many, it is a deeply embedded emotional feeling that something is not right in the current way in which both government and society function.

In one issue of the *Earth First! Journal*, Tim Haugen exemplifies the philosophical and rooted history of deep ecology. Arguing for a simpler, yet higher quality of living, Haugen describes his friend Roger, who adopted a different variation of the American dream. Instead of placing value on homes, vehicles, electronics, and so forth, Roger escaped the traditional American dream with its accompanying lifetime of debt and service as a wage slave. He valued quality over quantity. Roger also achieved self-realization through appreciation of all life. While others may have more "nice things" than Roger, Haugen states that most Americans would (and in fact do) view Roger's life with a sort of grudging jealousy. For they "learned the truth that Roger has known all along: a huge pile of trinkets cannot make up for the banality and drudgery of modern working life. Whenever they see Roger, they say, 'Man, you're doing it right.' And Roger agrees."[13] Such rhetoric and anecdotal stories found in the *Earth First! Journal* are reminiscent of many of the writings of John Muir and Henry David Thoreau (see Chapter 2).

This "back to the Earth" rhetoric is extended in an analysis of primal or native people, with whom the deep ecologists often identify. They point to the reluctance of peoples in the "fourth" world to adopt modern, "civilized" ways. Pointing to the Penan of Borneo, the Bushmen of Africa, the Aboriginal Australians, and Indians throughout the Americas, one article in the *Earth First! Journal* explained that numerous cultures have resisted assimilation even when the alternative has been genocide. The deep ecologists use such rhetoric and examples to support their call for a simpler way of life. They cite the works of M. Annette Jaimes of the University of Colorado and Jerry Mander, who offer an explanation for why these cultures have refused to assimilate, for "contrary to all conventional wisdom, the lives of the so-called 'primitive' are much easier than those of 'modern man' (not to mention modern woman)."[14]

Many who have written about deep ecology point to such rhetoric to support the notion that deep ecologists would rather separate themselves from the current political environment than strive to change it. Some deduce even further from such statements that deep ecologists are ignorant of politics and all that goes on in society, for they would rather spend their time in the wilderness. The latter statement is probably true. Deep ecologists would rather spend a day in the wilderness than in an office complex (they would argue that given the chance, just about anyone would choose likewise), but many deep ecologists have become actively involved in the political arena, amassing vast knowledge about current environmental, governmental matters.

---

[13]Tim Haugen, "The Wild Ranch Manifesto," *Earth First! Journal: The Radical Environmental Journal*. Available from gopher.ige.aoc.org:70/00/orgs/ef.journal/4; INTERNET.
    [14]Ibid.

Mixing in Politics

Deep ecologists are very aware of the fact that politics play a large role in determining and directing environmental policy. One place that these feelings are expressed is the *Earth First! Journal*. A contributor remarked that at a luncheon to promote the NCCP program, a member of the Alliance for Habitat Conservation said to him that environmental policy is more or less about politics and not science.[15] Another article, which actually supports the use of science, explains that if it were not for science, "courts would not have evidence to base injunctions on, and activists would not have a valuable tool to educate Congress and the public with. In the Northwest, the science has helped chip away at the politics of forest destruction for profit. (Unfortunately, as evidenced by the Clinton Forest Plan, politics still holds sway.)"[16] So, even though the deep ecologists see a gradual shift to science over politics, their experiences continue to reinforce the point that politics reign supreme.

Other examples of the importance of politics abound in deep ecological literature. One article recounted a 1992 memo from Barbara Boaz, Bear Valley Presale manager of the Malheur National Forest in eastern Oregon, to her timber planning staff. The memo relayed the orders from her superiors which stated that "even if a sale is totally green, as long as one board comes off that would qualify as salvage on the Salvage Sale Fund Plan, it should be called Salvage. It's a political thing."[17]

But such a representation of the almost blasé attitude of deep ecologists toward politics would not be correct. For the intrinsic political element of environmental policy can be used by the deep ecologists and not just by their foes. In describing conservation biology, one member of Earth First! (EF!) describes the field as something more than just science. By going beyond the mere study of nature, conservation biology has entered the field of advocacy and thus ultimately, the political arena.[18]

Despite the seeming overwhelming odds faced by deep ecologists to push their agenda in the political arena, the attitude by most is not to just grin at the so-called political realities. Chad Hanson wrote in the Mabon, 1995 edition of the *Earth First! Journal* about his experiences traveling to Washington, D.C., to lobby for a prohibition on clearcutting in national forests. He wrote, in response to those who have preached the power of politics, that his efforts were "the essential difference between those who would continue to offer up our forests to the chainsaw and those of us who advocate

---

[15]Craig Beneville, "ESA Takes a Licking," *Earth First! Journal: The Radical Environmental Journal* (Brigid, 1995). Available from http://envirolink.org/orgs/ef/Brigid.html; INTERNET.

[16]Mark Hubbard, "Zero-Cut: Ending Commercial Logging on Federal Lands," *Earth First! Journal: The Radical Environmental Journal* (Beltane, 1994). Available from gopher.ige.aoc.org:70/00/orgs/ef.journal/16; INTERNET.

[17]James A. Barnes, "Salvage Rider of the Apocalypse," *Earth First! Journal: The Radical Environmental Journal* (Lughnasadh, 1995). Available from http://envirolink.org/orgs/ef/Lughnasadh.html; INTERNET.

[18]Mike Roselle, "Conservation Biology Dons the Green Uniform," *Earth First! Journal: The Radical Environmental Journal* (Brigid, 1996). Available from http://envirolink.org/orgs/ef/Brigid96.html; INTERNET.

protecting all public forests from logging: The former insist that advocating an end
to logging on public lands is surely 'politically unrealistic,' the latter realize that just
about every worthwhile idea has been dismissed as such. Our job as citizen advocates
is to change political realities, not grin and bear them."[19] The idea of the citizen is
very prevalent in deep ecological literature. The citizen is more than just an individual
living legally within the United States; rather it is one who actively involves him or
herself in political affairs by holding the government to responsible behavior. As
will be seen later, citizen oversight is one of the major ways in which deep ecologists
are able to influence environmental policy.

Deep ecologists, however, go beyond citizen oversight in their actions to influence
public policy. One example of the mix of deep ecology and politics was when the
environmental group Ancient Forest Rescue gave the Grand Old Party a gala event
of its own at the Republican headquarters in Denver. One article in the *Journal* asked,
"What do you get when you mix bongos, bike locks and politics?" For one, you get
a good example of the mixture of deep ecology and politics and for another, you get
two hundred people demanding that Colorado's Republican delegation introduce
legislation to repeal the salvage logging/grazing laws.[20]

Increasing Environmental Awareness

Deep ecologists do not attempt to enter the political arena in a cloud of ignorance.
One reading of the *Earth First! Journal* illustrates their vast knowledge of current
and past government action. Thus when deep ecologists ask for the introduction of
legislation, it is with a thorough, though admittedly biased, background of past bills
and acts. Earth First! members are able to keep a close watch on environmental legislation through the use of the *Journal*. Nearly every issue has an article about some
piece of legislation that is on the threshold of adoption. When the Clinton Forest
Plan was announced, the *Journal* carried an article that was quick to provide an evaluation of the legislation. It stated, "The Final Environmental Impact Statement for
the Clinton Forest Plan (Option 9) is out and the news is not good for the life support
system. How bad is it? Bottom line is that the plan calls for cutting the habitat of
almost half of the surviving spotted owls based on the asinine premise that this is
OK because we'll grow more old growth in the future!"[21] This blunt and opinionated
tone is typical of much EF! rhetoric that not only seeks to tell it as it is, but is also
unashamed to express individual feelings.

---

[19]Chad Hanson, "Mr. Hanson Goes to Washington," *Earth First! Journal: The Radical
Environmental Journal* (Mabon, 1995). Available from http://envirolink.org/orgs/ef/Mabon.html;
INTERNET.

[20]Magpie, "Ancient Forest Rescue Takes Stand," *Earth First! Journal: The Radical
Environmental Journal* (Yule, 1995). Available from http://envirolink.org/orgs/ef/Yule.html;
INTERNET.

[21]Justin Time, "Clueless Bill's Extinction Plan," *Earth First! Journal: The Radical
Environmental Journal* (Beltane, 1994). Available from gopher.ige.aoc.org:70/00/orgs/
ef.journal/12; INTERNET.

The *Journal* is not just about voicing concerns and stating blunt opinions; rather it also provides thoughtful commentary about current bills before Congress. When the question came as to whether to support the Gilchrest bill, the *Journal* stated that while it may have some strategic value, "it sets a bad precedent for a bottom line standard for reauthorization. Support of the Gilchrest bill is yet another example of national environmental groups yielding to a false reality created by opponents of endangered species protection without attempting to influence it in anyway."[22] The *Journal* continues, stating that the national environmental groups must stand for nothing less than a stronger Endangered Species Act (see Chapter 5 for a detailed analysis of this legislation). It notes that the "big environmental groups need to stop talking about 'political reality' and start creating a new reality that reflects the overwhelming public support for preserving the environment!"[23] Again, there is the admission of the role of politics but also a call to change the current political environment.

The knowledge of laws and legislation is not limited to only the national level. Keeping with the grassroots beginnings and the idea of the citizen, deep ecologists are very informed on local and state laws. They keep track of recent votes in the state senates and local governance boards. They direct rallies to influence not only national policy but also local environmental programs. The *Earth First! Journal*, while concentrating on the West and Northwest (where a predominant number of its members are located, especially of those who contribute to the *Journal*), alerts "members" to upcoming votes in their bioregions and the chances that certain bills have of becoming signed into law.[24]

Keeping track of legislation is not the only way Earth First!ers stay on top of environmental policy. The *Journal* serves as a forum for detailed discussion of some of the more influential pieces of environmental policy. They explain the legislation while providing practical applications of how a certain regulation will affect wilderness areas. One example is Craig Beneville's article about the devaluation of the Endangered Species Act, which he wrote in the Brigid, 1995 edition of the *Journal*:

The FWS also issued new guidelines for dealing with Habitat Conservation Plans (HCP's) under section 10(a) of the act. The FWS uses HCP's to license private landowners to destroy endangered wildlife. If a private landowner has an endangered species "problem," they can apply for an "incidental take permit," which allows the landowner to destroy habitat as long as a plan has been approved to conserve the species. The obvious problem is that nearly all species are endangered due to habitat destruction. HCP's, which regularly allow 50–75 percent of an endangered species existing habitat to be destroyed, are clearly an absurd way to maintain a species, much less see it recover as the ESA mandates (For example, the HCP for the Coachella

---

[22]Karyn Strickler, "Environmental Politics Ain't for Sissies: Living Up to the Legend," *Earth First! Journal: The Radical Environmental Journal* (Samhain, 1995). Available from http://envirolink.org/orgs/ef/Samhain.html; INTERNET.

[23]Ibid.

[24]Randy Ghent, "Mass Action for Headwaters: 264 Arrested," *Earth First! Journal: The Radical Environmental Journal* (Mabon, 1995). Available from http://envirolink.org/orgs/ef/Mabon.html; INTERNET.

Valley fringe-toed lizard allowed for an incredible 89 percent of its extant habitat to be developed).[25]

For a group that frequently critiques environmental legislation, their use of environmental law is in many ways both astounding and paradoxical. Legislation such as the Endangered Species Act, the Clean Air Act, and the National Environmental Policy Act, are all treated as tremendous victories in the eyes of deep ecologists.[26] As will be seen later, it is very interesting that Earth First!ers would view these pieces of environmental policy as major victories, since each one of them contains definite anti–deep ecological provisions.

But nonetheless, deep ecologists do make use of such environmental legislation to hold up injunctions and stall policies designed to degrade the environment. Karyn Strickler wrote in the Samhain, 1995 issue of the *Journal* that "the Endangered Species Act (ESA) is our main line of defense against global extinctions that scientists predict may otherwise be up to 10,000 times the natural rate."[27] So not only are deep ecologists aware of environmental policy and the politics involved, but they also utilize this repertoire of legislation in their effort to further deep ecological goals.

Using the issue of biodiversity, this use of law on the part of deep ecologists may not be as far-fetched as it may seem if one considers the overall tone of much of the legislation and case law concerning biodiversity protection. It would almost seem that there is a de facto policy of biodiversity protection in the United States, especially on national forest lands.[28] While such an aura of policy may exist, the politics involved frequently interfere with the full protection of biodiversity. This has led many deep ecologists to supporting additional legislation. Dave Foreman, co-founder of EF!, says that he has supported "much wilderness legislation."[29] (It should be noted, though, that he has recently been at odds with the majority of EF! members in his new role as a member on the board of directors of the Sierra Club, a group that is deeply involved in the political arena. He has been criticized by many for compromising all too readily.)

Politics, Politicians, and Policies

While a lot of deep ecological rhetoric concerns making a difference in the current political environment, the largest category of political rhetoric pertains to criticism of politics, politicians, and policies. Kieran Suckling provided an interesting perspective

---

[25]Beneville, "ESA Takes a Licking."

[26]Jeffrey St. Clair, "Cashing Out: Corporate Environmentalism in the Age of Newt," *Earth First! Journal: The Radical Environmental Journal* (Eostar, 1995). Available from http://envirolink.org/orgs/ef/Eostar.html; INTERNET.

[27]Strickler,"Environmental Politics Ain't for Sissies: Living Up to the Legend."

[28]Hubbard,"Zero-Cut: Ending Commercial Logging on Federal Lands."

[29]Dave Foreman, "Dave Foreman on Zero Cut," *Earth First! Journal: The Radical Environmental Journal* (Mabon, 1995). Available from http://envirolink.org/orgs/ef/Mabon.html; INTERNET.

on environmental legislation in this country. Her social critique of the timing and events surrounding some of the largest environmental victories gives an insightful look into how deep ecologists view the larger issues:

Environmental laws have always been something of an anomaly in American culture. Remember, it was Nixon who signed the National Environmental Protection Act into existence—the same Nixon who incinerated Vietnamese villagers and poisoned our own troops with agent orange. While the National Forest Management Act and the Endangered Species Act were being written and authorized, the Marines were soaking Nicaraguan beaches in blood and the CIA was assassinating human rights activists in Chile and El Salvador. While the Clean Air and Water Acts were winding their way through Congress, timber cut volumes were increasing and dams were being thrown up on the few truly wild rivers left.[30]

Suckling's words may offend a number of people and strike some as a bit radical (an understatement). But, it is this style of "in-your-face, tell-it-as-it-is" writing that grabs people's attention and fuels the deep ecology movement.

Most criticism, however, is much more oriented toward solely ecological goals. Criticism of the government usually takes three forms. The first is anger directed against specific environmental actions. Such rhetoric usually takes the form of either sarcastic remarks or blunt criticism. The 104th Congress's attempt to weaken the Endangered Species act provoked a wide array of criticism in the *Earth First! Journal*.[31] Additional legislation and acts by the government also receive their fair share of criticism. In describing the Surface Mining Control and Reclaiming Act of 1977 (abbreviated SMSRA, or "smackra" by the deep ecologists), Whaley Mander (pseudo-name) stated that "as with many of our half-assed, half-implemented laws, the loopholes pass the buck to often-inept agencies."[32]

One policy, not totally unrelated to environmental regulation, and which has received a considerable amount of criticism from the deep ecologists, is fiscal conservatism. Many point to the current timber policies, describing them as nothing more than "a blank check to federal agencies to spend on the timber industry."[33] To deep ecologists, and particularly to Earth First!ers, real fiscal conservatism would consist of canceling the entire "federal timber welfare program," which, according to one contributor to the *Journal*, would save $700 million to $1 billion.[34] So not only do

---

[30]Kieran Suckling, "Beyond Litigation: What's Left After the Trashing of Environmental Laws?" *Earth First! Journal: The Radical Environmental Journal* (Beltane, 1995). Available from http://envirolink.org/orgs/ef/Beltane.html; INTERNET.

[31]Strickler, "Environmental Politics Ain't for Sissies: Living Up to the Legend."

[32]Whaley Mander, "What Do You Mean You Won't Arrest Us?" *Earth First! Journal: The Radical Environmental Journal*. Available from gopher.ige.aoc.org:70/00/orgs/ef.journal/7; INTERNET.

[33]Barnes,"Salvage Rider of the Apocalypse."

[34]Mark Ottenad, "Salvage: Timber Industry Welfare Is Ecological Disaster," *Earth First! Journal: The Radical Environmental Journal* (Beltane, 1995). Available from http://envirolink.org/orgs/ef/Beltane.html; INTERNET.

they criticize government policy and so-called goals, but they also are frequently quick to offer solutions, though not always the most politically viable ones.

Related to this first group of criticisms of specific governmental actions is the second group, which is conerned with the link between government and big business. Though most of this is centered on the cozy relationship between Republicans and big business, it has on occasion crossed party lines to include all politicians. One author in the *Journal* wrote about the still lingering environmental degradation as a result of the Exxon Valdez oil spill. He stated that the rich executives of the mega-business Exxon sit "smugly in their penthouse offices in Dallas, secure in the knowledge that their billions of dollars of yearly profits are guaranteed by their hired lackeys and compliant politicians in that quaint northern colony called Alaska."[35] The rhetoric of the *Earth First! Journal* is unlike most found in journals in that it does not stray away from being raw or blunt. Such rhetoric complements the publicity and shock-value nature of many of their actions.

Furthermore, the apparent contradiction of government (and more specifically Republican) spending is often discussed in the *Journal*. They claim that "although the Republicans offer fiscally conservative rhetoric wrapped in the flag, further examination of their actions reveals service to their true masters—large corporations and wealthy individuals that benefit from the free-spending of federal dollars and the give-away of public assets."[36] The social commentary continues as the author of the above quotation explains how governmental programs for the defenseless, such as the poor, minorities, the elderly, and wildlife, are drastically cut while corporate welfare subsidies are increased through misguided environmental policies. They describe politicians who give in to big business, and especially the "Timber Beast," as sell-outs.[37]

Their contempt and criticism of the government are perhaps only dwarfed by that for big business. One contributor wrote that the true deep ecologists should always avoid becoming employed in a big corporation or with the government, for these two entities are responsible for the destruction of wilderness. The author does qualify the statement, noting, that they do make excellent employers if you are an expert at internal sabotage.[38]

The final category of criticism deals with the government as a whole. Whether it be an entire framework for government, such as the Republican's Contract with America,[39] or for all of those who frame government, such as legislators and bureau-

---

[35]Michael Lewis, "Prince William Sound Five Years After the Exxon Valdez Oil Spill," *Earth First! Journal: The Radical Environmental Journal* (Beltane, 1994). Available from gopher.ige.aoc.org:70/00/orgs/ef.journal/12; INTERNET.

[36]Ottenad,"Salvage: Timber Industry Welfare Is Ecological Disaster."

[37]Mike Roselle, "The Man Without a Bioregion: The End of Humor," *Earth First! Journal: The Radical Environmental Journal* (Beltane, 1995). Available from http://envirolink.org/orgs/ef/Beltane.html; INTERNET.

[38]Randall Restless, "The Illusion of Security," *Earth First! Journal: The Radical Environmental Journal* (Beltane, 1994). Available from gopher.ige.aoc.org:70/00/orgs/ef.journal/19; INTERNET.

[39]Ottenad, "Salvage: Timber Industry Welfare Is Ecological Disaster."

crats,[40] this type of criticism takes aim at the entire political process. The U.S. government has been described as a malevolent central government and even deemed the enemy in some *Journal* articles.[41] Such rhetoric appears to run counter to the advice of Arne Naess, who advises against being overly critical of politicians. He asks supporters of deep ecology to praise politicians who are courageous enough to take a fairly radical green stance on controversial issues even when they do not go far enough. By the same token, politicians, according to Naess, have an obligation to admit that they as private persons entertain these green views, "even if it is *politically* suicidal to plan changes of this dimension as part of a political platform."[42] Perhaps the reason why politicians are targeted so often is due to the fact that they do not admit to privately sympathizing with deep ecological viewpoints.

Frequently called Freddies, the federal government takes the brunt of most EF! criticism.[43] Perhaps the large size and the commonality of the central government explain why local and state governments tend to get by with less criticism (or maybe it is that they are doing a better job than their older sibling). Many deep ecologists have a fundamental distrust of the government. These feelings show through in their rhetoric. Such expressions should be both expected and unusual; expected because the decentralized focus and environmental goals put the movement on an opposite pole from the federal government, unusual because of the growing utilization of the political system to advance deep ecological goals.

Earth First! and the Mainstream

In any case, the criticism of the federal government and big business often bleeds over into mainstream organizations. Mainstream environmental groups are frequently chastised in many scholarly writings about the deep/shallow ecology split, but such reproach is not as severe in the *Earth First! Journal*. This is not to say that the national environmental groups avoid being the subject of criticism, for many articles take passing shots at the beltway insiders. They are criticized for their compromise and comradeship with the Washington elite.[44] The dilution of the movement is often the topic of deep ecological discussion pertaining to the national environmental organizations. The Wilderness Society and the Sierra Club have received the most heat, for their "destruction of the environmental movement," according to one author in the *Journal*.[45] The roles of the shallow and deep ecological movements will be discussed in detail in the final chapter. It should be noted, however, that there is an emerging number of

---

[40]Barnes, "Salvage Rider of the Apocalypse."

[41]St. Clair, "Cashing Out: Corporate Environmentalism in the Age of Newt."

[42]Ibid., pp. 155–156.

[43]Missouri Transition Zone/Pink Planarians EF!, "Ozark Summer '94," *Earth First! Journal: The Radical Environmental Journal* (Beltane, 1994). Available from gopher.ige.aoc.org:70/00/orgs/ef.journal/18; INTERNET.

[44]Beneville, "ESA Takes a Licking."

[45]St. Clair, "Cashing Out: Corporate Environmentalism in the Age of Newt."

ecosystem-based groups that have adopted the radical agenda but share much in common with the structure of the more mainstream organizations. These groups, termed part of the "New Conservation Movement," are an interesting mutation of direct-action grassroots movements and the larger mainstream organizations.

Policy Initiatives

Regardless of what shape deep ecological groups take, the question invariably becomes, if deep ecologists could change current environmental practices, what types of policies would they endorse? Devall and Sessions provide some examples, stating that "advocates of deep ecology can work on large wilderness proposals, wilderness preservation on private lands, and public policy on pollution and land uses."[46] Policies within the current system that deep ecologists support include zoning all of Antarctica as wilderness, large wilderness proposals, and criminal sanctions of polluters.[47] While many view deep ecologists as those who only want to remake society, there is room within the status quo political arena to make positive changes in the spirit of deep ecology.

In order to make change in the political arena, deep ecologists, and Earth First!ers in particular, employ a wide range of tactics that extends beyond direct confrontation and publicity-gathering events. They are quick to point to public opinion in order to lobby the government for greater environmental protection. One article in the *Journal* cited an ABC News/Washington Post poll that showed 70 percent of the public thinks that the government has not gone far enough in protecting the environment. In the words of the author, "That's not 70 percent for maintaining the status quo, that's 70 percent for strengthening existing regulations. Relating specifically to the ESA, 75 percent in the ABC/Post poll say that the existing law has either struck the right balance or not gone far enough."[48] Such use of public opinion illustrates that at least some deep ecologists want to work within traditional political avenues to lobby the government to change its environmental policies.

In order to garner public support, deep ecology has gone on-line. Both EF! and the Institute for Deep Ecology maintain Web pages on the Internet. The Deep Ecology On-line Project, sponsored by the Institute for Deep Ecology and the Institute for Global Communication (EcoNet), encourages the use of communication technology to facilitate discussions among the deep ecology community. According to its founders, the listserv can be used for many purposes ranging from a chat center for the discussion of various environmental and social topics from a deep ecology perspective to a political place to share tidbits and updates on government legislation. The listserv is extensively used for the discussion of recent environmental legislation, of candidates for political office, and of new books and journals on the subject of deep ecology. Members put

---

[46]Bill Devall and George Sessions, *Deep Ecology: Living as If Nature Mattered* (Salt Lake City, UT: Gibbs Smith Publisher, 1985): 29.

[47]Ibid., pp. 30–31.

[48]Strickler, "Environmental Politics Ain't for Sissies: Living Up to the Legend."

out calls for letter-writing campaigns, rallies, and protests, and for workshops and lectures on the subject of deep ecology. Embracing the Internet and technologies would almost seem to go against the basic principles of deep ecology with its reverence for the natural world over the "techno-sphere." But Tara Strand-Brown, director of the Institute for Deep Ecology, states, "We are embedded in a time when technology rules. . . . If we forego the opportunity to use the Internet, we diminish the impact we can have."[49]

Another way EF! attempts to influence environmental politics is through letter writing. Many articles in the *Journal* have a concluding section that instructs "members" on how they can make a difference, and many list writing congresspersons, and as one author stated, "especially the Republicans." Some articles give a brief synopsis of what should be in the letter. For example, an article about the Snake and Columbia Rivers instructed EF!ers to

tell them you hate nothing more than corporate welfare schemes like the one run for the power companies in the Snake and Columbia Rivers. Tell them you think the chinook salmon is a mighty important part of your heritage and you want your grandchildren to be able to watch salmon leap waterfalls on their way home from the sea, and you don't care what it costs, because such a thing is priceless. Tell them you just don't really care much about jobs when it comes to keeping chinook salmon in Idaho.[50]

Influencing environmental politics does not just occur at the legislative branch of government. Articles in the *Journal* not only take shots at the president, but also argue for the initiation of change at the executive level. Referring to Al and Bubba (Al Gore and Bill Clinton), EF!ers state that it is time to set the executive branch straight.[51] Al Gore was originally viewed as someone who would change the tradition of an environmentally destructive White House, but after Clinton signed the Salvage Rider into law, both Gore and Clinton have been the center of much EF! criticism.[52]

Recently deep ecologists have turned to science in order to change existing forest policy while working within "the system." One contributor to the *Journal* described the invaluable lessons that science provides, arguing that each and every citizen must be aware of the scientific findings in their bioregion's ecosystem. Additionally, "activists must work with scientists to use the specific knowledge about their immediate ecosystem to educate, inform and influence public debate. Emotional appeals and

---

[49]Malcolm Howard, "Communications: 'Green' Groups See Internet as Mixed Blessing," *Inter Press Service* (April 25, 1996).

[50]Erik Ryberg, "Toughing It Out as the Lights Grow Dim: Chinook Salmon Nearly Gone from Idaho," *Earth First! Journal: The Radical Environmental Journal* (Eostar, 1995). Available from http://envirolink.org/orgs/ef/Eostar.html; INTERNET.

[51]Justin Time and the Mystery Riders Workshop, "The Only Forest Health Crisis Is the Deforestation Crisis," *Earth First! Journal: The Radical Environmental Journal* (Litha, 1995). Available from http://envirolink.org/orgs/ef/Litha.html; INTERNET.

[52]Gore has since publicly stated that this was the "worst mistake" of the Clinton administration.

political arguments are important, and should still be used, but sound science has proven to be most effective tool in changing forest policy under existing law."[53] The phrase "under existing law" indicates an effort to change environmental policy without a radical shift to a new political arena. In their book *Deep Ecology: Living as If Nature Mattered*, Bill Devall and George Sessions give some practical advice to the deep ecologists who try to influence environmental policy. They argue it is possible to work within the present political system, for "we can change the conventional political process by using it for deeper purposes."[54]

Despite the efforts to work within the system, there is a large amount of contempt surrounding the politics that govern how the system is run.[55] Thus many deep ecologists have shunned working within the system in favor of working outside of it. When a group of Earth First!ers took over a regional Bureau of Mining office, they were definitely working outside of the acceptable political tract. It is interesting, however, that the concessions sought by these individuals were nothing more than the ability to have a voice within the system. As one of the occupiers later remarked about what they were able to gain from their actions, "a meeting, a public hearing, clarification of valid existing rights issues, and an investigation. Not exactly a halt to the strip mine, but enough for a day's work."[56] In an interview, Mike Roselle remarked, however, that "it would be a big mistake to say that it is simply a matter of tactics [because] you can have radical tactics and not have radical politics. But if you have radical politics you may not need radical tactics."[57] While a lot of the "loud" actions by EF! or the Sea Shepherds is meant to grab media attention and sway the American public, Roselle insists that the more important goal must be to change public policy.[58]

Working Outside the System

Though many deep ecologists work within the system or strive to change the current system, in the background, there is always the belief that the system cannot be truly reformed. A totally new political system is need. Dave Foreman[59] describes the situation:

I'll go even further: I do not believe that reform of democratic society, political and social institutions, and human civilization is possible. I suppose this makes me a realist instead of an idealist, a pessimist instead of an optimist. Some would even say it makes me a misanthrope, or worse, a conservative. For this reason, I do not believe it is possible for us to achieve real

---

[53]Hubbard, "Zero-Cut: Ending Commercial Logging on Federal Lands."

[54]Devall and Sessions, *Deep Ecology: Living as If Nature Mattered*, p. 29.

[55]Justin Time, "Clueless Bil"'s Extinction Plan."

[56]Whaley Mander,"What Do You Mean You Won't Arrest Us?"

[57]Mike Roselle quoted in Dean Kuipers, "Eco Warriors; Environmental Activists," *Playboy* 40, no. 4 (April, 1993): 74.

[58]Ibid.

[59]It should be noted that this rhetoric is from the Dave Foreman who is now on the board of directors of the Sierra Club, and not the same rhetoric that characterized his days with EF!

reform of federal land management, or to arrive at any kind of sustainable economy and society. My fundamental political strategy is to protect as much biodiversity as we can, using whatever ethical means will work in each situation or particular time.[60]

Many who have written about EF! and other radical environmental groups have reached similar conclusions about the inability of such organizations to not only achieve true change but to also have their voices heard by the government.[61]

The paradox faced by many deep ecologists is that they want a remaking of civilization but also want to make as much of an impact as possible within the current political arena. The question then becomes, would politics exist in a deep ecological world? While some have characterized such a world as numerous self-sufficient communes with inhabitants living similar to primal people, some rhetoric points to a world in which politics would still reign supreme. Mike Roselle,[62] a frequent contributor to the *Earth First! Journal*, states that most Americans agree with the beliefs that characterize EF!. But "radical ecologists are still a small voice in the political wilderness. We should never doubt for a moment, though, that if our small voice is heard by reasonable people, we can change public perceptions and thereby change political reality."[63] A change in the political reality assumes some type of political reality in the aftermath of the change. What this political reality would consist of is still in question, but one could safely assume that it would be radically different, but probably just as powerful, as that which rules policy today.

The idea of the "citizen," as commented on previously, perhaps lies at the very heart of what many deep ecologists strive for in their calls for change in environmental policy. Many call for greater citizen oversight, whether it be in public hearings or in litigation. The radical environmental movement has become so successful in their citizen oversight efforts that some legislation now being passed limits, and in some cases completely restricts, such oversight. Needless to say, this has enraged many

---

[60]Dave Foreman, "Dave Foreman on Zero Cut."

[61]Martha F. Lee wrote in her book about EF! that "each of these groups [the two factions of EF!] believed that they had no institutionalized way of voicing their political grievances. The first generation of Earth First!ers was largely comprised of individuals who had once believed that the traditional political system could effectively address their concerns, they cherished the American founding, and many were longtime conservation lobbyists. They were moved to reject those assumption by 'the disaster' that was RARE II. It destroyed their hopes, their faith in American government, and their 'true society.' The second group, Earth First!'s millenian social justice faction, can also be understood this way. The majority of its adherents felt that the American political system had never, and would never, address their grievances." (Martha F. Lee, *Earth First!: Environmental Apocalypse* [Syracuse, NY: Syracuse University Press, 1995]: 147–148.)

[62]In one article, Roselle actually stated that he probably is not a deep ecologist, though much of his rhetoric and actions share in its philosophy.

[63]Mike Roselle, "A War of Words over Violent Analogies," *Earth First! Journal: The Radical Environmental Journal* (Litha, 1995). Available from http://envirolink.org/orgs/ef/Litha.html; INTERNET.

in the EF! "organization."[64] The main form of citizen oversight that has been most successful and thus has been limited the most is judicial review. When the recent timber salvage rider was signed, many argued that it effectively suspended federal laws while stripping away judicial review. Deep ecologists feel that this not only damages endangered fisheries and wildlife habitats but also destroys due process. As one EF! member wrote, "This kind of governmental activity—abusing public resources and suspending the laws for the benefit of a private industry, and preventing citizens from seeking justice in the courts—borders on fascism. Once the lawmakers become lawbreakers, it becomes ever more tempting to suspend other laws, such as those protecting civil rights, consumers, workers and even public safety."[65] Such statements are typical EF! rhetoric designed to alert people to what types of precedents environmental public policy sets for laws that also govern society as a whole.

Need for Government Intervention

Judicial review and citizen oversight are used to influence environmental politics, but contained in EF! rhetoric is also a call for greater government control. This is perhaps the most interesting paradox of them all, for in certain circumstances, deep ecologists are arguing for action from the very body for which they hold the most contempt. The dilemma faced by many deep ecologists is that while the government may need constant oversight and direction, it is better than if wildlife areas were in the hands of private business with no oversight and no constituents.[66] David Brower explains, "Too much forest is in private hands. Private owners can be nice, but governments last longer (except in Italy) and when reminded to do so, can concern themselves with future generations better than privatized institutions do, and history proves it."[67] Those who "remind" the government are the deep ecological activists.

Other contributors to the *Earth First! Journal* also support greater government action, especially with respect to the harvesting of timber. Mark Hubbard[68] writes that "not just environmental activists, but scientists, employees in the Forest Service and Bureau of Land Management, and everyday citizens, who upon learning what havoc has been wrought on our federal lands, are demanding that our federal govern-

---

[64]Barnes, "Salvage Rider of the Apocalypse."

[65]Ottenad, "Salvage: Timber Industry Welfare Is Ecological Disaster."

[66]Businesses do have constituents in the form of consumers, but because many of the companies that "harvest" wilderness areas are detached from the final consumer by two or three steps, the power of the consumer is less than it would be with a government that must answer directly to their consumers, the voting public.

[67]David Brower, "David Brower on Zero Cut," *Earth First! Journal: The Radical Environmental Journal* (Mabon, 1995). Available from http://envirolink.org/orgs/ef/Mabon.html; INTERNET.

[68]Mark Hubbard is an interesting contributor to the *Journal* with his experience of working within the system as a staff attorney for the Oregon Natural Resources Council. According to the *Journal*, he has won over one hundred timber sale appeals against the U.S. Forest Service in Oregon.

ment do better."[69] The merger of public opinion with the demands for the federal government to do better does show a support for government action, a position that would seem to contradict deep ecology's philosophy of de-centralization. Perhaps even more contradictory is the call by Devall and Sessions for global action.[70] While it is doubtful that many deep ecologists would endorse a world government to carry out environmental policies, the scholarly rhetoric of deep ecologists does point to a positive, instead of an adversarial, relationship with governments around the world. Unfortunately, "governments in Third World Countries (with the exception of Costa Rica and a few others) are uninterested in deep ecological issues."[71] Overall, whether it be in the United States or around the world, there is contempt yet also a reserved support of government action in deep ecology rhetoric.[72]

Government as a Threat

While many deep ecologists support federal action for the environment, they do view the government as a subversive threat to their existence (these feelings are probably mutual). One example was the FBI infiltration of a group of EF!ers who were allegedly planning to shut down a power station in Arizona. Although EF! maintains that it was a government setup,[73] the FBI arrested the five individuals involved, as well as Dave Foreman for supposedly supplying funds to the group. This bust effectively led to the end of Foreman's association with the group he helped to found.[74]

The most widely cited story of Federal Bureau of Investigation (FBI) involvement with the group was the car bombing of Judi Bari and Darryl Cherney. Immediately after the bombing, the mainstream press reported that the two EF!ers had been carrying a bomb when it exploded. This report came from FBI press releases that named the two as the only suspects, yet the many searches of Bari's home yielded no incriminating evidence. It has since been concluded that Bari and Cherney were bombed, but the FBI has yet to name a single suspect. Earth First!ers, however, are pretty sure they know who did it: the government of the United States through the FBI. Bari writes, "As we peel back the layers of lies and deception, we can begin to reconstruct what really happened. I have had plenty of time now to ponder the magnitude and the horror

---

[69]Hubbard, "Zero-Cut: Ending Commercial Logging on Federal Lands."

[70]Devall and Sessions, *Deep Ecology: Living as If Nature Mattered*, pp. 37–38.

[71]Ibid.

[72]Hubbard, "Zero-Cut: Ending Commercial Logging on Federal Lands."

[73]Judi Bari, "The Bombing Story—Part 1: The Set-Up," *Earth First! Journal: The Radical Environmental Journal.* Available from gopher.ige.aoc.org:70/00/orgs/ef.journal/10; INTERNET.

[74]This is not the only reason Foreman left the group, however. Foreman became alienated due to the group's growing acceptance of social issues as part of its platform. He thought that the group had steered away from its original defense of wilderness by adopting social issues.

of this attack. And I think it's important for all Earth First! activists to know this story."[75]

If it was indeed the FBI that was responsible for the bombing, it indicates not only the power of EF! but also the perceived threat on the part of the government to the status quo. Bari sees a connection between the actions of the FBI today toward EF! and those toward the Black Panthers twenty-five years ago. Earth First! claims that the same operation, called COINTELPRO, was responsible for the murders of Black Panther activists. Even though COINTELPRO was disbanded after a Congressional Judicial Committee in 1975 found its action to be illegal and unconstitutional, Bari and other radical environmentalists believe that though its target may have changed, the FBI operation has not.[76] Should the FBI be involved, and there is credible evidence they were, then the relationship between EF! and the government is not only one of the radical environmentalists trying to influence the government, but also of the government actively attempting to influence (and stifle) the radical environmentalists.

CONCLUSION

The rest of this book concerns itself with how effective deep ecologists have been in influencing environmental politics and policies in the United States. Those who have commented on this topic have made claims that while the deep ecologists have enjoyed a fair amount of publicity in the popular press, they have had little success in affecting the course of environmental action.[77] While it may be true that deep ecology has found its way into some of the popular press, there is the question of how the media treated the philosophy. Furthermore, what principles of deep ecology have penetrated the politics that govern environmental policy? Part II examines the relationship between deep ecology and politics, first by looking at major pieces of legislation for evidence of deep ecological philosophies and then by focusing on congressional testimony and the legislature's stance toward deep ecology. Because today's media often serves as both a guide and a watchdog of politics, Part III will take a look at how deep ecology is treated in the popular (and not so popular) press.

[75]Bari, "The Bombing Story—Part 1: The Set-Up."

[76]Ibid.

[77]Samuel P. Hays, review of *Toward Unity Among Environmentalists*, *Science* 258, no. 5089 (December 11, 1992): 1822.

II

Deep Ecology and Politics

In order to assure that an increasing population, accompanied by expanding settlement and growing mechanization, does not occupy and modify all areas within the United States and its possessions, leaving no lands designated for preservation and protection in their natural condition, it is hereby declared to be the policy of the Congress to secure for the American people of present and future generations the benefits of an enduring resource of wilderness.

—Wilderness Act of 1964

The Congress finds and declares that various species of fish, wildlife, and plants in the United States have been rendered extinct as a consequence of economic growth and development untempered by adequate concern and conservation.

—Endangered Species Act

4

Introduction to Deep Ecology and Politics

Part II, Deep Ecology and Politics, looks at both past legislation and current congressional testimony to measure the degree of influence that deep ecological principles have had on environmental politics. Before proceeding, however, it is important to define the term "politics." The definition of politics can be both precise and nebulous. For the purposes of this book, many different definitions will be examined. Harold Lasswell coined the famous phrase "Who gets what, when and how" in his definition of politics, while David Easton described it as the "authoritative allocation of values." Reinhold Niebuhr, in a little more lengthy definition, called politics "that realm where conscience and power meet, where the ethical and coercive factors of human life interpenetrate and work out their tentative and uneasy compromises."[1] Niebuhr's definition is perhaps most applicable in this study because the conscience and ethical factors of human life correlate to the battle between shallow and deep ecological principles to gain the most power.

THE RULES OF THE GAME

The political scientist James Q. Wilson describes many "rules" of politics that help illuminate why deep ecology has had a difficult time finding its way into environmental politics. According to Wilson, once policies are adopted, they tend to persist regardless of their value; for it is easier to start new programs than to end old ones. If this is true, then it is even amazing that shallow environmental philosophies have been adopted, for their predecessor was the absence of environmental policy. The momentum of the status quo can be illustrated in the following story. During the Persian Gulf crisis of the late 1980s, the United States grappled with how to protect

---

[1]Cathal J. Nolan, *The Longman Guide to World Affairs* (White Plains, NY: Longman Publishers, 1995): 301.

American oil tankers from mines. One Navy admiral suggested that helicopters fly over tankers and radio when a mine was spotted. One captain of an oil tanker quickly explained why such an option was out of question: in order to stop a fully loaded tanker, the captain would have to put all engines in full reverse, and even then, the tanker would not come to a stop for many hours, if not an entire day. This is also the case for environmental legislation. Because so much shallow ecological momentum has been amassed, it is quite difficult for deep ecologists to stop and reverse the trend of this political juggernaut.

Although many deep ecologists argue for local action, there is a grudging support for national environmental policy because of the lack of "responsible" environmental policies at the local level. This lack of local support also does not bode well for deep ecologists, for, according to Wilson, almost all electoral politics is local politics. When members of Congress ignore or forget their home base, they tend not to win reelection.[2] This helps to explain the large influence of the wise-use movement and big businesses that support local workers.[3]

Because "whatever the size of their staff and budget, Congress and the White House will always be overworked," deep ecologists must compete against other programs and interests in order to lobby for new legislation and regulations. Yet perhaps the element of politics that works most against the deep ecologists is that "proposals that seem to confer widespread and immediate benefits will be enacted whatever their long-run costs."[4] Many deep ecological concerns are long term in benefits, but short term in costs. Since most of the costs of deep ecological programs are known, and not concealed or deferred, traditional politics dictates that they would not be popular with the people (a fact that the deep ecologists disagree with, pointing to public opinion surveys) and thus not attractive to politicians.

CRISIS POLITICS

Another element of politics that is detrimental to the causes of deep ecologists is that planning in government frequently takes place only after a crisis.[5] Everything from antiterrorism to environmental policy often takes shape only after a crisis has occurred, such as a downed airliner or a massive oil spill. It would seem from the very outset, given the nature of politics, that deep ecological philosophies would have a difficult, if not impossible, task of influencing environmental policy in the United States. Even the fact that public opinion seems to favor more, instead of less, environmental policy, does not help as much as one might think, for the rules of the game

---

[2]James Q. Wilson, *American Government: Institutions and Policies* (fifth edition) (Lexington, MA: D. C. Heath, 1992): 619.

[3]This is not to say that deep ecologists do not support jobs. Many Earth First!ers have attempted to join with timber workers to band against their employers for both the exploitation of nature and the exploitation of the worker.

[4]Wilson, *American Government: Institutions and Policies*, p. 619.

[5]Ibid.

indicate why government policy will often be at odds with public opinion.[6] Further complicating the matter is that "the public does not typically react to current levels of environmental damage in an instantaneous fashion. There is usually a lag in public concern as people wait until the environmental damage begins to affect them directly."[7]

Despite the nature of the political system against the incorporation of deep ecological philosophies, many deep ecologists continue to propose changes at both the national and international level. Michael Zimmerman observes that "deep ecologists call for structural changes in social, economic, and political institutions. Sessions proposes that the United Nation establish an Environmental Council, analogous to the Security Council, which would provide an integrated ecospheric-protection approach to population issues, Third World economic development, and wildlife habitat preservation."[8] Such proposals not only face resistance from the shallow-ecological value system of those who make policies but also are "subject to the same fate of political trade-offs as is any other concern. The typical environmental trade-off is economic, as measured in terms of losses in gross domestic product or jobs."[9] The short-term costs often do not compensate for the long-term benefits in the eyes of many policy makers. Finally, many environmental problems are not clearly definable. While public concern, though lagging, has the ability to spur politicians to act, money will be allocated only when the policy maker can point to a specific problem that has a specific solution. This allows politicians to answer to public calls of accountability.[10]

EXAMPLE OF GORE AND THE 104th CONGRESS

An interesting political atmosphere to examine is the relationship between the White House and the 104th Congress. Within that political climate, many environmentalists saw two opposing forces at work. On one side there was the great environmental hope embodied by the Vice President Al Gore. On the other was the perceived anti-environmental members of the 104th and 105th Congress. Though both were criticized by the deep ecologists, many would rather have had environmental policy crafted by the former rather than the latter. Al Gore's book *Earth in the Balance* has a few striking similarities to deep ecological rhetoric. Consider these words from the Vice-President: "the evidence of an ecological Kristallnacht is as clear as the sound of glass shattering in Berlin. . . . It is not merely in the service of analogy that I have referred so often to the struggles against Nazi and communist totalitarianism, because I believe that the emerging effort to save the environment is a continuation of these

---

[6]Ibid., p. 95.

[7]Courtney Brown, "Politics and the Environment: Nonlinear Instabilities Dominate," *American Political Science Review* 88, no. 2 (June, 1994): 294.

[8]Michael E. Zimmerman, *Contesting Earth's Future: Radical Ecology and Post Modernity* (Berkeley: University of California Press, 1994): 28

[9]Brown, "Politics and the Environment: Nonlinear Instabilities Dominate," p. 292.

[10]Ibid., pp. 294–295.

struggles, a crucial new phase of the long battle for true freedom and human dignity."[11] Such lofty rhetoric could easily find its way into even the most radical of environmental journals.

James L. Huffman, in his review of the book, comments that primitive religion, Native American religion, ecofeminism, the Gaia hypothesis, the rule of law, liberty, freedom, social justice, democracy, community, and "even some deep ecology all contribute to Gore's ecumenical thinking on the environmental crisis."[12] Gore did criticize deep ecologists in his book, but later noted that "some Deep Ecologists . . . are more thoughtful."[13] Gore praised capitalism though he explained the need for government regulation of the the free market. His support for economic growth irritated many deep ecologists, but given Arne Naess's insight (see Chapter 3) pertaining to the political necessity for all politicians to take such a stance on economic growth, they may find ways to forgive him. Given the alternative, the Republican Congress, many deep ecologists (and environmentalists) had little choice.

As alluded to above, the alternative to the "Al Gore environmental perspective" was that of the Republican Congress. The *Earth First! Journal* was filled with fierce diatribes against many of the proposed programs of the Republican Contract with America and other Republican initiatives. Deep ecologists, and environmentalists in general, were terrified when proposals such as the one introduced by Senator Craig Thomas (R-Wyo.) were brought before Congress. Thomas introduced legislation to transfer Bureau of Land Management lands to the states, remarking, "We are talking about Bureau of Land Management lands. We are not talking about Forest Service. We are not talking about wilderness. . . . These are low production lands. These are not national parks. These are very low rainfall, low moisture content areas, so they are very unproductive."[14] As if such proposals were not enough to provoke deep ecologists, consider the words of Senator Slade Gorton (R-Wash.) as he introduced legislation to weaken the Endangered Species Act: "How important to society is this species? What is the biological significance of the species? Is it the last of its kind? Will it provide a cure for a deadly disease?"[15] It should be no surprise why deep ecologists were worried. This worry translated into increased political activity. It is such political acitivity that serves as the focus of this book.

---

[11]Albert Gore, *Earth in the Balance: Ecology and the Human Spirit* (New York: Houghton Mifflin, 1992): 275.

[12]James L. Huffman, "Book Review: Civilization in the Balance: Comments on Senator Al Gore's *Earth in the Balance*," *Environmental Law* 23 (Winter, 1993): 239.

[13]Gore, *Earth in the Balance*, p. 217.

[14]141 Congressional Record S9913 (daily ed. July 13, 1995) quoted in Kelly Nolen, "Residents at Risk: Wildlife and the Bureau of Land Management's Planning Process," *Environmental Law* 26 (Fall, 1996): 771.

[15]141 Congressional Record S6339 (daily ed. May 9, 1995) quoted in Nolen, "Residents at Risk: Wildlife and the Bureau of Land Management's Planning Process," 771.

PREVIOUS RESEARCH

Little has been written on the relationship between deep ecology and politics. The first instance of deep ecological principles becoming involved in politics in the West occurred in 1587 when the village of Saint-Julien brought suit against a colony of weevils that were attacking their vineyards. The court's verdict came out against the villagers with the judge declaring that "the insects, being creatures of God, possessed the same rights as people to live in the place."[16] While the verdict was based on religious principles, it is the first example of politics and laws conforming to the intrinsic worth of species, an idea at the very center of deep ecology.

A LOOK AHEAD

Such anecdotal stories are easy to pick out and explain how deep ecological principles have had an influence. But when measuring this influence on a grander scale, in terms of the laws and legislation of the United States, the problem becomes more complicated. In order to accomplish this task, a number of assumptions have been established to aid with this study. Chapter 5 examines major environmental legislation to trace the influence of deep ecological philosophies. Using a comprehensive understanding of the ecophilosophy, every section, paragraph, and sentence of selected environmental legislation is scrutinized. Even the title and the section of the legal code in which the particular law is found is examined to search for both deep and shallow ecological principles. The legislation reviewed has been selected based on its overall impact on environmental politics and its frequency of reference in deep ecological literature.

Chapter 6 attempts to decipher the language of legislative rhetoric, much like the previous chapter examined the rhetoric of deep ecologists. Because testimony and rhetoric play such important roles in the political process, congressional testimony for the last three years was examined to note how those who mentioned terms associated with deep ecology viewed the philosophy as a whole. Chapter 7 takes a more scientific approach by categorizing all testimony in the last three years in which the term "environment" was uttered. Each piece of testimony is graded in five different deep ecological subjects on a scale from one to five, ranging from superficial to very deep ecology. Finally, Chapter 8 examines the relationship between the legal system and deep ecology. It attempts to discern the influence deep ecology has already had on the courts and explores what the future may hold for radical environmental law. Together, the chapters of this part of the book will trace the interesting and intricate relationship between the deep ecology philosophy and the political process in the United States.

---

[16]Donald Worster; "The Rights of Nature; Has Deep Ecology Gone Too Far?" *Foreign Affairs* (November/December, 1995): 111.

5

Environmental Legislation

INTRODUCTION

One manner in which the federal government expresses its attitudes and desires is through legislation. This chapter examines major pieces of environmental legislation that provide clues as to the ecological attitude of the legislative branch of the U.S. federal government. During the second wave of environmentalism,[1] a plethora of legislation was passed. Many of these laws continue to form the legal framework of environmental policy today and thus deserve special attention. This was also a time when environmentalists were able to have a large influence over the actions of Congress. For example, when the construction of the Dinosaur Dam was being debated by the U.S. Congress, environmentalist David Brower made it his personal mission to put into the hands of every member of Congress the book *This Is Dinosaur*. This effort, combined with several trips to Washington to testify before congressional committees, helped to spare Dinosaur National Monument. Phyllis Stanley writes that "to environmentalists, the Dinosaur conflict demonstrated that environmental issues are political issues. To Brower, it confirmed that hard-nosed political clout and an informed public can take action and sway legislation."[2] Many now question

---

[1]According to writer Mark Dowie, we have now entered the fourth-wave environmental movement. According to Dowie, the first three waves of the environmental movement have run dry. The first wave encompassed land conservation in the early part of the century, the second, passage of federal legislation such as the Endangered Species Act in the '70s, and the third, economy-based policies such as pollution credits in the late '80s. For more information, see Mark Dowie, *Losing Ground: American Environmentalism at the Close of the Twentieth Century* (Cambridge, MA: MIT Press, 1995).

[2]Phyllis M. Stanley, *American Environmental Heroes* (Springfield, NJ: Enslow Publishers, 1996): 82.

whether today's environmentalists can have the same influence over congressional legislation.

Mark Dowie writes that when it comes to lobbying Congress, the environmental movement "has remained a mosquito on the hind quarters of the industrial elephant."[3] He points to the 10 to 1 advantage that big business has over environmentalists in both dollars and lobbyists. Though Dowie may think that the legislative path now leads to a dead end, the major environmental laws that now exist are critical in legally based environmental activism. The following analysis of environmental legislation discerns the ecological outlook in an attempt to measure the influence of deep ecology in environmental politics. Each piece of legislation is examined for its deep or shallow ecological tendencies.

Before proceeding, however, it should be noted that some readers may think that this analysis might not be doing the various pieces of environmental legislation justice in that it uses a 1990's deep ecological perspective to characterize 1960's and 1970's pieces of legislation. As a high school English teacher of mine would say, one must not forget the genre of a piece of writing, and in scholarly criticism, literature should be analyzed according to its appropriate genre. While this is very good advice, the reason that this study looks at these acts through the eyes of a different genre is that its purpose is to show the progression of deep ecological thought into the laws and legislation that govern this nation. Additionally, as noted previously, the ideas, though not always popular or well known, have existed for thousands of years.

CLEAN AIR ACT (1963)

The Clean Air Act was originally passed and signed into law in 1963, long before the term "deep ecology" was even coined. But as its history has shown, the ideas were prevalent long before they were given a specific name. This section takes a critical look at the act, which was subsequently amended in 1967, 1970, and 1990. The entire act has been reviewed for both deep and shallow ecological rhetoric and philosophy. For the purposes of this analysis, only the most pertinent parts of the act are discussed.

The first element one notices about the Clean Air Act is its place within the legal code. It is found in Chapter 85 under Title 42, The Public Health and Welfare. The intent, garnered from its name and placement, indicates it is for the public welfare, not for the welfare of the environment. The anthropocentric or human-centered placement indicates that this law was made by and for the shallow ecologists. But sometimes a title can be misleading, as illustrated later in the analysis.

---

[3]Kevin Berger, "Harsh Medicine for Environmentalism; Mark Dowie Takes On the Mainstream Movement in a Spirited Polemic," *San Francisco Examiner*, 27 April 1995, sec. C, p. 5.

§ 7401. Congressional findings and declaration of purpose (Subchapter I—Programs and Activities Part A—Air Quality and Emission Limitations)

The Congressional findings and declaration of purpose are found in the very beginning of the act and provide the legislative intent of the law. The act states, "(1) that the predominant part of the Nation's population is located in its rapidly expanding metropolitan and other urban areas, which generally cross the boundary lines of local jurisdictions and often extend into two or more States."[4] This finding would be embraced by the deep ecologists. However, their solution would be to stop this urban sprawl and actually reverse the trend of expanding metropolitan areas. The intent of the act runs counter to deep ecology because it attempts to remedy the effects of the problem rather than address the root causes. The act further states, "(2) that the growth in the amount and complexity of air pollution brought about by urbanization, industrial development, and the increasing use of motor vehicles, has resulted in mounting dangers to the public health and welfare, including injury to agricultural crops and livestock, damage to and the deterioration of property, and hazards to air and ground transportation."[5] It is significant that the ill effects of air pollution fall primarily on humans and society. The act fails to note the effects that air pollution, such as acid rain, has on trees and lakes. By centering on humans only, the act embraces shallow ecology and anthropocentrism.

The third finding of the Congress is supported by deep ecologists. Although Chapter 3 noted the grudging support of centralized action on the part of the federal government, much of the scholarly writing about deep ecology notes its emphasis on decentralization. The Congressional declaration of findings states that the control of air pollution at its source is the primary responsibility of the state and local governments.[6] Additionally, it remarks "that Federal financial assistance and leadership is essential for the development of cooperative Federal, State, regional, and local programs to prevent and control air pollution."[7] Despite their call for decentralization, many deep ecologists, especially those who are members of such groups as Earth First!, would probably push for such federal involvement. Remember, that one of the primary weapons Earth First!ers use is judicial injunction in federal courts to stop the actions of local governments. Thus the involvement of the federal government becomes their only institutionalized protection when surrounded by hostile local governments.

While the statement of findings provides a reasonable framework to determine the intent of the law, the declaration of purposes that follows the findings is perhaps even more telling. According to the act, the "purposes of this subchapter are—(1) to protect and enhance the quality of the Nation's air resources so as to promote the

---

[4]*Air Pollution Prevention and Control, U.S. Code*, title 42 (Public Health and Welfare), chapt. 85, sec. 7401.

[5]Ibid.

[6]Ibid.

[7]Ibid.

public health and welfare and the productive capacity of its population."[8] Because
this purpose is listed first and is the only significant statement of purpose pertinent
to this examination, it deserves very close scrutiny. Notice how it is entirely concerned
with public health and welfare. Nowhere in this declaration of purpose or any of
the other declarations, is the health and welfare of the natural environment even
mentioned. It should be noted that although the act was passed in 1963, it was sixty
years after the establishment of the national parks and fourteen years after the publication
of Leopold's *A Sand County Almanac*. There is no trace of deep ecological thoughts
whatsoever in the declaration of purposes. Even more unfavorable for the deep ecologists is the subscription to the economic growth mindset implied within the phrase
"productive capacity of its population."

§ 7402. Cooperative activities

§ 7402, entitled "Cooperative Activities," calls for a decentralized centralization,
which is significant for the deep ecologists. As seen, one of the primary means of
change and influence is citizen oversight. Thus the closer the Congress makes legislation
to the people, the greater the ability of the people will be to influence legislation.
Unfortunately for the deep ecologists, when environmental policy is put under local
control, the risk of increased influence by private land owners, unconcerned with
the environment in a deep ecological sense, is at its peak.

§ 7403. Research, investigation, training, and other activities

The section of the act on research, investigation, training, and "other" activities
is perhaps the most important, second only to the declaration of findings and purposes,
in the analysis of this piece of legislation. While it does later discuss research into
the environmental effects of air pollution, the first subsection concerns itself only
with public welfare. According to the act, the administrator shall "(1) conduct, and
promote the coordination and acceleration of, research, investigations, experiments,
demonstrations, surveys, and studies relating to the causes, effects (including health
and welfare effects), extent, prevention, and control of air pollution."[9] It is significant
that under the effects listed, there is no mention of damage to ecosystems or to the
environment. However, the use of science to guide future public policy, which appears
to be the intent of undertaking such research, has found its way into deep ecology
literature. In the Beltane (May 1), 1994 edition of *Earth First! Journal*, Mark Hubbard
argues that science is an important ally for radical and deep ecologists in their attempts
to influence public policy. Science should be embraced, according to Hubbard, for
it gives the deep ecologists substantiated and credible proof in the minds of legislators.

---

[8]Ibid.

[9]*Air Pollution Prevention and Control, U.S. Code*, title 42 (Public Health and Welfare),
chapt. 85, sec. 7403.

In order to carry out the research, the administrator is authorized to "(3) make grants to air pollution control agencies, to other public or nonprofit private agencies, institutions, and organizations, and to individuals, for purposes stated in subsection (a)(1) of this section."[10] This provision allows local organizations and individuals to perform their own pollution control activities through federal grants. Deep ecologists would support such an outreach to citizens, which allows those who are nearest to the land to have a voice in the formation of public policy. This is reminiscent of the decentralization called for by deep ecology.

Later within the same subsection, the act states that the administrator may "(6) collect and disseminate . . . basic data on chemical, physical, and biological effects of varying air quality and other information pertaining to air pollution and the prevention and control thereof."[11] Based on the apparent intent of the law, it makes one wonder whether the "biological" effects described will come to mean just those biological effects on humans, or those on all living species in the environment. A shallow ecological interpretation would assume the former, whereas a deep ecology interpretation would hope for the latter.

Subsection (c) of § 7403 centers around air pollutant monitoring, analysis, modeling, and inventory research. The subsection describes a program of research which shall include the "(1) consideration of individual, as well as complex mixtures of, air pollutants and their chemical transformations in the atmosphere."[12] Although this statement expresses neither a deep nor a shallow ecological bias, it does acknowledge the synergistic linkages between pollutants, something that many environmentalists today fight to have considered in public policy. Additionally, the subsection calls for the "(2) establishment of a national network to monitor, collect, and compile data with quantification of certainty in the status and trends of air emissions, deposition, air quality, surface water quality, [and] forest condition."[13] The mention of forest condition is the first time that the legislation has considered any other living entity other than humans. But this does not make it deep ecology, for the question has yet to be answered whether this protection is for the forests' own well-being, or the health of a natural resource for human use?

There is a distinct change within the act as the issue of ozone depletion is raised. Instead of referring to "man-made" sources of pollution, the term "anthropogenic" is used. The language about the ozone within this subsection was added later, and the rhetoric is much different. It calls for the improvement of "the understanding of the mechanism through which anthropogenic and biogenic volatile organic compounds react to form ozone and other oxidants."[14] This proposed study of the effects of humans on the environment comes much closer to deep ecological principles than any of the other rhetoric within the act to this point.

---

[10]Ibid.
[11]Ibid.
[12]Ibid.
[13]Ibid.
[14]Ibid.

Subsection (d), entitled "Environmental Health Effects Research," continues the shallow ecological and anthropocentric outlook of the act. It states that the "(1) the Administrator, in consultation with the Secretary of Health and Human Services, shall conduct a research program on the short-term and long-term effects of air pollutants, including wood smoke, on human health."[15] The deep ecologists would ask, "What about the health of other species and of the ecosystem as a whole?" The concentration, as seen in other parts of the act, is still very shallowly ecological in outlook. The second plank of the subsection is equally anthropocentric. It remarks that "the Administrator shall develop methods and techniques necessary to identify and assess the risks to human health from both routine and accidental exposures to individual air pollutants and combinations thereof."[16]

All of the research called for within the act, while beneficial to supporting future legislation, is seen by many deep ecologists as a stalling act. Radical environmentalist would sooner assume that air pollution is harmful to humans and ecosystems alike and take any necessary steps to reduce and eliminate it from the source. Only after the elimination of pollution should time and energy even be spent on determining what levels of pollution have what effects on humans and the environment.

Subsection (e), "Ecosystem Research," is the first to concentrate solely on the natural environment. It in fact helps to counterbalance some of the above anthropocentric criticism. It directs the administrator to "conduct a research program to improve understanding of the short-term and long-term causes, effects, and trends of ecosystems damage from air pollutants on ecosystems."[17] Although many deep ecologists would applaud such research, the distinction that the act makes, in terms of both placement of the provisions and the wording of the provisions themselves, indicates a separation of humans from the environment. This represents a shallow ecological approach. As noted previously, the call for "(2) evaluation of risks to ecosystems exposed to air pollutants, including characterization of the causes and effects of chronic and episodic exposures to air pollutants and determination of the reversibility of those effects"[18] should almost be foregone, for the deep ecologists would just as soon assume that pollution has an adverse effect upon the ecosystem. A truly deep ecological policy would strive to stop all of it.

Subpoint (4) of the subsection, does show some deep ecology influence. Here, the act authorizes the "evaluation of the effects of air pollution on water quality, including assessments of the short-term and long-term ecological effects of acid deposition and other atmospherically derived pollutants on surface water (including wetlands and estuaries) and groundwater."[19] The inclusion of wetlands and estuaries does show some deep ecological approach because they usually are not considered water resources for human use. Subpoint (5) exhibits an even deeper ecological influence when it

---

[15]Ibid.
[16]Ibid.
[17]Ibid.
[18]Ibid.
[19]Ibid.

calls for the "evaluation of the effects of air pollution on forests, materials, crops, biological diversity, soils, and other terrestrial and aquatic systems exposed to air pollutants."[20] Biological diversity is one of the chief concerns for deep ecologists and while there are substantial hints of shallow ecology (materials and crops are inherently for human use alone), the mention of terrestrial and aquatic systems does show an ecological understanding on the part of the policy makers.

But just as it may seem that deep ecology was having an influence on this important early piece of legislation, the very next statement highlights the predominance of shallow ecology. Subpoint (6) calls for the estimation of economic costs, both direct and associated, of ecological damage. There is no mention of intrinsic worth, but rather an anthropocentric outlook concerned with human welfare. Only the shallow ecologists would be concerned with the economic costs of such damage. The deep ecologists would be more concerned with the actual damage and the loss of life that accompanies environmental pollution.

Subsection (f), "Liquefied Gaseous Fuels Spill Test Facility," exhibits even more of the influence of shallow ecology over deep ecological concerns. It states that the "highest priority shall be given to those chemicals that would present the greatest potential risk to human health as a result of an accidental release."[21] No mention is made of other species, and this human-first attitude is very characteristic of anthropocentrism and a shallow ecology outlook on environmental policy. Subsection (g), "Pollution Prevention and Emissions Control," is also anti–deep ecology. Instead of dismantling the industrial complex that has created the problem of pollution, as many deep ecologists would advocate, the subsection merely argues for "improvements in nonregulatory strategies and technologies for reducing air emissions from area sources."[22] This is not to say that deep ecologists would fail to support strategies aimed at reducing air emissions, but it is arguing that such programs are frequently seen by the more radical environmentalists as piecemeal measures that merely push back, instead of preventing, an environmental Armageddon.

Further evidence of an anthropocentric influence can be found in subsection (h), "NIEHS Studies," which states that the "Director of the National Institute of Environmental Health Sciences may conduct a program of basic research to identify, characterize, and quantify risks to human health from air pollutants."[23] Again, calls for more research on the effects of air pollutants on human health and welfare without mention of ecosystems or the environment.

There was a substantial change in wording and intent when the section was further modified in 1990. Subsection (j), "Continuation of National Acid Precipitation Assessment Program," illustrates the growing influence of deep ecological philosophies. For example, the subsection argues for the "maintenance, upgrading, and application of models, such as the Regional Acid Deposition Model, that describe the interactions

---

[20]Ibid.
[21]Ibid.
[22]Ibid.
[23]Ibid.

of emissions with the atmosphere, and models that describe the response of ecosystems to acid deposition."[24] It does not even mention human health and welfare; rather it concentrates solely on ecosystems. One possible interpretation of this wording is that humans are part of this ecosystem (a belief that many deep ecologists share). However, the amendment still puts a price tag on ecosystem protection by calling for an "analysis of the costs, benefits, and effectiveness of the acid deposition control program."[25] But to the deep ecologists' comfort, the wording of the subsection indicates that environmental policy will be guided by science, which the deep ecologists feel will lead to better environmental policy. Deep ecologists advocate the elimination of all acid deposition, and, though the act does not go nearly that far, it does call for the reduction in acid deposition rates in order to prevent adverse ecological effects.

§ 7470. Congressional declaration of purpose (Part C—Prevention of Significant Deterioration of Air Quality Subpart I—Clean Air)

§ 7470, the Congressional declaration of purpose for the prevention of significant deterioration of air quality, is very similar to the previous declaration of purpose already examined. The second purpose states, "to preserve, protect, and enhance the air quality in national parks, national wilderness areas, national monuments, national seashores, and other areas of special national or regional natural, recreational, scenic, or historic value."[26] Deep ecologists would ask, "Why not protect all wilderness areas?" But the most significant observation to be gained from this section is that the purpose mentioned first is human welfare and health. The juxtaposition of humans first and wilderness second indicates a sense of priority in the minds of those who make and enforce the legislation. In this position hierarchy, it is also noteworthy that national monuments are given the same standing as parks and wilderness areas.

The third purpose listed in the section is to "insure that economic growth will occur in a manner consistent with the preservation of existing clean air resources."[27] This purpose is very shallow in its ecological outlook for two reasons. First, there is the mandate for the continuation of the economic growth mindset, which is embraced by the shallow ecologists and shunned by the deep ecologists. Second, the term "resources" indicates a non-intrinsic worth assigned to the environment. Although it is significant that national parks and wilderness are singled out for protection, the overall tone and rhetoric of the section is decidedly shallow ecological.

The final purpose examined here (number five overall) and found in this subsection is treated with contempt by deep ecologists, for its allows selected increases in air pollution. The act seeks "to assure that any decision to permit increased air pollution in any area to which this section applies is made only after careful evaluation of all

---

[24]Ibid.

[25]Ibid.

[26]*Air Pollution Prevention and Control, U.S. Code*, title 42 (Public Health and Welfare), chapt. 85, sec. 7470.

[27]Ibid.

the consequences of such a decision and after adequate procedural opportunities for informed public participation in the decision making process."[28] Even though the act calls for careful evaluation, it still allows for increases in pollution levels, a position that few, if any, deep ecologists would ever support.

§ 7521. Emission standards for new motor vehicles or new motor vehicle engines

§ 7521, which sets the emission standards for new motor vehicles and new motor vehicle engines, has gone through many modifications and amendments in the last twenty-five years. Despite these amendments, the section as a whole still remains both anthropocentric in outlook and ecologically shallow in its philosophy. It calls for the administrator to "prescribe (and from time to time revise) in accordance with the provisions of this section, standards applicable to the emission of any air pollutant from any class or classes of new motor vehicles or new motor vehicle engines, which in his judgment cause, or contribute to, air pollution which may reasonably be anticipated to endanger health or welfare."[29] While the shallow ecologists focus on public health and welfare, the deep ecologists would look at the larger environmental picture. But even more, this subsection calls for making the system better by reforming while maintaining the current reliance on motor vehicles. The deep ecologists would favor a change from motor vehicles altogether in favor of zero emission vehicles such as bicycles.

This anthropocentric outlook can be found elsewhere in section (e) when it mentions only public health and safety with no mention of the environment. When the section discusses new technology (7521[a][6]), it can be categorized as shallow ecology because it entrenches the use of "resources" by using them more efficiently. The deep ecologists do embrace certain technologies that are non-dominating, but maintain that most technological "fixes" merely prolong the inevitable and make real policies changes that much more difficult. Subsection (b)(1)(C) states that "the Administrator may promulgate regulations under subsection (a)(1) of this section revising any standard prescribed or previously revised under this subsection, as needed to protect public health or welfare, taking costs, energy, and safety into account."[30] Not only does this provision not mention the environment, but it also allows the economic mindset of current society to circumvent the regulations in order to preserve growth. This is classic shallow ecology.

The influence of the pro-economic growth influence can be found elsewhere in this section. When discussing high altitude regulations, it mandates the consideration of "the economic impact upon consumers, individual high-altitude dealers, and the automobile industry of any such regulation, including the economic impact which

---

[28] Ibid.

[29] *Air Pollution Prevention and Control, U.S. Code*, title 42 (Public Health and Welfare), chapt. 85, sec. 7521.

[30] Ibid.

was experienced as a result of the regulation imposed during model year 1977 with respect to high altitude certification requirements."[31] The deep ecologists shun the economic growth mindset, for, according to most followers, it is economic growth that has led to the current environmentally destructive policies. Overall, this section has proven to be very shallow in its ecological perspective because instead of doing away with the motor vehicle, it does everything possible to maintain its use and predominance in American society.

§ 7554. Urban bus standards

It is peculiar from a deep ecology standpoint that § 7554, which regulates emissions from urban buses, never takes any steps to encourage the use of buses and public transportation as a way to further cut down on pollutants. The subsection does call for the use of low-polluting fuel such as methanol, ethanol, propane, and natural gas. To the deep ecologists, however, practically any fuel is polluting because it is based on some measure of extracting a natural resource from the environment and burning it, ultimately producing pollutants in the process.

§ 7612. Economic impact analyses

Section 7612 provides instruction for economic impact analysis of the costs and benefits of pollution mitigation. The section opens by remarking that "the Administrator . . . shall conduct a comprehensive analysis of the impact of this chapter on the public health, economy, and environment of the United States."[32] The first thing that deep ecologists would notice is that the environment is mentioned third on the list, behind public health and the economy. If this was not enough to indicate a shallow ecological influence, the manner in which cost-benefit analysis is defined later in the same subsection (a) indicates a clear shallow ecological bias.

This same juxtaposition of terms can be found in subsection (b), which describes and defines the applicable benefits. It states, "in describing the benefits of a standard described in subsection (a) of this section, the Administrator shall consider all of the economic, public health, and environmental benefits of efforts to comply with such standard. . . . The Administrator shall assess how benefits are measured in order to assure that damage to human health and the environment is more accurately measured and taken into account."[33] Again, economic and public health benefits are listed before environmental ones. But it should be noted that the mere listing of environmental benefits is an "improvement" from the very beginning of the act, when the environment was not even mentioned. The wording is vague concerning whether the damages to the environment are based on what it costs humans in terms of economic and public

---

[31]Ibid.

[32]*Air Pollution Prevention and Control, U.S. Code*, title 42 (Public Health and Welfare), chapt. 85, sec. 7612.

[33]Ibid.

health, or if they are based on "pure" environmental damage, acknowledging some intrinsic right of the natural environment to be free from pollution.

Subsection (c) describes and defines the applicable costs associated with economic impact analysis. The provision states, "In describing the costs of a standard described in subsection (a) of this section, the Administrator shall consider the effects of such standard on employment, productivity, cost of living, economic growth, and the overall economy of the United States."[34] It needs no pointing out that all of the "costs" are economic (this should be expected for a section entitled "Economic Impact Analyses"). The consideration of economic factors, and the placement of these above environmental factors, indicates a shallow ecological approach.

§ 7641. Noise abatement

The penetration of economic-based thought into environmental policy, as seen above, is also prevalent in section 7641, "Noise Abatement." The section mandates research into the problem of noise pollution, mentioning first the effects on humans and then on wildlife and property. But the economic growth mindset can be illustrated when the act calls for research into the "effect on wildlife and property (including values)."[35] Wheras deep ecologists give wildlife intrinsic worth and do not measure its worth according to its usefulness or monetary value to humans, shallow ecologists measure species worth according to its value to humans. The use of "values" in the above statement is referring to the latter, shallow ecological interpretation rather than the former, deep ecological meaning of the term "value."

§ 7651. Findings and purposes (Subchapter IV-A—Acid Deposition Control)

Section 7651 states the findings and purposes of acid deposition control. The first finding listed by the Congress is significant in that it mentions ecosystems. It states that "the Congress finds [that] the presence of acidic compounds and their precursors in the atmosphere and in deposition from the atmosphere represents a threat to natural resources, ecosystems, materials, visibility, and public health."[36] It is very significant that ecosystems are mentioned before public health, indicating either a heightened concern for natural ecosystems or that the threat to public health has been weakly established (unfortunately, the evidence points more to the latter than the former explanation). The biggest clue as to the ecological outlook of this section is the use of the term "natural resources." This is decidedly shallow ecology because it measures the environment according to its value to humans.

---

[34]Ibid.

[35]*Air Pollution Prevention and Control, U.S. Code*, title 42 (Public Health and Welfare), chapt. 85, sec. 7641.

[36]*Air Pollution Prevention and Control, U.S. Code,* title 42 (Public Health and Welfare), chapt. 85, sec. 7651.

Acid deposition has found its way into deep ecological literature, and based on remarks about this environmental hazard, deep ecologists would definitely agree with the third finding of the Congress, which states that "the problem of acid deposition is of national and international significance."[37] Finding number six takes a larger look at the problem of sulfur dioxide and nitrogen oxides in the atmosphere, noting that a reduction of total atmospheric loading of these pollutants will improve the protection of public health and welfare and the environment. Unlike finding number one, public health and welfare are again ahead of the environment in listing of priority.

Subsection (b) lists the purposes of action to control acid deposition. The act states that it is "the purpose of this subchapter to encourage energy conservation, use of renewable and clean alternative technologies, and pollution prevention as a long-range strategy, consistent with the provisions of this subchapter, for reducing air pollution and other adverse impacts of energy production and use."[38] This purpose has both deep and shallow ecological elements. It is deep ecology in that it promotes non-dominating technology but shallow in that it merely extends the current consumption habitats of humans.

§ 7651b. Sulfur dioxide allowance program for existing and new units

Section 7651b was added in the revision of the Clean Air Act in 1990. Subsection (c), entitled "Interpollutant Trading," states that "not later than January 1, 1994, the Administrator shall furnish to the Congress a study evaluating the environmental and economic consequences of amending this subchapter to permit trading sulfur dioxide allowances for nitrogen oxides allowances."[39] One can notice a change throughout the sections that were added in 1990 from those that were written in 1963. Note how environment is now listed first. Still, to the deep ecologists' dismay, the subsection calls for the evaluation of economic consequences.

Subsection (e) that regulates new utility units is also shallow in its ecological outlook. While it does limit sulfur dioxide tonnage, it still allows for new utility units. Deep ecologists would argue that instead of an energy or pollution problem, Americans face a consumption crisis. They advocate regulation that prevents the need for new utility units, unless, of course, these new units were renewable and designed to replace fossil fuel, nuclear, or hydro-electrical power units.

§ 7671b. Monitoring and reporting requirements

Section 7671b, another recently added section, also exhibits more of a deep ecological influence than its older relatives. For example, subsection (d), "Monitoring and Reports to Congress," notes that "not less frequently than every 6 years the Admin-

---

[37]Ibid.

[38]Ibid.

[39]*Air Pollution Prevention and Control, U.S. Code*, title 42 (Public Health and Welfare), chapt. 85, sec. 7651b.

istrator shall report to Congress on the environmental and economic effects of any stratospheric ozone depletion."[40] It is significant that the environment is mentioned first and that public health is not mentioned. A favorable, deep ecological interpretation would state that this provision is very deep ecological in that it incorporates human health into effects on the environment. Subsection (e), which mandates a technology status report in 2015, describes efforts to incorporate non-dominating technology into the mainstream. This is favored by deep ecologists, but the intent of the subsection seems to encourage continued economic growth, a shallow ecological principle.

§ 7671m. Relationship to other laws

Section 7671m discusses the relationship of the ozone regulations of the Clean Air Act. This section, again added in 1990, establishes in subsection (b) the supremacy of the Montreal Protocol.[41] The Montreal Protocol was supported by such groups as Earth First!, and this concession to international law can be considered, at least to some degree, deep ecological. Subsection (c) also exhibits a deep ecological influence. Throughout the Clean Air Act, economic impacts have been placed in high regard. But, according to this subsection on technology export and overseas investment, the President shall as of November 15, 1990 "prohibit the export of technologies used to produce a class I substance."[42] Nowhere is there an economic cost qualifier. This prohibition appears absolute, reminiscent of the resolve of the deep ecologists.

Overall, the Clean Air Act is a piece of environmental legislation based on shallow ecological principles and an anthropocentric outlook. There is a noticeable change in language from the original 1963 legislation to subsequent amendments, which illustrates a greater deep ecological influence. For example, the 1970 Clean Air Act has been hailed by many environmentalists as a victory.[43] But this praise and change in language away from shallow ecology could also be due to a more ecological perspective that is neither shallow nor deep, but one that understands the effects of human activity on the environment.

WILDERNESS ACT OF 1964

The Wilderness Act of 1964 is viewed by many environmentalists as an important, early piece of legislation and a forerunner for much of the environmental laws that would follow. Its passage was no easy process. It took eight years of consideration

---

[40]Ibid.

[41]The Montreal Protocol was an international treaty on ozone-depleting substances (primarily chlorofluorocarbons [CFCs]) adopted in 1987. It has been hailed by many as the premier example of effective global environmental governance through international negotiation and agreement.

[42]*Air Pollution Prevention and Control, U.S. Code*, title 42 (Public Health and Welfare), chapt. 85, sec. 7671m.

[43]Berger, "Harsh Medicine for Environmentalism; Mark Dowie Takes on the Mainstream Movement in a Spirited Polemic," p. C-5.

and debate on reintroduced bills before Congress passed the act. In the words of Representative Walter P. Riehlman of New York, "This bill, I am happy to say, will preserve for present and future generations, land in its original state to be used and enjoyed by all who are interested in outdoor life and conservation."[44] Mention of the Wilderness Act can be found in deep ecological literature. For example, Bill Devall and George Sessions note that "the Wilderness Act of 1964 provides a framework for legally designated wilderness."[45] Additionally, the Wilderness Act was the first, perhaps, to be utilized by both mainstream and deep ecologists in the judicial arena to influence public policy. David Brower was able to steer the Sierra Club toward using the courts to protect the environment after the passage of the act. This led to a very historic and deep ecologically significant court decision regarding Storm King Mountain in New York, which "upheld the concept that parts of nature (canyons, rivers, lakes, mountains, old forests) could be represented and defended in courts."[46] While the Wilderness Act has been remembered by many deep ecologists as a historically significant piece of environmental legislation, its language and rhetoric deserve a closer analysis.

The Wilderness Act of 1964, then called the National Wilderness Act, can be found under chapter 23 of title 16 (Conservation). While the placement of the Clean Air Act under Public Health and Welfare set the tone for the entire act, so too does the placement of the Wilderness Act. The act is relatively short compared to later legislation, such as the Endangered Species Act, which is based upon it. The Wilderness Act is divided into six sections, beginning with § 1131, the National Wilderness Preservation System.

§ 1131. National wilderness preservation system

Subsection (a) deals with the establishment of the wilderness preservation system. It describes the needs for such an establishment, stating:

In order to assure that an increasing population, accompanied by expanding settlement and growing mechanization, does not occupy and modify all areas within the United States and its possessions, leaving no lands designated for preservation and protection in their natural condition, it is hereby declared to be the policy of the Congress to secure for the American people of present and future generations the benefits of an enduring resource of wilderness.[47]

---

[44]110 Congressional Record 17,437 (1964) (statement of Rep. Walter P. Riehlman) quoted in Edwin McCullough, "Through the Eye of a Needle: The Earth's Hard Passage back to Health," *Journal of Environmental Law and Litigation* 10 (1995): 389.

[45]Bill Devall and George Sessions, *Deep Ecology: Living as If Nature Mattered* (Salt Lake City, UT: Gibbs Smith Publisher, 1985): 230.

[46]Stanley, *American Environmental Heroes*, p. 84.

[47]*National Wilderness Preservation, U.S. Code*, title 16 (Conservation), chapt. 23, sec. 1131.

This opening declaration and finding of facts has a hint of deep ecology. It cites the growing human population along with its associated development that threatens natural areas. This tenet is central to deep ecological thought. But after agreeing with the reasons for environmental destruction, the provision takes on a shallow ecological flavor by treating the environment as a resource for the benefit of future generations. The subsection continues by stating that the National Wilderness Preservation System is to consist of federally owned areas designated by Congress as "wilderness areas." These areas, according to the act, will be administered for the use and enjoyment of the American people. This is clearly anthropocentric. But the act does qualify the above statements by arguing for a type of concerned and careful stewardship of the wilderness. Stewardship of the land is one of the main tenets of shallow ecology.

Subsection (c) provides for a definition of wilderness. One of the more interesting phrases used to define wilderness by the act is "an area of underdeveloped Federal land retaining its primeval character and influence, without permanent improvements."[48] One would never find such a statement in deep ecological literature, for there is no way to improve the perfection of natural wilderness. The idea of improving under-developed land is one unique to shallow ecology and its offshoots. There is a Thoreau-esque phrase in the definition that is worth noting. Thoreau wrote frequently about the power of nature to awake the dead soul, and Congress obviously took this into consideration when defining wilderness. One of their requirements for wilderness designation included land that had "outstanding opportunities for solitude or a primitive and unconfined type of recreation."[49] But overall, the Congressional definition of wilderness is shallow in ecological outlook. It concentrates on anthropocentric reasons for protection such as scientific, education, scenic, or historical value. There is no mention of critical habitats or biodiversity.

§ 1132. Extent of system

Section 1132 concentrates on the execution of the act and has elements of both deep and shallow ecology. Subsection (b) describes a system that is very centralized, utilizing only the executive and legislative branch. As discussed before, deep ecologists favor more public input into environmental policy decision making and execution, but do acknowledge the need for federal legislation. In contrast to subsection (b), subsection (d)(1) calls for public notification, hearings, and involvement. Deep ecologists push for greater public input into the laws and legislation that govern environmental policy. Thus, the policies stated here are very appealing to deep ecologists, though they have been frequently disenchanted with the system of public hearings because of the lack of incorporation of local opinion in policy directives. In addition to the hearings, the act mandates that at least thirty days prior to the date of a hearing, everyone from the governor to county executives to federal officials be invited to submit their opinions either at the hearing or up to thirty days after the

---

[48]Ibid.
[49]Ibid.

date of the hearing. Soliciting a wide array of local opinions while educating everyone about the proposed actions is supported by most deep ecologists.

§ 1133. Use of wilderness areas

The debate over the use of wilderness areas has always been a contentious issue in environmental politics. It began in the early 1900s when two schools of thought competed. Conservationism, led by Gifford Pinchot, supported a multiple-use policy governing the national parks, while preservationism, led by John Muir, wanted national parks to be put aside for preservation only. The National Wilderness Act appears to take the Muir approach to national forests, but section 1133 states that "nothing in this chapter shall be deemed to be in interference with the purpose for which national forests are established as set forth in the Act of June 4, 1897 (30 Stat. 11), and the Multiple-Use Sustained-Yield Act of June 12, 1960 (74 Stat. 215) (16 U.S.C. 528-531)."[50] Thus the Wilderness Act does not overturn the multiple-use sustained-yield policy that treats the forests as natural resources instead of an entity worthy of intrinsic value.

Subsection (c) does, however, make it clear that once areas are designated for wilderness, they will indeed be protected from development. The act states, "There shall be no temporary road, no use of motor vehicles, motorized equipment or motor-boats, no landing of aircraft, no other form of mechanical transport, and no structure or installation within any such area."[51] This is very far reaching and would be supported by many deep ecologists. The only aspect that deep ecologists would have trouble accepting is that more federal (and private) land is not given the same protection. But there are more troubling aspects for deep ecologists.

Although subsection (c) makes it appear that these areas are safe from any development, subsection (d) lists special provisions, one of which allows for both mining prospecting and mining operations. Deep ecologists would ask, "Why allow mining prospecting, even if it is 'carried on in a manner compatible with the preservation of the wilderness environment,' if these areas are to be forever protected?" The catch is that if the land is found to be of value, it can be then taken out of the program and used for mining. This is very disheartening to deep ecologists. It illustrates a shallow ecological approach that sets aside land that is currently "worthless" to humans but notes that if such land should be found of some economic benefit, it would then be exploited. Mining is not the only activity that could be allowed. The act states:

The President may, within a specific area and in accordance with such regulations as he may deem desirable, authorize prospecting for water resources, the establishment and maintenance of reservoirs, water-conservation works, power projects, transmission lines, and other facilities needed in the public interest, including the road construction and maintenance essential to

---

[50]*National Wilderness Preservation, U.S. Code*, title 16 (Conservation), chapt. 23, sec. 1133.
   [51]Ibid.

development and use thereof, upon his determination that such use or uses in the specific area will better serve the interests of the United States and the people thereof than will its denial.[52]

This "special provision" of the act definitely puts human interests first by allowing for the use and development of wilderness areas. The phrase "better serve the interests of the United States" is very shallow in its ecological outlook in that it puts wilderness areas at the whim of human needs and interests. It should be noted that "interests" are not even defined by the act, allowing the President broad latitude in deciding the fate of wilderness areas when human interests are concerned.

Although the Wilderness Act is significant in that it takes a more ecological approach to environmental protection than any previous act, it still fails to show a predominantly deep ecological influence. The language is decidedly from the philosophies and principles of shallow ecology.

NATIONAL ENVIRONMENTAL POLICY ACT OF 1970

The National Environmental Policy Act (NEPA) was signed into law by Richard Nixon in 1970. Like the Wilderness Act of 1964, it too has been referred to in deep ecological literature for its role in including the requirement for legal environmental assessment.[53] But unlike the Wilderness Act, the NEPA is found under Title 42 ("The Public Health and Welfare"). From a deep ecological point of view, it is very significant that an act solely for environmental policy should fall under the domain of public health and welfare, denoting an anthropocentric, and thus shallow ecological, outlook on the environment and on environmental policy.

§ 4321. Congressional declaration of purpose

The Congressional declaration of purpose found under section 4321 provides the greatest amount of insight as to the ecological leaning of the act. The first of the four purposes listed by the section aims "to declare a national policy which will encourage productive and enjoyable harmony between man and his environment."[54] This statement lacks a deep ecological influence for two reasons. First, it separates humans from the environment by calling for a "productive harmony" between the two. Second, it implies an ownership of the environment by humans. Both are signs of a shallow, rather than a deep, ecological influence.

The second purpose is "to promote efforts which will prevent or eliminate damage to the environment and biosphere and stimulate the health and welfare of man."[55] This purpose, too, exhibits a shallow ecological influence. It is not good enough

---

[52]Ibid.

[53]Devall and Sessions, *Deep Ecology: Living as If Nature Mattered*, pp. 29–30.

[54]*National Environmental Policy, U.S. Code*, title 42 (The Public Health and Welfare), chapt. 55, sec. 4321.

[55]Ibid.

to merely prevent or eliminate damage to the environment; it must also stimulate the welfare of human beings. This is not only anthropocentric but it also denies the intrinsic right for the environment to be free from anthropogenic pollutants. Additionally, it again makes the distinction between the environment and human beings.

The third purpose, and final one that is of any relevance to this analysis, seeks "to enrich the understanding of the ecological systems and natural resources important to the Nation."[56] Deep ecologists would favor a policy that enriches human understanding of the environment, but would never use such rhetoric as "natural resources important to the nation." The term "resources" has a different connotation to the deep ecologists than to the shallow ecologists. The former group views resources as Earth supplies for all living beings, while the latter group sees them as for human use only. The Congressional rhetoric illustrates a clear shallow ecological influence.

§ 4331. Congressional declaration of national environmental policy

Section 4331 also provides insight into the motivations and intentions of Congress in creating the NEPA. It states that "the Congress [recognizes] the profound impact of man's activity on the interrelations of all components of the natural environment, particularly the profound influences of population growth, high-density urbanization, industrial expansion, resource exploitation, and new and expanding technological advances."[57] Deep ecologists would agree very much with this statement, arguing that these human forces are perhaps the root cause of environmental degradation. But just as it would seem that the NEPA bares a deep ecological influence, it remarks, "and [recognizes] further the critical importance of restoring and maintaining environmental quality to the overall welfare and development of man."[58] This is very anthropocentric in that it mentions only the effects that environmental degradation has on humans. There is no intrinsic worth assigned to species that co-habitate the same environment as humans.

The subsection continues, describing policy steps to ensure the protection of the environment. It calls for the use of whatever means practically possible to protect the environment. Although this is deep ecological in outlook, the ideas of a productive harmony and the fulfillment of economic "requirements," also found in the language, are very shallow ecological in outlook. This especially applies when one considers the current growth mind set that seems to be assumed in the legislation.[59] Subsection (b)

---

[56]Ibid.

[57]*National Environmental Policy, U.S. Code*, title 42 (The Public Health and Welfare), chapt. 55, sec. 4331.

[58]Ibid.

[59]The act specifically directs the "Federal Government, in cooperation with State and local governments, and other concerned public and private organizations, to use all practicable means and measures, including financial and technical assistance, in a manner calculated to foster and promote the general welfare, to create and maintain conditions under which man and nature can exist in productive harmony, and fulfill the social, economic, and other requirements of present and future generations of Americans."

helps to define the practical means mentioned above. It provides six quasi-mandates to be carried out by the "Nation."

The first directive is to "fulfill the responsibilities of each generation as trustee of the environment for succeeding generations."[60] Deep ecologists would definitely agree that each generation has an obligation to those that follow. Yet this language seems to indicate more of a stewardship than a peaceful coexistence. The idea of humans as responsible stewards of the land is very shallow in its ecological outlook. The second provision argues for the assurance "for all Americans safe, healthful, productive, and esthetically and culturally pleasing surroundings."[61] This mandate is anthropocentric in that it treats the environment as a resource for human use and consumption instead of an entity worthy of intrinsic value.

The third mandate calls for the attainment of "the widest range of beneficial uses of the environment without degradation, risk to health or safety, or other undesirable and unintended consequences."[62] Though the language describes the environment as an entity to be used by humans, it does argue for this use to have a minimal impact on the environment. This is somewhat reminiscent of deep ecology, but it does not go as far as the deep ecologists in advocating simple material needs.

The fourth directive is the preservation of "important historic, cultural, and natural aspects of our national heritage, and [to] maintain, wherever possible, an environment which supports diversity and variety of individual choice."[63] This goal is quite interesting in that it embraces the deep ecological idea of identification with minority traditions but also seems to embrace property rights and other individual rights that might run counter to environmental preservation.

The penultimate provision directs the nation to "achieve a balance between population and resource use which will permit high standards of living and a wide sharing of life's amenities."[64] This statement is very shallow in ecological outlook. Deep ecologists make an important distinction between the standard of living and the quality of life. Whereas the standard of living is a shallow ecological term in that it measures life according to quantity (usually monetary), quality of life is measured by the non-materialistic caliber of one's life. A high quality of life can emanate from a low standard of living as defined by the shallow ecologists. The above goal seems to prescribe a type of sustainable development, an idea that many deep ecologists reject.

The final directive is to "enhance the quality of renewable resources and approach the maximum attainable recycling of depletable resources."[65] Recycling and "doing with enough" are tenets central to deep ecological philosophy, but this goal seems

---

[60]*National Environmental Policy, U.S. Code*, title 42 (The Public Health and Welfare), chapt. 55, sec. 4331.

[61]Ibid.
[62]Ibid.
[63]Ibid.
[64]Ibid.
[65]Ibid.

to allow for further development, albeit less environmentally destructive, and not a return to the environment as many deep ecologists embrace.

Subsection (c) of the Congressional declaration of national environmental policy is a call to empower the American people to take individual responsibility to contribute to the preservation and enhancement of the environment. This call for individual responsibility is deep ecological. But when the act mentions humans as those who are the only beneficiaries of a healthful environment, the act again exhibits a shallow ecological influence.

§ 4332. Cooperation of agencies; reports; availability of information; recommendations; international and national coordination of efforts

Section 4332 basically ties together the loose ends of the NEPA. Four of its nine mandates are significant to this analysis and three of the four show a shallow ecological influence. According to 4332(a), humans have possession of the environment. Combined with 4332(b), which argues for the inclusion of economic and technical considerations into environmental policy, the entire section is colored with a shallow ecological influence. Furthermore, the act describes "the relationship between local short-term uses of man's environment and the maintenance and enhancement of long-term productivity."[66] It still views the environment as a resource for human consumption. But it should also be noted that it does incorporate a long-term outlook that is characteristic of deep ecology.

Further evidence of a limited deep ecological influence is the recognition of the "worldwide and long-range character of environmental problems" and support of "initiatives, resolutions, and programs designed to maximize international cooperation in anticipating and preventing a decline in the quality of mankind's world environment."[67] The recognition of the global reach of environmental problems is found in deep ecological literature. So although there is limited deep ecological influence, the overall flavor of the section is one influenced by shallow ecological principles.

§ 4341. Reports to Congress; recommendations for legislation

Section 4341 provides a very inclusive list of environmental matters that the President must discuss in his or her annual report to the Congress. The report should also include "current and foreseeable trends in the quality, management and utilization of such environments and the effects of those trends on the social, economic, and other requirements of the Nation."[68] This requirement appears to entrench the notion that economic growth is a national "requirement," which is very shallow in its ecological

---

[66]*National Environmental Policy, U.S. Code*, title 42 (The Public Health and Welfare), chapt. 55, sec. 4332.

[67]Ibid.

[68]*National Environmental Policy, U.S. Code*, title 42 (The Public Health and Welfare), chapt. 55, sec. 4341.

outlook. The final Congressional mandate states that the report shall include "the adequacy of available natural resources for fulfilling human and economic requirements of the Nation in the light of expected population pressures."[69] This reinforces the shallow ecological influence because the anthropocentric nature of the above statement views resources as those for use by only humans. Additional sources of anthropocentrism can be found in the remaining sections of the act. For example, section 4362 focuses solely on the relationship of environmental pollution with human cancer and heart and lung disease.

Though regarded by many environmentalists as an important statement about environmental policy in the United States, the overall tone and nature of the act is decidedly shallow in its ecological outlook. Certain concepts are borrowed from deep ecology, but the overriding anthropocentrism within the act characterizes it as shallow ecology. The NEPA provides little, if any, weight to non-economic value to the environment. Though many, including deep ecologists, have attempted to use NEPA to stop environmentally destructive agency action, the "courts have interpreted NEPA to be a purely procedural statute which does not proscribe detrimental environmental actions.[70] However, the publicity created by the disclosure of harmful effects, and the interactions of NEPA with other environmental laws have stopped or modified many projects."[71]

NEPA has been further criticized. One critic wrote, "As written, NEPA is a 'Non-Environmental Policy Act.' It merely requires disclosure of adverse environmental consequences, but not mitigation. And as administered, NEPA currently requires public participation only in its narrowest sense, not 'protection of the community' in its broadest sense, including human beings."[72] This had led some to call for an amendment to NEPA that would require "federal agencies to reject project alternatives whose benefits to a single segment of the biotic community (human beings) are outweighed by the adverse impacts on the 'whole community.'"[73] Such an amendment would create an environmental bill of rights.

Even without an amendment, some do contend that NEPA has made a difference. William H. Rodgers argues that NEPA can bring about subtle changes in institutional behavior by drawing out different voices on the subject of the environmental conse-

---

[69]Ibid.

[70]McCullough explains that "because NEPA only provides procedural requirements to disclose consequences, it does not provide grounds for challenging an agency's actions merely due to resulting environmental harm." See also, John V. Cardone, "Substantive Standards and NEPA: Mitigating Environmental Consequences with Consent Decrees," *Boston College Environmental Affairs Law Review* 18 (1990): 159, 160.

[71]Edwin McCullough, "Through the Eye of a Needle: The Earth's Hard Passage back to Health," *Journal of Environmental Law and Litigation* 10 (1995): 389.

[72]Beverly McQueary Smith, "The Viability of Citizens' Suits Under the Clean Water Act After Gwaltney of Smithfield v. Chesapeake Bay Foundation," *Case Western Reserve Law Review* 40 (1990): 1.

[73]Ibid.

quences and appropriate responses to them.[74] Likewise, Michael Blumm and Steve
Brown illustrate in the *Harvard Environmental Law Review* that environmental groups
can only win a NEPA case if aligned with individuals or agencies of the government.[75]
Thus when environmental groups such as Earth First! recruit support from within
government circles, litigation under the NEPA is a practical tool for environmental
protection.

CLEAN WATER ACT (1972)

The Clean Water Act of 1972, which followed the Water Pollution Control Act
of 1948 (amended 1956), grew out of a need for better regulation of water pollution.
The act can be found under title 33, "Navigation and Navigable Waters," of the United
States Code. The act, which is considerably more lengthy than either the NEPA or
the Wilderness Act of 1964, extends from sections 1251 to1387 of the U.S. code.
Despite the length, the overall tone of the language of the act can be best examined
in four primary sections of the act. These sections are less regulatory and bureaucratic
than the rest of the act and illustrate the various ecological influences.

§ 1251. Congressional declaration of goals and policy

Subsection (a) of the section lists the primary objective of the Clean Water Act.
A deep ecological influence is very noticeable. Whereas each of the previous three
laws examined all described the underlying goal as the protection of human health
and welfare, the Congressional declaration of goals states clearly, "Restoration and
maintenance of chemical, physical and biological integrity of Nation's waters."[76]
In order to fulfill this objective, the section names seven provisions to restore the
integrity of the nation's waters.

The second of the seven directives is significant in that it states it is the national
goal that "wherever attainable, an interim goal of water quality which provides for
the protection and propagation of fish, shellfish, and wildlife and provides for recreation
in and on the water be achieved by July 1, 1983."[77] Although it does mention recreation
in and on the water for humans, it is not treating waters as solely for human use. Rather,
fish and wildlife are listed first, a noticeable departure from the text of previous environmental legislation. If not a deep ecological influence, then an ecocentric influence
is definitely at work. The third provision states that "it is the national policy that

---

[74]William H. Rodgers, Jr., "Symposium on NEPA at Twenty: The Past, Present and
Future of the National Environmental Policy Act: Keynote: NEPA at Twenty: Mimicry and
Recruitment in Environmental Law," *Environmental Law* 20 (Fall, 1990): 485.

[75]Michael Blumm and Steve Brown, "Pluralism and the Environment: The Role of Comment
Agencies in NEPA Litigation," *Harvard Environmental Law Review* 14 (1990): 277.

[76]*Water Pollution Prevention and Control, U.S. Code*, title 33 (Navigation and Navigable
Waters), chapt. 26, sec. 1251.

[77]Ibid.

the discharge of toxic pollutants in toxic amounts be prohibited."[78] The very first thing one notices is the lack of the factorization of economics into the above goal. Deep ecologists would agree very much with the language so far put forth in this section.

The fourth goal says that "it is the national policy that Federal financial assistance be provided to construct publicly owned waste treatment works."[79] Instead of addressing the underlying causes of the vast production of waste, the act treats the problem according to a shallow ecological outlook by using technology to "solve" the effects, rather than the causes, of pollution. Directive number six also embraces technological fixes. It remarks that "it is the national policy that a major research and demonstration effort be made to develop technology necessary to eliminate the discharge of pollutants into the navigable waters, waters of the contiguous zone, and the oceans."[80] While the use of technology to encourage current habits of consumption and waste is very shallow in its ecological perspective, the call for non-dominating and appropriate technology, which seems to be applicable in the aforementioned provision, is reminiscent of a deep ecological influence.

The final statement of goals, number seven, exhibits a high degree of deep ecological influence. It states that "it is the national policy that programs for the control of nonpoint sources of pollution be developed and implemented in an expeditious manner so as to enable the goals of this chapter to be met through the control of both point and nonpoint sources of pollution."[81] This statement shows a deep ecological influence because it addresses the root causes of pollution as well as dealing with the problem in a comprehensive and holistic manner.

Subsections (b) and (c) also exhibit a deep ecological influence. The former, which aims to protect the primary responsibilities and rights of states, argues for limited decentralization in the execution of policy, a goal favored by many deep ecologists. The latter, which directs Presidential activities with foreign countries, is an example of thinking globally and acting locally. The only significant non–deep ecological outlook expressed in the section is found in subsection (g), which introduces the idea of water resource management. This exemplifies a shallow ecological influence because it attempts to separate humans from the environment while establishing humans as responsible stewards of the water.

§ 1252. Comprehensive programs for water pollution control

Section 1252, which describes the development of comprehensive programs for water pollution control, highlights a much greater shallow, rather than deep, ecological influence. The subsection states, "Due regard shall be given to the improvements which are necessary to conserve such waters for the protection and propagation of fish and aquatic life and wildlife, recreational purposes, and the withdrawal of

---

[78]Ibid.
[79]Ibid.
[80]Ibid.
[81]Ibid.

such waters for public water supply, agricultural, industrial, and other purposes."[82] It treats water as a natural resource to fuel growth and consumption. While this runs counter to deep ecological thoughts, it should be noted that aquatic life and wildlife are mentioned first. While this is not exactly putting the Earth first, it is designating them as a top priority of national policy. Subsection (b)(2) however, allows for waters that may not be suitable for fish and wildlife in favor of more anthropocentric priorities.

§ 1281. Congressional declaration of purpose (Subchapter II—Grants for Construction of Treatment Works)

Section 1281, which provides the Congressional declaration of purpose for subchapter two, combines elements of both deep and shallow ecology. It begins with the declaration that "it is the purpose of this subchapter to require and to assist the development and implementation of waste treatment management plans and practices which will achieve the goals of this chapter."[83] This statement of purpose allows for a deep ecological approach in the use of waste water treatment plants as well as in the exploration of the source and underlying causes of waste water. Subsection (b) applies to the application of technology. It supports the use of non-dominating and appropriate technology, which is endorsed by the deep ecologists when not used as a mask for the continuation of overconsumption.

Subsection (d) also exhibits a deep ecological influence because it supports the recycling of potential sewage pollutants "through the production of agriculture, silviculture, or aquaculture products, or any combination thereof."[84] Subsection (g)(5) calls for efficient use of energy and resources. This is characteristic of both shallow and deep ecology, but the apparent hard-line stance against pollution, also in this subsection, is deep ecological in environmental outlook.

§ 1313. Water quality standards and implementation plans

Section 1313 reveals a lot about the ecological influence of the entire act. The section establishes the supremacy of federal laws. But as discussed previously, this could actually favor the deep ecologists in striving for tougher environmental standards. The section describes standards to be used in evaluating water quality. These standards "shall be such as to protect the public health or welfare, enhance the quality of water and serve the purposes of this chapter. Such standards shall be established taking into consideration their use and value for public water supplies, propagation of fish and wildlife, recreational purposes, and agricultural, industrial, and other purposes,

---

[82] *Water Pollution Prevention and Control, U.S. Code*, title 33 (Navigation and Navigable Waters), chapt. 26, sec. 1252.

[83] *Water Pollution Prevention and Control, U.S. Code*, title 33 (Navigation and Navigable Waters), chapt. 26, sec. 1281.

[84] Ibid.

and also taking into consideration their use and value for navigation."[85] It is very significant that human needs are listed first and are given the highest priority. Such anthropocentrism exhibits more of a shallow, than a deep, ecological influence. Although the standards do include fish and wildlife provisions, these are hardly the primary concerns of the standard. This lack of deep ecological influence is dissimilar to the overarching influence found in the original declaration of purposes and findings. Additional remarks about water as a resource for human use can be found in this section. It states, "The State shall establish a priority ranking for such waters, taking into account the severity of the pollution and the uses to be made of such waters."[86]

But there is one instance when the environment is put first in section 1313. Subsection (d)(1)(B) explains that "each State shall identify those waters or parts thereof within its boundaries for which controls on thermal discharges under section 1311 of this title are not stringent enough to assure protection and propagation of a balanced indigenous population of shellfish, fish, and wildlife."[87] While this statement does exhibit a deep ecological influence, it is the only example within the entire section. Section 1342, which governs the national pollutant discharge elimination system, echos the above deep ecological influence when it describes the impact of pollution on other species and not just humans.

Overall, the Clean Water Act of 1972 illustrates a greater degree of deep ecological influence than any other previous piece of landmark environmental legislation that has been considered. Although the rest of the act did not reflect the amount of influence exhibited in the declaration of purposes, the change in tone from previous legislation should be considered a small yet significant victory for deep ecological ideas.

ENDANGERED SPECIES ACT (1973)

The Endangered Species Act (ESA) is perhaps the most widely quoted and cited piece of environmental legislation in deep ecological rhetoric. The act is an important exception to the manner in which most environmental legislation was written because it shifts the burden of proof to businesses, which must demonstrate that a proposed economic activity will not further endanger a species in danger of extinction. Tricia Andryszewski describes the uniqueness of the act:

Not only does the Endangered Species Act take a different approach from most American environmental legislation, it is a significant departure from earlier wildlife legislation as well. Most of the federal laws to protect wildlife, passed piecemeal since the days of Theodore Roosevelt, were meant to ensure a reliable supply of game for hunters. The 1973 Endangered Species Act, like the 1964 Wilderness Act, was based instead on the belief that nature has

---

[85]*Water Pollution Prevention and Control, U.S. Code*, title 33 (Navigation and Navigable Waters), chapt. 26, sec. 1313.

[86]Ibid.

[87]Ibid.

intrinsic value beyond its potential economic value—and that it is worth preserving not only if this costs money but even if it makes certain economic activities impossible.[88]

Holism underlies the field of ecology, which highlights the essential role of each part of an ecosystem. These parts combine to produce a healthy and functioning whole. According to Max Oeslchlaeger, from this understanding, there "arose 'the necessity of protecting the ecosystem from collapse due to the extinction of vital members,' as in endangered species legislation."[89]

Unlike previous environmental legislation, the ESA imposes a total ban on those activities that threaten the well-being of endangered species. This protection is granted even when doing so results in economic losses. This prompted one legal scholar to remark that the "ban is a political and legal reflection of the feelings of many people in the United States and throughout the world who value the mere existence of a species and suffer a deep sense of regret at its passing."[90] The ESA partially implements Leopold's land ethic by protecting non-economic values within limited contexts, for "it requires us to examine non-economic values. We cannot place a dollar value on maintaining species and intact ecosystems. Many species would probably not have survived in the last twenty years without the ESA."[91] Like its precursor, the National Wilderness Act, the ESA is located under chapter 35 of title 16, "Conservation." Its text is relatively short; comprising only fifteen sections with almost every single section providing clues as to its ecological influence.

§ 1531. Congressional findings and declaration of purposes and policy

Overall, section 1531, the Congressional findings and declaration of purposes and policy, appears to have a greater deep, than shallow, ecological influence. The Congress "finds and declares that various species of fish, wildlife, and plants in the United States have been rendered extinct as a consequence of economic growth and development untempered by adequate concern and conservation."[92] It would be difficult to find a deep ecologist who did not agree. It is significant that the Congress has indicted economic growth and development. This should be seen as a major policy victory by deep ecological ideas.

The third Congressional finding, however, shows a greater shallow, than deep, ecological influence. It states that "these species of fish, wildlife, and plants are of esthetic, ecological, educational, historical, recreational, and scientific value to the

---

[88]Tricia Andryszewski, *The Environment and the Economy: Planting the Seeds for Tomorrow's Growth* (Brookfield, CT: The Millbrook Press, 1995): 44.

[89]Max Oeslchlaeger, *The Idea of Wilderness: From Prehistory to the Age of Ecology* (New Haven, CT: Yale University Press, 1991): 289–290.

[90]Jeffrey C. Dobbins, "The Pain and Suffering of Environmental Loss: Using Contingent Valuation to Estimate Nonuse Damages," *Duke Law Journal* 43 (February, 1994): 879.

[91]McCullough, "Through the Eye of a Needle: The Earth's Hard Passage back to Health," p. 389.

[92]*Endangered Species, U.S. Code*, title 16 (Conservation), chapt. 35, sec. 1531.

Nation and its people."[93] This statement is a mix of both deep and shallow ecological perspectives. It does hint to the fact that species have some type of intrinsic worth, but it also describes them according to their extrinsic worth to humans.

Subsection (c), which lays forth the declaration of policy, is also indicative of both shallow and deep ecological influences. First, it states that "it is further declared to be the policy of Congress that all Federal departments and agencies shall seek to conserve endangered species and threatened species and shall utilize their authorities in furtherance of the purposes of this chapter."[94] This declaration is very sweeping in its reach. It seems to place the protection of species and biodiversity at the forefront of all public policy. This is why deep ecologists find so much hope in the act. But the second policy declaration waters down the first directive. It states that "it is further declared to be the policy of Congress that Federal agencies shall cooperate with State and local agencies to resolve water resource issues in concert with conservation of endangered species."[95] While this does not totally overshadow the deep ecological influence, the provision does subscribe to a shallow ecological outlook in viewing water as a resource for human consumption while also hinting toward more of a Pinchot-type of conservation than a deep ecological one.

§ 1532. Definitions

Terms are very important and the manner in which they are defined is perhaps more important than how they are used. The definition of a word or phrase is central to the understanding of the motivations of those who frame the legislation. Section 1532 provides twenty-one definitions for the critical terms of the act, nine of which will be examined here. The first term defined is "alternative course of action," which, according to the act, "means all alternatives and thus is not limited to original project objectives and agency jurisdiction."[96] This is a very broad definition of the term and thus is compatible with the first declaration of policy stated above.

In defining the term "commercial activity" as "all activities of industry and trade, including, but not limited to, the buying or selling of commodities and activities conducted for the purpose of facilitating such buying and selling,"[97] the framers view species as a resource, denying them their intrinsic worth. Many deep ecologists would take issue with such an implication. Additional traces of a shallow ecological influence can be found in the definitions of "conserve," "conserving," and "conservation," which all hint toward the idea of humans as stewards of the land, a very shallow

---

[93]Ibid.
[94]Ibid.
[95]Ibid.
[96]*Endangered Species, U.S. Code*, title 16 (Conservation), chapt. 35, sec. 1532.
[97]Ibid.

ecological belief. But it should also be noted that these definitions also place a high priority on biodiversity (a concept held dear by deep ecologists).[98]

The idea of a connection between a species and its habitat is found in the definition of the term "critical habitat." It is defined as "specific areas outside the geographical area occupied by the species at the time it is listed in accordance with the provisions of section 1533 of this title, upon a determination by the Secretary that such areas are essential for the conservation of the species."[99] One of the primary applications of the ESA is the preservation of old growth forests. The case of the spotted owl illustrates how the protection of "critical habitat" is used by deep ecologists and other environmentalists to save entire ecosystems.

It appears that the 1587 court decision, pertaining to the suit brought by the villagers of Saint-Julien against a colony of weevils that were attacking their vineyards, was fresh in Congress's mind when it defined an endangered species as "any species which is in danger of extinction throughout all or a significant portion of its range other than a species of the Class Insecta determined by the Secretary to constitute a pest whose protection under the provisions of this chapter would present an overwhelming and overriding risk to man."[100] The definition is fairly broad for any species not in the class Insecta, which does show a deep ecological influence. But the exclusion of certain species (in this case insects) that cause harm to "man" definitely illustrates a shallow ecological influence.

The term "plant," however, is given a very broad definition, including everything from "weeds" to house plants. It states that "the term 'plant' means any member of the plant kingdom, including seeds, roots and other parts thereof."[101] Not only is this a broad definition, but it is also focuses on the entire plant. This holistic outlook is further evidence of a deep ecological influence. Just as the act defines plants in a very broad manner, it defines species likewise. Species are defined as including "any subspecies of fish or wildlife or plants, and any distinct population segment of any species of vertebrate fish or wildlife which interbreeds when mature."[102] This definition is very inclusive. It makes no distinction between species and subspecies by granting protection to all plants and animals. The deep ecologists would want it no other way.

---

[98]The actual definition of these terms, as found in the text of the act, states, "The terms 'conserve,' 'conserving' and 'conservation' mean to use and the use of all methods and procedures which are necessary to bring any endangered species or threatened species to the point at which the measures provided pursuant to this chapter are no longer necessary. Such methods and procedures include, but are not limited to, all activities associated with scientific resources management such as research, census, law enforcement, habitat acquisition and maintenance, propagation, live trapping, and transplantation, and, in the extraordinary case where population pressures within a given ecosystem cannot be otherwise relieved, may include regulated taking."

[99]*Endangered Species, U.S. Code*, title 16 (Conservation), chapt. 35, sec. 1532.

[100]Ibid.

[101]Ibid.

[102]Ibid.

To protect both species of plants and of animals, the legislators chose to define "take" as "to harass, harm, pursue, hunt, shoot, wound, kill, trap, capture, or collect, or to attempt to engage in any such conduct."[103] This, like many of the definitions in the section, is very broad in scope. It is significant that "harass" and "harm" are included in the definition. The fact that they are mentioned first gives added emphasis to all that is included under the definition of "take."

Although many of the above terms have been defined in a deep ecological manner, the term "threatened species" is an exception. A threatened species is one "which is likely to become an endangered species within the foreseeable future throughout all or a significant portion of its range."[104] This definition indicates that the act is concerned with species only when they have reached the threshold of extinction. Deep ecologists would frown at policies that condone the extinction of a species in less than a "significant portion of its range."

§ 1533. Determination of endangered species and threatened species

Section 1533 gives further insight into the ecological influences at work within the ESA. Subsection (a) discusses how the Secretary shall determine whether any species is an endangered or a threatened species. The first factor is "the present or threatened destruction, modification, or curtailment of its habitat or range."[105] It is significant from a deep ecological stand point that the ESA is in effect providing protection to the ecosystem and not just the individual species. The second factor concerns the "overutilization for commercial, recreational, scientific, or educational purposes."[106] The act does not limit the human use of species as long as they are not overutilized. This approach is more shallow, as is the third factor: disease or predation. Although it does protect species, it elevates humans to stewards of the Earth attempting to govern nature. The fifth factor (fourth omitted purposely as it was non sequitur) includes "other natural or manmade factors affecting its continued existence."[107] This final factor is also shallow in ecological outlook because it makes a conscious separation between nature and humans, which further reinforces the idea of humans, as above or separate from the environment instead of part of it, as deep ecologists believe.

Subsection (b) discusses bases for determinations. It states that "the Secretary shall designate critical habitat, and make revisions thereto, under subsection (a)(3) of this section on the basis of the best scientific data available and after taking into consideration the economic impact, and any other relevant impact, of specifying any particular area as critical habitat."[108] The inclusion of an economic impact factor is not deep ecology and seems to counter the original findings and purposes estab-

---

[103]Ibid.

[104]Ibid.

[105]*Endangered Species, U.S. Code*, title 16 (Conservation), chapt. 35, sec. 1533.

[106]Ibid.

[107]Ibid.

[108]Ibid.

lished in the beginning of the act. Additionally, the Secretary is given the ability to exclude "any area from critical habitat if he determines that the benefits of such exclusion outweigh the benefits of specifying such area as part of the critical habitat, unless he determines, based on the best scientific and commercial data available, that the failure to designate such area as critical habitat will result in the extinction of the species concerned."[109] This exception seems to seriously weaken the act. It also means that the enforcement of the act will depend on the ecological outlook of the individual Secretary of the Interior. Additionally, the act calls for a review of all species included on the endangered species list at least once every five years. Deep ecologists would just as soon protect as many species and ecosystems as possible by keeping all species on the list while adding as many new ones as possible.

In order for the public (including deep ecologists) to keep track of proposed regulations, the Secretary must publish the proposal in a newspaper of general circulation "in each area of the United States in which the species is believed to occur; and promptly hold one public hearing on the proposed regulation if any person files a request for such a hearing within 45 days after the date of publication of general notice."[110] These two provisions appear to open listings of endangered species to public review and comment, if not just notification. Educating and involving the public in environmental policy is one of the goals of the deep ecologists. Public involvement is also mandated in subsection (f), which deals with recovery plans. It too calls for "public notice and an opportunity for public review and comment on such plan. [Additionally], the Secretary shall consider all information presented during the public comment period prior to approval of the plan."[111] Though this is popular with deep ecologists, it should also be noted that it gives opportunities to private land holders, interested in economic growth, to have a say in the formation of recovery plans for endangered species.

Just as there are apparent loopholes for the exclusion of certain species, there are loopholes that do work in favor of deep ecologists. The act states that "treatment of an unlisted species will substantially facilitate the enforcement and further the policy of this chapter."[112] It appears deep ecologists could use this provision to have other species in critical habitats listed to have the eco-region protected. Subsection (f)(1)(A) gives priority to endangered or threatened species "without regard to taxonomic classification, that are most likely to benefit from [recovery] plans, particularly those species that are, or may be, in conflict with construction or other development projects or other forms of economic activity." While it may seem that this provision puts diversity ahead of development and economic growth, it actually tries to minimize the economic loss by moving species off the endangered lists as fast as possible.

---

[109]Ibid.
[110]Ibid.
[111]Ibid.
[112]Ibid.

§ 1534. Land acquisition

Section 1534 governs federal acquisition of land. It authorizes the appropriate Secretary "to acquire by purchase, donation, or otherwise, lands, waters, or interest therein, and such authority shall be in addition to any other land acquisition authority vested in him."[113] This places diversity and species protection ahead of property rights, a concept championed by the deep ecologists but shunned by the shallow ecologists.

§ 1536. Interagency cooperation

Section 1536 describes more than just interagency cooperation. It describes provisions for the taking of endangered species and the granting of exceptions. Subsection (c) states procedures for the taking of endangered or threatened marine species. It argues, as do deep ecologists, for a minimal impact on the environment. But the act does not totally exclude exemptions. For example, subsection (h) notes that exemptions may be granted if "the action is of regional or national significance."[114] Deep ecologists would take issue with this loophole that allows potentially environmental damaging activity. Subsection (j) notes that exemptions shall be granted if the Secretary of Defense finds that such exemption is "necessary for reasons of national security."[115] This again places the value of humans above that of any other species. Furthermore, the term "national security" is difficult to define precisely. Other exemptions are reserved in the case of a presidentially declared disaster area. These exemptions, however, must go through normal means unless the President determines it "(1) is necessary to prevent the recurrence of such a natural disaster and to reduce the potential loss of human life, and (2) to involve an emergency situation which does not allow the ordinary procedures of this section to be followed."[116] Although it would be difficult even for deep ecologists to criticize the above exemption, it does illustrate a firm commitment to human life over all else.

The committee that determines and grants exemptions is called the "Endangered Species Committee." The seven member committee is comprised of the Secretaries of Agriculture, of the Army, and of the Interior, the Chairman of the Council of Economic Advisors, the Administrator of the Environmental Protection Agency and of the National Oceanic and Atmospheric Administration as well as the President of the United States. This is an interesting choice of members for the committee. Deep ecologists would probably object to both the Secretary of the Army and the Chairman of the Council of Economic Advisors in favor of someone with a specialty in the field of biodiversity protection.

[113]*Endangered Species, U.S. Code*, title 16 (Conservation), chapt. 35, sec. 1534.
[114]*Endangered Species, U.S. Code*, title 16 (Conservation), chapt. 35, sec. 1536.
[115]Ibid.
[116]Ibid.

§ 1537. International cooperation and § 1537a. Convention implementation

Subsection (b), which encourages foreign programs, mandates that the Secretary of the Interior, through the Secretary of State, encourage "foreign countries to provide for the conservation of fish or wildlife and plants including endangered species and threatened species listed pursuant to section 1533 of this title."[117] This extension of the reach of biodiversity protection is very deep ecological in outlook (remember Devall and Sessions call for global action through the United Nations). Section 1537a also calls for international cooperation and action to ensure that migratory birds are given the same treatment across state lines as they are given within them.

§ 1538. Prohibited acts

The most significant aspect of section 1538 from a deep ecology point of view is that many of the prohibited acts are economically oriented. For example, the act prohibits the selling or offering for sale in interstate or foreign commerce any species that is either threatened or endangered. Furthermore, the act states that "it is unlawful for any person, without first having obtained permission from the Secretary, to engage in business—as an importer or exporter of fish or wildlife . . . or plants; or as an importer or exporter of any amount of raw or worked African elephant ivory."[118] To the delight of deep ecologists, these provisions all place the protection of species above trade and economic growth.

§ 1539. Exceptions

Exceptions to tough environmental legislation are feared by deep ecologists. The most notable of the exemptions listed in this section is the hardship exemption. It states:

If any person enters into a contract with respect to a species of fish or wildlife or plant before the date of the publication in the Federal Register of notice of consideration of that species as an endangered species and the subsequent listing of that species as an endangered species pursuant to section 1533 of this title will cause undue economic hardship to such person under the contract, the Secretary, in order to minimize such hardship, may exempt such person from the application of section 1538(a) of this title to the extent the Secretary deems appropriate if such person applies to him for such exemption and includes with such application such information as the Secretary may require to prove such hardship.[119]

Despite the deep ecological influence found throughout this act, especially when economic issues are involved, the hardship exemption is characteristic of a shallow ecological influence. It is anthropocentric in outlook but probably politically necessary

---

[117]*Endangered Species, U.S. Code*, title 16 (Conservation), chapt. 35, sec. 1537.
[118]*Endangered Species, U.S. Code*, title 16 (Conservation), chapt. 35, sec. 1538.
[119]Ibid.

for the passage of the act. The act does define "undue economic hardship," but in such a manner as to entrench a shallow ecological perspective by viewing species as a resource.[120] The debates over the spotted owl in the Pacific Northwest a few years ago illustrate how economic and political costs have "whittled away at the Act's near-absolute commitment to species survival."[121]

Deep ecology shares an identification with primal and native peoples. This identification can also be found in the ESA. It allows Alaskan village natives to take endangered fish and wildlife for consumption or for the "creation and sale of authentic native articles of handicrafts and clothing."[122] This faith in the ability of native peoples to live in harmony with the land is singled out in the ESA and by the deep ecologists.

§ 1540. Penalties and enforcement

Section 1540 of the ESA is the teeth of the legislation. For example, "all guns, traps, nets, and other equipment, vessels, vehicles, aircraft, and other means of transportation used to aid the taking, possessing, selling, purchasing, offering for sale or purchase, transporting, delivering, receiving, carrying, shipping, exporting, or importing of any fish or wildlife or plants in violation of this chapter, any regulation made pursuant thereto, or any permit or certificate issued thereunder shall be subject to forfeiture to the United States upon conviction of a criminal violation pursuant to subsection (b)(1) of this section."[123] When it comes to penalties and means of enforcement, biodiversity is placed much higher than economic interests.

§ 1544. Annual cost analysis by Fish and Wildlife Service

The final section of the ESA bears more of a shallow than a deep ecological approach. It calls for an annual accounting "on a species by species basis of all reasonably identifiable Federal expenditures made primarily for the conservation of endangered or threatened species pursuant to this chapter."[124] A deep ecological approach would rather save the money from such an accounting and use it for more land acquisition and better programs to protect species and ecosystems.

Overall, the ESA is unlike any piece of environmental legislation that preceded it. There is a very noticeable deep ecological influence in both its purpose and policies. While species are still not given intrinsic worth under the act, they and their respected ecosystems are given broad protection, even at the expense of economic development.

---

[120]For a discussion of the ethical choices represented in the act and other environmental statutes, see Mark Sagoff, "Economic Theory and Environmental Law," *Michigan Law Review* 79 (1981): 1393, 1396–1397.

[121]Dobbins, "The Pain and Suffering of Environmental Loss: Using Contingent Valuation to Estimate Nonuse Damages," p. 879.

[122]*Endangered Species, U.S. Code*, title 16 (Conservation), chapt. 35, sec. 1538.

[123]*Endangered Species, U.S. Code*, title 16 (Conservation), chapt. 35, sec. 1540.

[124]*Endangered Species, U.S. Code*, title 16 (Conservation), chapt. 35, sec. 1544.

Still, the act is not what it could be according to law professor Oliver A. Houck. Houck, after reviewing its provisions and the history of its implementations, concludes that the ESA, through a series of amendments, has become a discretionary permit system. He believes that these compromises may serve to only slow down, instead of abate, the rate of species decline. Perhaps even more ominous for deep ecologists are the prospects of new taking legislation, touted by many conservative lawmakers. Such legislation would compensate landowners when "'regulatory takings' diminish their ability to make a profit. Since the staff and funds are not available to implement such requirements, the ESA would not be enforced on private lands."[125]

CONCLUSION

For some, including many deep ecologists, the environmental picture looks gloomier than ever. They acknowledge the beneficial legislation of the '60s and '70s starting with the Wilderness Act, but take issue with the current bureaucratic and piecemeal approach to environmental protection. Conservation biologists Reed F. Noss and Allen Y. Cooperrider note that "we have laws, regulations, and agencies set up to protect aspects of the environment, yet none of them has measured up to the challenge of protecting biodiversity as a whole."[126] Despite this gloomy outlook, this analysis of major environmental legislation provides evidence of an increasing deep ecological influence. For instance, the Clean Water Act and the ESA illustrate a much greater deep ecological outlook than the Clean Air Act or the National Wilderness Act. The five pieces of environmental legislation examined in this study are fairly representative of Congressional environmental acts. In addition, they also serve as the basis of environmental policy today, even though they were first written twenty to thirty years ago.[127]

The Clean Air Act centered on human needs by singling out public health and welfare. It entrenched the economic growth mindset as well as the extrinsic worth of species (forests in particular). The act called for the inclusion of economic costs into the execution of environmental policy. This early piece of environmental legislation exhibits anthropocentric ideals and a shallow ecological influence. The National Wilderness Act hinted of some deep ecological ideas, but embraced the concept of stewardship and human ownership of the land. It incorporated the Pinchot school of conservationism and took an overall shallow stance toward ecological issues. The NEPA also exhibited a shallow ecological influence. It was more concerned with public health and welfare than with ecological well-being. This statement of environ-

---

[125]McCullough, "Through the Eye of a Needle: The Earth's Hard Passage back to Health," p. 389.

[126]Reed F. Noss and Allen Y. Cooperrider, quoted in McCullough, "Through the Eye of a Needle: The Earth's Hard Passage back to Health," p. 389.

[127]Though these acts were often written more than twenty years ago, many have subsequently been amended. The wording and language of these amendments also help to illustrate the evolving influence of deep ecological thought.

mental policy separated humans from nature while buying into the ideas of human ownership of land and extrinsic worth of species.

The Clean Water Act represents a turning point in environmental legislation. Its statement of intent is deep ecological in outlook. While the act does not go as far as the opening may suggest, the overall change in tone is significant and should be considered as a small victory by the deep ecologists. Finally, the ESA exhibits many deep ecological tenets. It is perhaps the most popular piece of federal legislation with the deep ecologists. To some degree, the act indicts economic growth and development and calls for global action to preserve endangered species. The act does, however, continue to subscribe to some shallow ecological perspectives. The hardship exemption is one example of placing the economic needs of humans above those of the environment. Thus, the progression of deep ecological ideas in federal legislation is apparent in this study. Not only were later pieces of legislation more deep ecological, but subsequent amendments to individual pieces of legislation were also more deep ecological than the original act. While this analysis of legislation has provided clues as to the influence of deep ecology on environmental politics, it supplies no statistical evidence to quantify this influence. Chapters 6 and 7 will attempt to fill this void as well as examine the influence of deep ecology over the past three years.

6

Congressional Testimony: Politics of Words

This chapter examines congressional hearings in an attempt to find clues as to the effects of deep ecology on environmental politics. Congressional hearings have been an intrinsic part of the political process throughout the history of American government. When senators or representatives have wanted to make changes in policy, one of their first actions has traditionally been to call for hearings on the matter. And though those called upon to testify are usually experts in their field, it is politics that determines who is selected to testify, why the hearing is called, and what is said at the hearings. Law makers have significant influence on congressional hearings. Thus it is possible to learn many things from these hearings. While the subject and subjects of hearings provide insight into the motivations and beliefs of the legislature, the actual testimony given provides insight into the direction of public policy. For example, when Representative John D. Dingell (D-Mich.) wanted action on a particular environmental matter, he called a hearing that he expected would "establish a factual predicate for, and demonstrate the necessity of a top-level reexamination of the role of the Department of Justice headquarters in environmental criminal enforcement."[1]

Many famous environmentalists have testified before congressional committees. Rachel Carson's testimony in 1963 led to the formation of a government-appointed, special panel of scientists to investigate her claims of pesticide poisoning (which found them to be 100 percent correct).[2] David Brower testified against the construction of the Dinosaur Dam.[3] Congressional testimony can thus illuminate the relationship between deep ecology and environmental politics. It can also display the current

---

[1]John D. Dingell, quoted in "Politics Suspected in Environmental Prosecutions," *Chemical and Engineering News* (November 22, 199): 26.

[2]Phyllis M. Stanley, *American Environmental Heroes* (Springfield, NJ: Enslow Publishers, 1996): 74.

[3]Ibid., p. 82.

"pulse of America" by providing a window into the thoughts and actions of those involved in the political process throughout the country. The questions which need to be answered include:

- Are deep ecologists selected to testify and express their views?
- What deep ecological ideas are introduced into the minds of legislators?
- What do individuals say regarding deep ecology?

This chapter is in some respects a tedious analyzation of the rhetoric and syntax of congressional testimony. It combines both content analysis and communication research to produce a comprehensive study of the language of congressional hearings. Though some may feel this examination to be too laborious, it does allow the reader the ability to gain an in-depth understanding of environmental congressional testimony without having to trudge through thousands of pages him or herself.

SURVEY METHOD

To answer these questions, all Congressional testimony between July of 1993 and June of 1996 was examined. This allowed a sample divided between two different Congresses. Using Lexis/Nexis to examine the full text of every piece of testimony, various deep ecological terms and ideas were located. Such terms included "deep ecology," "anthropocentrism," "environmental ethic," "Earth First!," and many others. Should a term find its way into a piece of rhetoric, that testimony would be examined and analyzed to answer the questions set out above. The search terms were categorized into four groups: (1) deep ecological language, (2) environmental ethics, (3) environ-mental consciousness, and (4) deep ecological groups and individuals.

DECIPHERING THE LANGUAGE OF CONGRESSIONAL TESTIMONY

Deep Ecological Language

This section examines the usage of certain terms associated with deep ecology. These include "deep ecology," "shallow ecology," "anthropocentrism," "ecocentrism," "biocentrism," and others. In congressional testimony since July 1993, the term "deep ecology" is mentioned only once. This one mention was by Doug Crandall, who testified before the Subcommittee on the National Park, Forests, and Public Lands. Crandall blasted a recent book entitled *Clearcut—The Tragedy of Industrial Forestry*, for its deception and its basis in a spiritually crazed unscientific belief of deep ecology. He stated, "This fits (so to speak) as much of the text of the book seems to be founded in deep—I would say very, very deep—ecology."[4] Crandall sarcastically remarks that the book, edited by the deep ecologist Bill Devall, asks readers "to 'think like

---

[4]Doug Crandall, "H.R. 1164, The National Parks, Forests and Public Lands, Subcom-mittee," *Federal Document Clearing House Congressional Testimony* (May 5, 1994).

a forest' and . . . to engage in 'tree meditations.'"[5] As the only reference to deep ecology in a three-year time span, this shows either that deep ecology has taken on such a negative connotation that even deep ecologists won't utter the term, or that deep ecologists and sympathizers of ecological beliefs have been excluded from the political process (in terms of congressional hearings).

There has been only one mention of the term "deep ecology;" the term "shallow ecology" fared even worse. Even though it would seem that many of those who testify before Congress have shallow ecological outlooks (see Chapter 7), the lack of any mention of the term is not surprising because it is used primarily by deep ecologists to describe the "other half." Anthropocentrism (and derivatives there of) was mentioned twice in Congressional hearings during the three-year time period. The first piece of testimony was a statement by the Honorable Gerry E. Stubbs, Chairman of the Subcommittee on Environment and Natural Resources.[6] It would be difficult to find a deep ecologists who did not agree with Stubbs' rhetoric. He testified that current anthropocentric attitudes toward wetlands should be replaced with a more environmentally centered perspective like the ones shared by John Muir and Aldo Leopold. The Congressman stated that society must reverse its disastrous past efforts to make the wetlands productive by extending to them the intrinsic worth they deserve as being part of the Earth. There is a definite deep ecological influence in the testimony of Congressman Stubbs. Because Stubbs is directly involved in the making of environmental legislation, the deep ecological ideas he expressed are perhaps very illuminating as to the effect deep ecology has had on environmental politics. It shows that at least certain members of the Congress hold deep ecological viewpoints.

The second individual to testify before Congress and use the term "anthropocentric" was Clifton Curtis of Greenpeace.[7] Curtis discussed the need for action concerning sunken nuclear Soviet submarines in the Arctic Ocean. His language incorporated a number of deep ecological perspectives such as an identification with indigenous people as well as with all species that inhabit the environment. The Oceans Advisor of Greenpeace International argued for international action, just as Devall and Sessions did in their ground-breaking book. Curtis's references drew from primarily anthropocentric language, describing the human health risk as well as the economic benefits of cleaning up the site. This is the same language used by shallow ecologists. While Curtis did express some deep ecological thoughts, he did not fully subscribe to the ecophilosophy. Nevertheless, the negative connotation toward the term "anthropocen-

---

[5]Ibid.

[6]Gerry Studds, "Statement of the Honorable Gerry E. Studds, Chairman Subcommittee on Environment and Natural Resources H.R. 4308," *Federal Document Clearing House Congressional Testimony* (June 8, 1994).

[7]Clifton Curtis, "Statement of Clifton Curtis, Ocean Advisor, Political Unit, Greenpeace International, Before the Subcommittee on Oceanography Committee on Merchant Marine and Fisheries, U.S. House of Representatives Concerning Radioactive Contamination in the Arctic Ocean," *Federal Document Clearing House Congressional Testimony* (September 30, 1993).

tric" exhibited by both Stubbs and Curtis illustrates at least a growing dissatisfaction with shallow ecology and perhaps a welcoming of a more deep ecological perspective.

A search for the terms "ecocentrism" and "biocentrism" found no mention of the former and only one of the latter. The single reference to biocentrism was in the testimony of Mark A. Davidson, an upset and angry property owner.[8] He was upset with the Endangered Species Act (ESA) (which has already been determined to have a deep ecological influence) because it precludes the development of his land if an endangered species has a habitat either on or near his property. His narrative makes a compelling case that the federal environmental law is too inflexible. Davidson feels the federal government is being bullied by groups with a radical biocentric outlook (deep ecologists). According to the property owner, the biocentric outlook of the ESA is turning people from nature lovers into endangered species haters. Davidson's testimony is definitely anti–deep ecology, but it is important because it illustrates that deep ecological principles have influenced environmental politics and policies.

The final term under this subheading of deep ecological terms is "radical environmental" and its derivatives. Since July of 1993, the term was used in four separate pieces of congressional testimony. All four criticized radical environmental groups and policies. The first testimony was by William Perry, the President and Chief Legal Officer of the Mountain States Legal foundation (James Watt's organization;[9] this alone should give a good idea of Perry's ideological background). Perry testified before the House Judiciary committee about the harmful effects and inherent injustices of affirmative action. He never even mentions environmental issues except for a tangential remark that Americans are rebelling against "the philosophy of social engineering that underlies radical environmental policies."[10] His language is anti–deep ecology, though probably more anti–social ecology, in outlook. Overall, he discusses the environment very little and one wonders why he decided to insert such a denunciation in a 7,500-plus–word statement on affirmative action.

Congressman Robert K. Dornan (affectionately known by some as "Crazy Bob" or "B2 Bob") opened his testimony on a bill he authored to increase the integrity of the government by halting all federal payments to non-profit organizations that

---

[8]Mark A. Davidson, "Testimony of Mark A. Davidson Before the Subcommittee on Clean Water, Fisheries and Wildlife, Senate Committee on Environment and Public Works, Endangered Species Conservation on Private Property," *Federal Document Clearing House Congressional Testimony* (July 19, 1994).

[9]James Watt was the Secretary of the Interior under President Ronald Reagan. Watt became a bitter enemy of most all environmentalists and is credited with turning back much of the environmental gains made in the 1970s. Ironically, he is also credited with dramatically increasing membership in environmental groups by providing environmentalists with an easy target to rally its cause.

[10]William Perry, "House Judiciary Committee, Justice Department's Civil Rights Division," *Federal Document Clearing House Congressional Testimony* (July 20, 1995).

lobby Congress.[11] Within his testimony was an attack against radical environmentalists and consumer groups who clog the judicial system with a plethora of "citizen" suits. According to Dornan, these suits are a form of "legal extortion." As discussed in Chapter 3, the utilization of the court system is one of the preferred ways deep ecologists are able to influence environmental politics. Such tactics have caught the eye of Congress and those who oppose the radical environmentalists are searching for ways to stop these actions.

Radical environmental groups were targeted as the scapegoat in a speech given before the House Committee on Resources by Gaylan Precott.[12] Precott, the President of the Longview Federated Aluminum Council, argued that radical environmental groups were causing the federal government to protect a sub-species of salmon that will cost up to a billion dollars a year. This would significantly increase the price of electricity to the residents of the Northwest as well as hurt the global competitiveness of the aluminum manufacturers in the area. The language was extremely anthropocentric to the extent that it went beyond shallow ecology to anti-ecology. Ironically, Precott says that he supports the salmon but does not want his company to have to absorb any of the costs. This testimony illustrates that deep ecologists have had great success using the ESA. Precott's statement is a tribute to the success of radical environmental groups in protecting habitats even when economic interests are high. But the testimony also parallels a change in the mood of Congress, from one of firm support of the ESA under the Democrats to a less supportive environment under the control of Republicans.

The final mention of the term "radical environmental" is found in a 1993 piece of testimony by Robert MacMullin, a consulting forester.[13] His statement clearly treated the environment as something to be used and harvested by humans. Coupled with his anthropocentric outlook was his opposition to any further government purchase of land that would preclude more logging. He blames radical environmental groups that have already shut down many mills and cost hundreds of job. MacMullin is perhaps a good example of the antithesis of deep ecology. This testimony also acknowledges the impact and influence that deep ecologists have had on environmental policy in the United States. It is significant that all four mentions of radical environmental groups were negative and from pro-business advocates. These instances illustrate where the battle lines are frequently drawn. But each of the statements also testifies to the influence that deep ecology has had in recent years in the political arena. Every piece of congressional testimony found in this section spoke to the rise of radical

---

[11]Robert K. Dornan, "Remarks by Congressman Robert K. Dornan Before the House Judiciary Subcommittee on the Constitution," *Federal Document Clearing House Congressional Testimony* (May 23, 1995).

[12]Gaylan Prescott, "Testimony of Gaylan Prescott, President of the Longview Federated Aluminum Council, Before the House Committee on Resources," *Federal Document Clearing House Congressional Testimony* (April 24, 1995).

[13]Robert MacMullin, "Testimony by Robert MacMullin, Consulting Forester, MacMullin Forestry and Logging, Before the Subcommittee on National Parks, Forests and Public Lands, Committee on Natural Resources, H.R. 2866 Headwaters Forest Act," *Federal Document Clearing House Congressional Testimony* (October 12, 1993).

environmentalism as a serious player in environmental politics. However, the small number of times in which deep ecology terms were mentioned indicates that the movement still has much further to go.

Environmental Ethics

The term "environmental ethic" has been used by many to describe deep ecology and other philosophies that argue for a more value-oriented and responsible environmental outlook. The term itself was used on thirty-two different occasions before congressional committees. Twenty-three of these statements were made by individuals who shared a shallow ecological outlook. Of these, only nine were non-military related.

The first of the non-military testimonials was by George D. Caruolo, the majority leader of the Rhode Island House of Representatives.[14] He testified about the harmful effects that possible de-regulation of the power production industry could have on the environment. The majority leader described the "pulse" of Rhode Island and New England as sharing a strong environmental ethic. His testimony certainly did not match the tenets of deep ecology, but the idea of having an environmental ethic is a first step nonetheless. However, Caruolo did seem to embrace the notion of competition and economic development, which is very shallow in ecological outlook. As will be seen later, the predominance of an economic development mindset is shared by the majority of those who testify before Congress.

The testimony delivered by Dan V. Bartosh, Jr., was also shallow in its ecological outlook. Bartosh, who is the corporate environmental manager of Texas Instruments (TI), commented that "TI believes that a strong economy and a healthy environment are mutually reinforcing goals."[15] He finds fault with the current Environmental Protection Agency (EPA) Clean Air regulation, which he described as bureaucratic and as having a negative effect on the environment. Bartosh believes that TI goes above and beyond current environmental standards by decreasing and preventing pollution. The group he represents "also share a strong and proactive environmental ethic and support the fundamental premise of the Clean Air Act—clean air for every American."[16] Although the environmental manager is very in-tune with the deep ecologists' belief in decentralization, he is a firm supporter of the industrial society and economic competitiveness. Bartosh has embraced a shallow ecological outlook.

---

[14]George D. Caruolo, "Testimony of George D. Caruolo, Majority Leader, Rhode Island House of Representatives, Before the House Energy and Power Subcommittee," *Federal Document Clearing House Congressional Testimony* (February 27, 1996).

[15]Dan V. Bartosh, Jr., "The Operating Permit Program Requirements of the Clean Air Act, the Subcommittee on Clean Air, Wetlands, Private Property and Nuclear Safety, of the Senate Committee on Environment and Public Works," *Federal Document Clearing House Congressional Testimony* (August 1, 1995).

[16]Ibid.

James E. Loesel, of the Southern Appalachian Forest Coalition, shares that same outlook.[17] He does make reference to some deep ecological ideas such as regional control and the preservation of cultural heritage, but his overriding reasons for the preservation of forests were rather anthropocentric. His language indicated a separation between humans, the forests, the environment, and the ecosystem. Another individual to use the term "environmental ethics" was Dr. Saul Fenster, President of the New Jersey Institute of Technology.[18] He testified before the Senate Appropriations committee about the work of the Institute, which is primarily concerned with pollution prevention. The text of the testimony contains largely evidence of a shallow ecological approach to the environment. Perhaps most telling is the definition Fenster contextually provides of the term "environmental ethics." He describes it as the notion that pollution prevention is an important part of professional decision making. Such environmental ethics are being taught in an undergraduate student program sponsored by the Institute. This does not sound very biocentric, but rather is an anthropocentric idea of environmental ethics; after all, "professional decision making" indicates an industrial society.

The Chemical Manufacturers Association (CMA), in a written statement to the Senate Subcommittee on the Environment and Toxic Substance, argued that voluntary compliance and environmental action is better than regulation and that partnership is better than subservientship.[19] The wording of the statement is very anthropocentric and subscribes to the "greatest good for the greatest number (of humans)" moral framework. It does share deep ecology's decentralization ideal as well as the idea of an environmental ethic that is practiced by people and not imposed by the government. But this could also be attributed to the capitalistic nature of the chemical industry. The CMA describe themselves as product stewards but point to a changing environmental ethic in which those who make the products examine the life cycle of the chemicals. Nonetheless, stewardship and perpetuation of human progress are very shallow ecological ideas.

Business representatives and politicians are not the only ones who use the term "environmental ethics." Lori Garver, the executive director of the National Space Society, also employed the term in her testimony.[20] Rather than supporting deep

---

[17]James E. Loesel, "Testimony of James E. Loesel, Representative of the Southern Appalachian Forest Coalition, Before the Senate Energy Committee, Forests and Public Land Management Subcommittee, on the matter of Forest Service Land Management," *Federal Document Clearing House Congressional Testimony* (April 5, 1995).

[18]Saul Fenster, "Testimony of Saul Fenster, President New Jersey Institute of Technology, Senate Appropriations/Va, HUD and Independent Agencies, FY 95 VA/HUD Appropriations," *Federal Document Clearing House Congressional Testimony* (May 20, 1994).

[19]Chemical Manufacturers Association, "Written Statement of the Chemical Manufacturers Association, Senate Environment/Toxic Substances, Research and Development," *Federal Document Clearing House Congressional Testimony* (May 17, 1994).

[20]Lori Garver, "Testimony of Lori Garver Before the U.S. House of Represenatives Committee on Science, Space and Technology, Subcommittee on Space," *Federal Document Clearing House Congressional Testimony* (February 23, 1994).

ecology, Garver's statement is the antithesis of deep ecology. She advocates a space-faring civilization as remedy to the current environmental destruction. In what deep ecologists would describe as a twisted interpretation of the Gaia Hypothesis, Garver says it is up to the human race to seed new environments with life. Her approach is very shallow in ecological outlook by looking to space to fulfill the human appetite for resources.

The concept of zoos and aquariums is an inherently shallow ecological approach to the environment. Robert Jenkins, who testified on the behalf of the American Zoo and Aquarium Association and the Alliance of Marine Mammal Parks and Aquariums, discussed the many benefits that zoos and aquariums bring to both local communities (financial) and the global environment (species restoration).[21] The mood and tone of the testimony are very anthropocentric despite highlighting a care for animal species. The approach is shallow, not deep, from an ecological perspective, and the term "environmental ethic" is not even used to describe a new approach to environmental policy.

The final two pieces of non-military congressional testimony that used the term environmental ethic were presented by senior officials in U.S. businesses. Gerald M. Keenan, Senior Vice President of the Bellevue Corporation, testified to the effectiveness of market-based environmental policies.[22] Though his arguments in favor of decentralization and of a guiding environmental ethic subscribe to the tenets of deep ecology, his anthropocentric outlooks as well as vested interest in the success of the industrial society make him a definite shallow ecologist. Dr. Joseph Sullivan, of the Ciba-Geigy Corporation, also testified about the need for market-based environmental policies.[23] He described the new environmental ethic of businesses and of the government, which realizes that environmental excellence and jobs go hand-in-hand. This approach to the environment is inherently shallow because its main focus is growth and the perpetuation of the industrial society. Deep ecological literature has a lot to say about the industrial society. Many view it as the primary source of both human and environmental degradation, for it separates humans from their natural environment while preaching progress through continued development of the land. It is interesting that those promoting economic growth describe themselves or their organization as

---

[21]Robert Jenkins, "Testimony of the American Zoo and Aquarium Association and the Alliance of Marine Mammal Parks and Aquariums Presented Before the Subcommittee on Environment and Natural Resources," *Federal Document Clearing House Congressional Testimony* (February 10, 1994).

[22]Gerald M. Keenan, "Testimony of Gerald M. Keenan, Senior Vice President, Palmer Bellevue Coporation, Senate Environment/Clean Air Implementation of Acid Rain Provisions of the Clean Air Act," *Federal Document Clearing House Congressional Testimony* (October 21, 1993).

[23]Joseph Sullivan, "Testimony of Dr. Joseph Sullivan Before the Senate Environment and Public Works Committee, Implimentation of the Clean Air Act Amendments of 1990," *Federal Document Clearing House Congressional Testimony* (September 23, 1993).

adhering to an environmental ethic. Needless to say, deep ecologists define the term very differently.

Thus, although each of the previous nine individuals who testified before Congress used the term "environmental ethic" in a positive manner, it does not make their testimony deep ecological. In fact, each of those who presented statements shared a shallow ecological outlook on environmental policy. While those who testified above were predominantly representatives of businesses, the military has come to incorporate the term "environmental ethic" into their testimony as well. The Air Force, Army, and Navy all used the term on more than one occasion when testifying before Congress during the three-year period.

The three instances where the Air Force incorporated the term all bore striking similarities. Though the three pieces of testimony were given by three individuals, they all basically shared the same wording when it came to environmental matters. Major General Eugene A. Lupia's speech writer probably originated the wording, which also found its way into the statement of the Deputy Assistant Secretary of the Air Force Jimmy G. Dishner, as well as into the testimony of Rodney A. Coleman, the Assistant Secretary of the Air Force.[24] In each statement, the Air Force official describes how their branch of the military instills an environmental ethic in its personnel. Although this does hint of deep ecology, other sections of their testimonies illustrate a shallow ecological outlook. They discuss the restoration of the environment for the sake of humans only. Examples include the building of sewers and other types of sanitary equipment designed to ensure human health and welfare. The texts talk about an environmental ethic in the same paragraph as they do about leveraging resources and putting "people first." In all, the official position is one of ownership and stewardship of the land, an idea very far from the beliefs of deep ecologists.

"Environmental ethic" has also found its way into Army rhetoric. Lewis D. Walker, then Deputy Assistant Secretary of the Army, testified before the Military Installations and Facilities Subcommittee of the House Committee on Armed Services on April 19, 1994.[25] He talked about an environmental ethic that the Army ingrained into its distinguished men and women. He states that "environmental stewardship, both here and overseas, is our responsibility, our legacy and our future." Walker's idea of an environmental ethic, one in which humans include the environment in their moral and value frameworks, would classify as deep ecological rhetoric. But the testimony rings heavily of shallow ecology and anthropocentrism. Humans are stewards, not part of the environment. Furthermore, the reasons behind saving the environment stem from practical human needs such as ensuring that natural resources and training grounds be available to the armies of tomorrow. Walker's ideas and almost exact

---

[24]Though many accuse the government of waste, when it comes to wording, they are among the leaders in recycling and reusing.

[25]Lewis D. Walker, "Testimony of Lewis D. Walker, Deputy Assistant Secretary for Environment and Safety Department of the Army, House Armed Services/Military Installations and Facilities, FY '95 Defense Authorization," *Federal Document Clearing House Congressional Testimony* (April 19, 1994).

words would find themselves before Congress on six additional occasions within fourteen months of the original testimony.

Not to be outdone by either the Air Force or the Army, Cheryl A. Kandaras, of the U.S. Navy, with some help from the honorable Dave McCurdy, also testified about an environmental ethic. The Kandaras speech would be used on three separate occasions before congressional committees.[26] It discusses institutionalizing and instilling an environmental ethic into the daily operations of the men and women of the Navy. She mentions compliance to environmental regulations, new environmental cleanup technologies, further recycling efforts, and environmental training as the cornerstones of the Navy's environmental programs. The wording is mostly anthropocentric with humans as stewards of the environment. The principal benefactors of these efforts are humans. Additionally, Kandaras describes environmental technologies as "paying off" not in terms of species saved but in monetary terms. The Air Force, Army, and Navy all shared a shallow ecological outlook on environmental issues, but an environmentally sensitive one nonetheless.

Of the thirty-two instances where the term "environmental ethic" was used in congressional testimony, none had a deep ecological outlook and only six had a mix of both deep and shallow ecological perspectives.[27] What is perhaps even more significant is that not a single one of those six who testified represented a business. The split between shallow and deep ecology almost mirrors the split between pro-business and con-business advocates. The most notable of those who testified on behalf of regulated business was Carol M. Browner, the Administrator for the EPA.[28] Browner testified alongside Richard Rominger, Deputy Secretary of the U.S. Department of Agriculture, and David A. Kessler, Commissioner of the Food and Drug Administration. After a close consideration of their lengthy testimony, there do seem to be traces of deep ecology in the testimony. They talk about the phasing out of pesticides in favor of more environmentally friendly farming techniques (that is, integrated pest management) as well as market-based incentives and decentralized initiatives.

The fact that they each represent a federal agency entrenches the centralization of current environmental policy counter to the deep ecologists' wishes. However, since these administrators seem to be at least allowing decentralized pilot programs, it is a move toward a greater deep ecological influence in environmental policy. The reason that this testimony cannot be considered entirely deep ecological was that it still relied on anthropocentric ideals and motivations. Executive agencies charged

---

[26]Kandaras testified before Congress on April 20, 1994, May 4, 1994, and May 17, 1994.

[27]The remaining three instances were neutral and not applicable to this analysis, and thus, although counted as part of the thirty-two overall mentions, they are not reviewed here.

[28]Carol Browner, et al., "Testimony of Carol M. Browner, Administrator, U.S. Environmental Protection Agency, Richard Rominger, Deputy Secretary, U.S. Department of Agriculture, and David A. Kessler, Commissioner, Food and Drug Adminstration before Subcommittee on Department Operations and Nutrition, Committee on Agriculture, U.S. House of Representatives," *Federal Document Clearing House Congressional Testimony* (September 22, 1993).

with the enforcement of broad congressional mandates have a large influence over environmental policy in the United States. The direction of these agencies is often affected by the personalities of their chief administrator. Thus the ideals and motivations of these individuals are extremely important in determining the effect of deep ecology on environmental politics. The mix of both shallow and deep ecological beliefs held by Browner, Rominger, and Kessler indicates a penetration of deep ecological thought into policy making.

Lynn R. Goldman, M.D., also a government official, testified before the Senate Subcommittee on the Environment and Toxic Substances in May of 1994.[29] The assistant administrator in the Office of Prevention had some very deep ecology–like ideas when it came to empowering people and making environmental ethics a part of everyone's decision calculus. Her framework was both anthropocentric and bio-centric. Though it appears Goldman's focus is mainly a safe environment for humans, the administrator does acknowledge the need to protect the environment for the environment's sake. The talk of an expanding environmental ethic is interesting and acknowledges that environmental issues have come to the forefront of policy making in recent years.

It is interesting that although two environmental activists testified from a shallow ecological perspective, not a single one testified from a deep ecological point of view. Dunwood Zaelke did, however, present a mixed statement to Congress.[30] Zaelke, the President of the Center for International Environment, came very close to espousing the philosophies of deep ecology before Congress. His distrust for the free market due to its inability to preserve the environment (though he believes it is the strongest engine for such environmental reform), as well as his belief in an environmental ethic through increased education, both point to a deep ecological perspective. Zaelke argues that the Earth is no longer sustainable due to human environmental degradation and references both Robert Kaplan's article on the "Coming Anarchy" and Lester Brown's "Vital Signs of the Environment" as proof. Zaelke does not go as far as many deep ecologists, but his testimony is many steps beyond any other statement so far examined.

Dr. Donald M. Waller, the only professor to testify before Congress who used the term "environmental ethic," is a botanist and conservation biologist at the University of Wisconsin.[31] He testified on two different occasions about the unwillingness of

---

[29]Lynn R. Goldman, "Testimony, Lynn R. Goldman, M.D., Assistant Administrator, Office of Prevention, Senate Environment/Toxic Substances, Research and Development," *Federal Document Clearing House Congressional Testimony* (May 17, 1994).

[30]Dunwood Zaelke, "Testimony, Dunwood Zaelke, President, Center for International Environmental Law, House Banking/Intnernational Development, Finances, Trade and Monetary Policy, International Labor and Environmental Standards," *Federal Document Clearing House Congressional Testimony* (March 23, 1994).

[31]Donald M. Waller, "Testimony, Dr. Donald M. Waller, Botanist, University of Wisconsin, Madison, Joint Natural Resources/National Parks, Forests and Public Lands and Oversight and Investigations, Reform of the Forest Service," *Federal Document Clearing House Congressional Testimony* (February 1, 1994). .

the U.S. Forest Service to listen to and incorporate the principles of conservation biology into its workings. Waller shares some of the tenets of deep ecology such as a holistic understanding as well as a respect for all species. He also places the value of the land and of the entire environment above monetary and human-centered activities. His recommendations were a mix of both shallow and deep ecology approaches. Although he heavily favors species diversity even when it comes at the expense of economic development or recreation, he does view the Forest Service as stewards of the land. Conservation biology is a topic that is frequently discussed in deep ecological literature. Waller's analysis that the Forest Service does not act according to the principles of conservation biology suggests a lack of deep ecological influence in this government agency.

The final piece of testimony examined here came from Youngstown Bishop James Malone who used rhetoric much like the deep ecologists to argue for a new environmental ethic.[32] But his message is much more like Bookchin's social ecology than Naess's deep ecology. The bishop is part of the environmental justice movement that seeks to help the poor and impoverished who are frequently the victims (besides the environment) of environmental degradation. The fusion of the church and religion into an environmental ethic is very interesting because the rhetoric is very similar to the deep ecologist's except that the underlying motive is different. It should not be surprising that deep ecology has been described as a religion in and of itself.

Each of the individuals who used the term "environmental ethic" can be classified as an environmentalist. For the environmental movement, overall, this is a promising sign. But for the deep ecology movement, the institutionalization of the mainstream can often be the worst enemy of the radical fringe. The overwhelming majority of these environmentalists discussed here subscribed to a shallow ecological outlook. None endorsed a complete deep ecological perspective and only six exhibited signs of both ecological viewpoints. Deep ecologists believe that the only way to save both the environment and humankind is through a change in ethics. Thus what becomes the meaning of "environmental ethics" will be of utmost importance.

Environmental Consciousness

Another term that has been used to describe deep ecology is "environmental consciousness." Although hardly synonymous with deep ecology, the term does suggest a deeper environmental perspective. During the time span from July of 1993 to June of 1996 there were ten instances in which the term was used in congressional testimony. Seven of the ten shared a shallow ecological outlook, with only two exhibiting a mix of both shallow and deep ecological rhetoric. The remaining piece of congressional testimony did not fall into any category because it was neutral and not applicable to this study.

---

[32]James Malone, "Testimony, Rev. James Malone, Bishop, Youngstown, House Energy–Transportation, Environmental Justice," *Federal Document Clearing House Congressional Testimony* (November 18, 1993).

Becky Doyle, Director of the Illinois Department of Agriculture, testified on behalf of the National Association of State Departments of Agriculture about a new environmental consciousness that was manifesting itself in the need for renewable agriculture.[33] The idea of a self-sustaining agricultural industry as well as of a renewable food and energy supply is deep ecological. But Doyle's overall tone is anthropocentric, putting people first by doing what is best for humans. There also seemed to be an overriding economic message that "green" crops were good because consumers were willing to pay more for such food (evidently due to a new environmental consciousness). Doyle's testimony was based on a statement submitted to the Senate Agriculture, Nutrition, and Forestry Subcommittee on Research, Nutrition, and General Legislation, by the National Association of State Departments of Agriculture. In that statement, the Association argued for successful local and regional agricultural markets as well as for the decentralization of governmental programs. Alan T. Tracy, Secretary of the Wisconsin Department of Agriculture, Trade, and Consumer Protection, also testified before Congress on this subject from this same perspective.[34]

Another state official who testified before Congress was John P. Carey, of the Alabama State Docks Administration.[35] His perspective was very anthropocentric as he testified before the House about the need for continued federal funding of local programs to offset the cost of environmental consciousness. Carey's concern was primarily for humans and his thoughts were primarily economically centered. Deep ecologists would take issue with the Secretary's solely economic explanation of the cost of environmental consciousness.

David L. Karmol, on behalf of the National Spa and Pool Institute, testified in June of 1994 about his opposition to certain aspects of the current Federal Insecticide, Fungicide, and Rodenticide Act.[36] Karmol favored raising environmental consciousness and decreasing federal regulations and authority. While this sounds very much like deep ecology, Karmol's overall tone is anthropocentric. He specifically separates "man" from the environment and seems more interested in economic freedom than a truly deep ecological world.

---

[33]Becky Doyle, "Testimony on Behalf of the National Association of State Departments of Agriculture Before the Senate Agriculture, Nutrition and Forestry Subcommittee on Production and Price Competitiveness, United States Senate," *Federal Document Clearing House Congressional Testimony* (June 19, 1995).

[34]Alan T. Tracy, "Testimony on Behalf of the National Association of State Departments of Agriculture Before the House Agriculture Subcommittee on Resource Conservation, Research and Forestry, U.S. House of Representatives," *Federal Document Clearing House Congressional Testimony* (May 18, 1995).

[35]John P. Carey, "Summary of Statements by John P. Carey and J. Edgar Brister Before the House Appropriations Subcommittee on Energy and Water Development," *Federal Document Clearing House Congressional Testimony* (March 21, 1995).

[36]David L. Karmol, "Testimony of David L. Karmol Representing the National Spa and Pool Institute on H.R. 4329 'to Amend the Federal Insecticide, Fungicide and Rodenticide Act and for Other Purposes,'" *Federal Document Clearing House Congressional Testimony* (June 15, 1994).

Another individual who shares the same ecological perspective as those reviewed so far is Paul O'Connell, Director of the Alternative Agricultural Research and Commercialization Center.[37] O'Connell testified about recent breakthroughs in the development of renewable energy from agriculture. He argued against fossil fuels, much like deep ecologists do, for three reasons. The director supports a decrease in pollution, less reliance on foreign countries, and greater local autonomy in this country, all of which are perspectives shared by deep ecologists. Despite this deep ecological influence, his outlook was anthropocentric with respect to the economic rationale for human comfortability.

Robert L. Foster, Vice Chairman at Agri-Mark, also testified before the Senate Committee on Agriculture, Nutrition, and Forestry.[38] The subject was not agriculture, but rather the North American Free Trade Agreement (NAFTA). He argued that the NAFTA would not only help business but also increase environmental consciousness in all three countries. Though Foster claims that resources are finite, he does not take a deep ecologist–type stance. Rather, he argues for the perpetuation of big business but in such a way as to ensure a future supply of resources for human consumption.

Each of these seven examples of congressional testimony all urged the Congress to act in a shallow ecological manner. While many of these individuals could be considered environmentalists, their use of the term "environmental consciousness," though usually positive, did not connote the same meaning of the word found in deep ecological literature. For deep ecologists, environmental consciousness requires a fundamental shift in the way most people think. It calls for an ecocentric as opposed to an anthropocentric outlook. As in the case of the meaning of environmental ethics, what becomes the linguistic meaning of environmental consciousness will be of utmost importance to the ability of deep ecology to influence politics.

The term "environmental consciousness" (and derivatives thereof) was used twice by individuals who took neither a shallow nor a deep ecological viewpoint. Gary A. Mucha, Vice President of GEC-Marconi Electronic Systems Corporation, testified about his company's environmental progress in recycling and energy efficiency.[39] The overall tone of Mucha's speech was pro-environmental as long as being environmental meant remaining competitive in the global marketplace. The approach described by Mucha incorporated both the ideas of deep ecology (getting by on the very least amount of resources), and of shallow ecology (still using resources for human needs but more efficiently). Mucha argued for more partnerships between

[37]Paul O'Connell, "Testimony Before a Joint House of Representatives Hearing of the Subcommittee on Foreign Agriculture and Hunger and the Subcommittee on Information, Justice, and Agriculture, Committee on Government Operations," *Federal Document Clearing House Congressional Testimony* (November 16, 1993).

[38]Robert L. Forster, "Testimony Submitted to the Senate Committee on Agriculture, Nutrition and Forestry," *Federal Document Clearing House Congressional Testimony* (September 21, 1993).

[39]Gary A. Mucha, "Testimony Before Subcommittee on Technology, Environment and Aviation, U.S. House of Representatives," *Federal Document Clearing House Congressional Testimony* (October 18, 1993).

private industry, academia, and the government, a concept that both shallow and deep ecologists would support.

The other example of a mixed perspective is a statement by Peter F. Romero, the nominee for Ambassador to the Republic of Ecuador.[40] Romero listed the goal of raising Ecuador's environmental consciounesss if he was confirmed for the ambassadorship. Though it was listed last, it was very significant that it was included in a semi-official declaration of policy.[41] While this indicates a move toward greater environmentalism on the part of U.S. foreign policy, the question is yet to be answered whether it is a deep or shallow environmental ethic.

Overall, the majority of testimony that incorporated the term "environmental conscious" directed the House and Senate toward shallow, rather than deep, ecological policies. It is worth noting that only one environmental activist was among the ten who testified and used the term "environmental consciousness," and this activist had a shallow ecological perspective. The definition and context of terms are very important. If deep ecologists constantly push for an environmental consciousness, the manner in which policy makers interpret this term is very important. If lawmakers interpret this term from a shallow ecological perspective, as those discussed here did, then they will feel that there is no need for massive change because they already possess an environmental consciousness.

Deep Ecological Names and Groups

Searching for the terms "environmental ethic" and "environmental consciousness" gave insight into the ecological perspective of those who testified, but it did not provide the same degree of insight as the deep ecological terms. This section, dealing with deep ecological names and groups, not only provides insight into the ecological perspectives of those testifying, but it also gives the reader a better idea of the influence of deep ecology on environmental politics.

In the past three years, the term "Earth First!" was mentioned on five occasions before congressional committees. Stuart L. Pimm, Professor of Ecology at the University of Tennessee at Knoxville, gave the only positive view of the group.[42] He provided an extremely thorough and condemning review of the book *A Moment in Time*, by Greg Easterbrook. His tone is almost deep ecological, strongly arguing

---

[40]Peter F. Romero, "Testimony Before the Senate Committee on Foreign Relations on Nomination to Be Ambassador to Republic of Ecuador," *Federal Document Clearing House Congressional Testimony* (September 29, 1993).

[41]While ambassadorial nominees are supposed to speak for themselves and have little outside knowledge of official policy before confirmation, the process at the Department of State is quite intense. Frequently the Country Desk Officer in conjunction with other area specialists prepare extensive nomination booklets that contain official policy answers to anticipated questions.

[42]Stuart L. Pimm, "Testimony Before the Senate Environment/Drinking Water, Fisheries and Wildlife Subcommittee, Endangered Species Reauthorization," *Federal Document Clearing House Congressional Testimony* (July 13, 1995).

for the protection of species and the preservation of biological diversity. Pimm's analysis of Easterbrook's severe misinterpretation of Leopold's idea of "thinking like a mountain" is directly on target. Pimm discounts the anthropocentric views of Easterbrook and debunks many of the author's statistics. It was interesting that one of the individuals, a professor at the University of Oregon, quoted by Pimm stated that when he claims that jobs are not lost by the spotted owl episode, he is accused of being some Earth First!er. This obviously indicates a negative connotation given to the deep ecological movement. Such a negative connotation of being a deep ecologist must weigh heavily on the minds of legislators and explain why the term is not used in statements made before the Congress.

On two occasions, individuals testifying before Congress gave critical statements about Earth First! Dennis T. Avery, the director of global food issues at the Hudson Institute, makes the case for high-yield agriculture before Congress.[43] Along the way he praises the environmental movement for raising awareness but condemns it for many of its actions. He snubs groups like Earth First!, claiming that unless we adopt new technology for a growing population then their apocalyptic future will come true. Many of his arguments would upset even the shallow ecologists. Avery justifies the use of DDT, the logging of trees, and the raising of cows. Another critic of the group Earth First!, Richard Pombo, compared environmentalists to Nazis.[44] What makes this even more unfavorable to deep ecologists is that Pombo is the Chairman of the House Resources Committee. His statement was submitted by the Oregon Cattlemen's Association. Pombo also remarked that the environmental group Earth First! is on the same level as those who bombed the federal building in Oklahoma. According to the congressman, preservationists have vested interests in endangered species and make a living by hyping false propaganda and pseudo-science. These two critical assessments of Earth First! illustrate just how many obstacles deep ecologists face in lobbying government officials. Based on his statements, it is doubtful that Pombo, a very prominent and powerful politician, would even sit down or agree to meet with anyone who espoused deep ecological beliefs.

The final two references to the group Earth First! were largely incidental. In one, a member of Earth First! was referred to and in another the name Earth First! was listed as part of a list of organizations that were opposed to a certain policy. But if one considers the negative connotation mentioned by Professor Pimm and the negative remarks by both Avery and Pombo, the group definitely has an image problem (whether deserved or not) in circles around Washington (if not throughout America).

Unlike the group Earth First!, many prominent individual deep ecologists went without mention in Congressional testimony between July 1993 and June 1996. Co-founder Dave Foreman, philosopher Arne Naess, and authors George Sessions

---

[43]Dennis T. Avery, "Testimony Before the House Resources Committee, Endangered Species Act," *Federal Document Clearing House Congressional Testimony* (May 25, 1995).

[44]Richard Pombo, "Testimony Before the Task Force on Endangered Species, Submitted by the Oregon Cattlemen's Association," *Federal Document Clearing House Congressional Testimony* (April 24, 1995).

and Christopher Manes are among the notable names in deep ecology that were not mentioned. There is one mention of Bill Devall. This piece of testimony by Doug Crandall, already reviewed for its reference to deep ecology, fiercely criticized a recent book edited by Devall entitled *Clearcut—The Tragedy of Industrial Forestry.*

One name associated with deep ecology has, however, found its way into congressional testimony. The originator of the land ethic, Aldo Leopold, is mentioned on eighteen different occasions during the three-year time span. The first eight that will be examined are from individuals who support the principles of deep ecology and Leopold's land ethic. Douglas L. Honnold, an attorney for the Sierra Club, testified to the importance of biological diversity as well as of a holistic approach to our nation's forests.[45] His tone was very similar to deep ecology ideals; though he did not go so far as promoting the downfall of the industrial state, he did discuss species as having some type of intrinsic worth (a concept that most humans have been unwilling to accept). While Honnold did talk about the medicinal benefits of biodiversity, this was not his primary justification for species preservation. He quoted Aldo Leopold's statement about the importance of maintaining all the cogs of the wheel. Finally, the attorney touched on the role of states in the ESA, arguing for partnership and local decision making. Another individual who quoted Leopold was Professor Stuart L. Pimm, whose testimony has already been analyzed. Pimm took issue with Greg Easterbrook's misinterpretation of Leopold's idea of "thinking like a mountain."

Roger Schlickeisen, President of the Defenders of Wildlife, testified for the reintroduction of the wolf into Yellowstone.[46] He used Aldo Leopold's arguments from his days as a game manager. Schlickeisen sounds very much like a deep ecologist by arguing for species diversity as well as for the restoration of an ecological balance. He has full confidence, as do deep ecologists, in nature and its ability to be its own steward. All three of these individuals have lobbied the government for environmental policies that abide by the principles of deep ecology

Testifying in December of 1995, Murray Lloyd refers to Aldo Leopold as the father of the land ethic.[47] He explains how the Tensas River National Wildlife Refuge is an example of this ethic in which people and land are able to form a healthy relationship. Lloyd says that while he is usually in favor of private land ownership, the Tensas River National Wildlife Refuge shows how effective state and federal ownership can work with a community to foster a sense of a land ethic. Not only is Lloyd influencing legislators as to the practicality and effectiveness of deep ecology,

---

[45]Douglas L. Honnold, "Statement Before the Senate Subcommittee on Forests and Public Land Management," *Federal Document Clearing House Congressional Testimony* (April 26, 1995).

[46]Roger Schlickeisen, "Written Testimony Before the House Natural Resources Committee, Canadian Gray Wolves," *Federal Document Clearing House Congressional Testimony* (January 26, 1995).

[47]Murray Lloyd, "Testimony of Murray Lloyd Before the House Resource Committee, Subcommittee on Fisheries, Wildlife and Oceans," *Federal Document Clearing House Congressional Testimony* (December 14, 1995).

but he also gives an example where deep ecological ideas have already had an influence on environmental policy.

Dale Pontius, director of the Southwest Regional Office of the American Rivers, testified about the neglect and ignorance of past policies governing the Colorado River.[48] Pontius states that there is a definite need for government action to at least attempt to restore the natural ecosystem. He quotes Aldo Leopold's visit to the area in which Leopold explained how man always kills what he loves, referring to the pioneers who ravaged the wilderness. Pontius is both ecocentric and anthropocentric. He mentions some of the benefits to humans as a rationale for acting, but his primary concern rests with the ecosystem and the species that inhabit the rivers and the lands. He is highly critical of past development and urban sprawl, which has come at the expense of the environment. This piece of testimony not only shows the lack of a deep ecological influence in current policy, but it also illustrates the beginning of a new direction in environmental programs (to the extent that this perspective gets anywhere).

One of the three government employees who testified using Leopoldian rhetoric was Gerry Studds, Chairman of the Subcommittee on Environment and Natural Resources.[49] As explained earlier, it would be difficult to find a deep ecologist who did not agree with his policy for wetland restoration. Mike Bader, of the Alliance for the Wild Rockies, gave compelling testimony in the spring of 1994, as to why local autonomy can hurt, not help, the environment.[50] While deep ecologists support local autonomy, they are aware of the current political reality and need for federal programs. According to Bader, the Northern Rockies need a federal law to protect the politically weak locals from industrial giants and from inconsistent state-to-state policies. Bader quotes Leopold about preserving all of the parts, meaning the preservation of all of the species of an ecosystem. Bader's testimony does not rely on anthropocentric reasons to save forests, but rather asserts ecocentric reasoning by placing the highest priority on ecosystems. The overall mood and tone of his testimony sound very much like those of a deep ecologist. Bader is another individual who is lobbying the government for changes from policies based on shallow ecological principles to ones based on deep ecological principles.

The final individual to testify with a pro–deep ecological stance is Roger G. Kenny, the Director of the National Park Service.[51] Though the mood of his testimony

---

[48]Dale Pontius, "Oversight Hearing on the Lower Colorado River Basin, Testimony Before the Subcommittee on Water and Power, Senate Energy and Natural Resources Committee," *Federal Document Clearing House Congressional Testimony* (June 9, 1994).

[49]Gerry Studds, "Statement Before House Merchant Marines/Environment and Natural Resources Subcommittee, Wetlands Conservation," *Federal Document Clearing House Congressional Testimony* (June 8, 1994).

[50]Mike Bader, "Testimony on Behalf of the Alliance for the Wild Rockies, Hearing on H.R. 2638, the Northern Rockies Ecosystem Protection Act," *Federal Document Clearing House Congressional Testimony* (May 4, 1994).

[51]Roger G. Kenny, "Statement Before the Subcommittee on National Parks, Forests and Public Lands, House Committee on Natural Resources, Concerning H.R. 3707 and H.R. 2416, Bills to Establish an American Heritage Areas Partnership Program in the Department

does not seem to be that of a deep ecologist, the ideas most certainly are. Kenny supports greater local autonomy. He also supports the ideas of Aldo Leopold—that if humans are able to form a community bond with the land, they will treat it much better. The idea of a land ethic formed through an attachment to the land seems to be heavily favored by the Director of the National Park Service. Kenny is the third example of a government employee in a position of power who supports Leopold's land ethic. This bodes very well for the influence of deep ecological ideas on environmental policy.

While eight of the individuals who referred to Aldo Leopold shared a deep ecological perspective, four who mentioned Leopold exhibited a mix of both deep and shallow ecological ideals. The first of these individuals was William J. Snape, Director of the Defenders of Wildlife.[52] He quoted Aldo Leopold, arguing that we should do what is ethically and aesthetically right as well as economically expedient. It appears that perhaps Snape underestimates Leopold's ideas by giving too much attention to the economics of the issue. While Leopold is ecocentric in his overall outlook, Snape seems to border between anthropocentrism and biocentrism. He does argue very persuasively for the preservation of biological diversity but economic issues shape most of his testimony.

Another environmentalist with a similar outlook is Karl Gawell of the Wilderness Society.[53] Gawell testified about the need for restrictions on aircraft flights over the national parks. His argument stemmed from early pioneers of the wilderness ethic, such as John Muir and Aldo Leopold, who strove to protect at least some of this country's land from mechanical noises and pollution. Gawell definitely sounds like a deep ecologist in putting the needs of the wilderness first and primarily for its own well-being. But he never goes as far as most deep ecologists, merely arguing for the protection of some land while industrial society may continue to expand. As previously expounded upon, support for industrial society is a main determinant in one's ecological perspective. The main criticism of mainstream environmental organizations by deep ecologists is their willingness to compromise and play the Washington game. Most of the environmental activists who have been called upon to testify before Congress are members of these national groups, which seldom take a deep ecological stance on the issues. Thus the predominant environmental voice heard by the legislators is that of the shallow ecologists.

---

of the Interior," *Federal Document Clearing House Congressional Testimony* (March 22, 1994).

[52]William J. Snape, "Testimony Before the Subcommittee on Clean Water, Fisheries and Wildlife, U.S. Senate Committee on Environment and Public Works," *Federal Document Clearing House Congressional Testimony* (March 7, 1995).

[53]Karl Gawell, "Testimony Before the Subcommittee on Aviation Regarding Legislation and Regulations Affecting Scenic Overflights Above National Parks," *Federal Document Clearing House Congressional Testimony* (July 27, 1994).

Jack Ward Thomas, Chief of the Forest Service, made his core values very clear when he testified in February and March of 1994.[54] He specifically stated that he subscribes to Leopold's land ethic and sees the necessity of short-term constraint on human action in order to preserve the biosphere. Furthermore, Thomas states that humans are part of the environment, a belief very much ingrained into deep ecology. It was difficult to determine whether Thomas's overall testimony, however, supported his claim that he shared a land ethic. He described the need to harvest resources for human consumption, a very shallow ecological perspective. Nonetheless, Thomas, like his counterpart of the National Park Service, looks favorably upon Leopold's land ethic, which bodes well for a deep ecological influence in the political arena.

The last group of individuals examined are those who have anthropocentric outlooks but still refer to Leopold in some capacity. The first is Robert Irvin, who called Aldo Leopold "the father of scientific wildlife management."[55] Irvin testified that the very first principle of wildlife management should be the preservation of every cog in the wheel, or species in the ecosystem. Though Irvin is a very strong advocate of biological diversity, his reasons are anthropocentric (that is, medicine, food, and jobs). It is interesting that he calls Leopold the father of the scientific wildlife management, but never mentions that we should preserve species for their intrinsic worth. It almost seems as though Irvin would believe in such a concept, but felt an obligation to rely on human-centered benefits to appeal to an anthropocentric Congress (that is, 'good politics'). Should this be true, it may explain why many of those who testify appeal to anthropocentric reasons for preserving the environment. This also tells us that those who make the laws predominantly share a shallow ecological outlook.

One of these law makers is Bruce Babbitt, Secretary of the Interior.[56] When testifying about the reintroduction of the gray wolf into Yellowstone National Park and central Idaho, the Secretary made no mention of the need to restore ecological balance nor of the concept of the intrinsic worth of species. Perhaps he was also trying to appeal to the congressional committee by discussing the wolf in mainly economic terms. His quote of Aldo Leopold, who argued for the reintroduction of the wild wolf almost fifty years ago, seemed to make this distinction clear between the two schools of conservationism. Leopold wanted to restore balance for ecological reasons; Babbitt wants to preserve a species for monetary reasons.[57]

---

[54]Jack Ward Thomas, "Statement Before the Subcommittee on Specialty Crops and Natural Resources, Committee on Agriculture, United States House of Representative Concerning H.R. 2153, Giant Sequoia Preservation Act," *Federal Document Clearing House Congressional Testimony* (March 9, 1994).

[55]Robert Irvin, "Statement Before the Committee on Resources, United States House of Representative Concerning H.R. 2275, the Endangered Species Conservation and Management Act," *Federal Document Clearing House Congressional Testimony* (September 20, 1995).

[56]Bruce Babbitt, "Testimony Before the House Resources Committee Regarding the Reintroduction of the Gray Wolf into Yellowstone National Park and Central Idaho," *Federal Document Clearing House Congressional Testimony* (January 26, 1995).

[57]Recent actions, however, such as the imposition of a $100,000 fine for the unlawful killing of an endangered wolf, do point toward considerable concern for a balanced ecosystem.

Yet another department head who testified before Congress was Paul W. Johnson, Chief of the Soil Conservation Service in the U.S. Department of Agriculture.[58] He presented evidence of the effectiveness of current soil conservation programs. Highlighting both a new environmental consciousness in farming as well as an increase in local partnerships and autonomy, he sounded like a deep ecologist. But Johnson's ends were decidedly anthropocentric and overall shallow in ecological outlook. So too was the outlook of the Honorable John D. Dingell.[59] The Congressman testified why hunters and fishers must be continually allowed to hunt and fish on national wildlife refuges. It is peculiar that he quotes Leopold saying that we should strive to have the finest national wildlife management system in the world. From this statement, Dingell leaped to the conclusion that hunters and fishers must be allowed on national land. The argument is inherently anthropocentric and shallow ecological if not a total misinterpretation of Leopold's ideas.

The final piece of testimony examined is yet another government employee. Robert M. Sussman, Deputy Administrator of the EPA, touted the benefits of environmental science.[60] His overall outlook was a shallow ecological perspective that viewed environmental degradation as a problem to be solved through technology and science, not by changing life patterns. Sussman seemed human-centered when it came to the environment, concentrating on risk to human health and welfare. His references to Aldo Leopold and Rachel Carson were an attempt to illustrate how past U.S. government employees have had a large impact on our environmental perspective. From a deep ecological perspective, it is unfortunate that Sussman and other government employees do not share the philosophies of Leopold and Carson.

Overall, the ten pieces of testimony that referred to Aldo Leopold provided many clues about the influence of deep ecology on environmental politics. It was significant, but not surprising, that the majority of those who testified about Leopold with a deep ecological perspective were environmental activists whereas the majority of those who shared a shallow ecological outlook were government employees who either made or carried out the laws.

CONCLUSION

The first set of testimonies illustrated the negative perception of deep ecology and radical environmentalists. The only mention of the term "deep ecology" was extremely negative. Not a single statement before Congress during the three-year

---

[58]Paul W. Johnson, "Testimony Before the Subcommittee on Environment, Credit and Rural Development of the Committee on Agriculture, U.S. House of Representative," *Federal Document Clearing House Congressional Testimony* (August, 11, 1994).

[59]John D. Dingell, "Testimony Before the Subcommittee on Environment and Natural Resources, Committee on Merchant Marine and Fisheries, U.S. House of Representative," *Federal Document Clearing House Congressional Testimony* (August 9, 1994).

[60]Robert M. Sussman, "Statement Before the Subcommittee on Technology, Environment and Aviation, Committee on Science, Space, and Technology, House of Representative," *Federal Document Clearing House Congressional Testimony* (April 19, 1994).

time period contained the term "shallow ecology." The two mentions of the term "anthropocentric" did, however, show signs of deep ecological influence. Another way to measure the influence of deep ecology on legislation is to note the instances (which were a few) when angry property and business owners testified about the radical environmental nature of the nation's laws. Though the term "environmental ethic" was used on thirty-two occasions in the three-year time span, not a single person who testified fully subscribed to deep ecological ideas. The statements did indicate a growing environmental influence in both business and government. Unfortunately for the deep ecologists, this environmental influence is decidedly shallow in its ecological outlook.

Another term that was frequently employed by those testifying was "environmental consciousness." It appears that many business representatives incorporate the term to describe their heightened environmental concerns. By comparison, only once did an environmental activist use the term to describe his or her organization or set of beliefs. Finally, the last set of search terms, deep ecological groups and individuals, yielded some important findings. Every mention of the group Earth First! was negative. Though this may seem to support the conclusion that deep ecology has had little influence, the context of the testimonies proves otherwise. Earth First! was criticized primarily for its effectiveness in changing and affecting environmental policy.

Although the examination of this testimony is a bit tedious, it does illustrate the place that deep ecological ideas hold in overall environmental policy. The overall lack of individuals who had a deep ecological perspective is disheartening to the movement, but one must remember that testifying before Congress to change policy is not exactly their primary tactic. On many occasions, those testifying referred to deep ecologists vehemently for the impact that they are having on environmental policy. Additionally, the fact that effective persuasion involves telling an audience what it wants to hear means that witnesses perhaps tailored their remarks to suit the audience (Congress). If this was the case, then it illustrates the dominant leaning of congressional Senators and Representatives toward shallow ecology.

7

Congressional Testimony: Politics of Perspectives

Chapter 6 provided valuable insight into the scope of deep ecology rhetoric in congressional testimony. It also explored how hearings operate within the overall political process. Those who testified provided not only a reflection of the pulse of America, but they also served as a mirror of those before whom they were testifying. People chosen to testify are selected by congressional committees for a specific purpose, and when they speak, they attempt to persuade Congress by appealing to their values and biases. Arne Naess asks environmentalists to keep track of various politicians and evaluate how they talk and vote on "green" policies.[1] This study does not profess to support green policies, nor does it critically examine voting records, rather it uses congressional testimony as a tool to pry open a window into the thoughts and actions of Congress. This chapter examines congressional testimony in a methodical manner to discern the rhetoric employed during hearings. During the time span from July 1993 to June 1996, the term "environment" was used on over 16,000 occasions. In order to determine the ecological perspective of those who were called upon to testify before Congress, and thus gain a perspective on the prevailing values of the congressional committee, every fiftieth piece of testimony that mentioned the term "environment" was examined and graded according to a five prong deep ecological scale.

SURVEY METHOD

First, each piece of testimony was categorized according to its broad subject heading. These headings included everything from trade to tourism and from the

---

[1]Arne Naess and David Rothenberg, *Ecology, Community and Lifestyle: Outline of an Ecosophy* (New York: Cambridge University Press, 1989): 135.

weather to the water. Additionally, environmentally related subjects were separated from non-environmental subjects. This proved useful for comparison of the two sets of data. Each testimonial was ranked on an ordinal scale ranging from one to five for each of the five deep ecological tenets. The first tenet asked whether the congressional statement favored either dominance over or harmony with the environment. If it discussed stewardship or human ownership of the environment, then a score of one or two was assigned. But if it discussed living with nature in a harmonious manner, then a four or five was assigned. Should both ideas be present equally, a three was given. The one-to-five scale basically equates with superficial,[2] shallow, mixed, deep, and very deep ecology.

The second element of deep ecology that was evaluated concerned the extrinsic versus intrinsic worth of species. A superficial ecological perspective would treat species existence solely for their use to humans, thus warranting a one. A very deep ecological perspective would assign species absolute intrinsic worth, perhaps even placing them above humans, and thus warrant a five. The third category of deep ecological thought contrasted economic growth and consumerism with simple needs and "doing with enough." Testimony that supported current economic growth and encouraged continued development was given a one or two, and testimony that shunned economic growth and supported the deep ecological definition of "simple needs" was assigned a four or five.

The fourth tenet of deep ecology used in this study pitted the belief in ample resources versus the belief that the Earth's "supplies" are limited. Should an individual testify that action was not needed to preserve the environment because resources were plentiful, his or her statement received a one. Testimony that claimed action was critically needed because of the lack of earthly "supplies" was assigned a five. The last ecological category determined whether testimony embraced high technological solutions and centralized control or supported appropriate, non-dominating technology and local control. Statements that endorsed the former were given a one or two while those that supported the latter received a four or five.

The full range of numbers on the ordinal scale was used whenever appropriate, with only those that took absolute positions receiving categorical numbers at the extremes of the range. No matter what the testimony concerned, every fiftieth instance was examined (even if it was a witness list).[3] When testimony was not applicable to a particular ecological tenet, no number was assigned (N/A was thus used). After the analysis of all the testimony was completed, it was broken up according to six-month increments. The purpose of this last step was to look for a progression of deep ecological

---

[2]The term "superficial" is used here without a negative connotation. The term provided a convenient one to contrast with "shallow." Its meaning should be interpreted as "on the surface only."

[3]The primary reason for this strict standard of evaluating the fiftieth piece of testimony regardless of its content was to preserve the randomness of the sample. Had witness lists and other pieces of testimony that contained little substantive information been omitted, it would have led to infinite regression and the injection of researcher bias.

influence as well as to examine possible differences in testimony between the 103rd and 104th Congresses.

FINDINGS

This section illustrates the findings of the study of congressional testimony. It employs some basic statistics to ascertain certain progressions or trends in the political process. For each of the five tenets, two tables are provided that contain the findings for both the overall set of data and the environmental-specific subset of data. First, the total number of pieces of congressional testimony is provided. This is basically the sample size for each six-month time period. The mean provides the numerical average of all testimony in the sample for a given time span. Additionally, the median and the mode are provided. Finally, the standard of deviation is noted to give the reader an idea of the variance within the sample size. In additional to the tables, each subsection includes a line graph that traces the progression of the mean averages. Each subsection is broken up according to the five tenets discussed above.

Tenets of Deep Ecology

Dominance vs. Harmony. Tables 7.1 and 7.2 highlight the major findings for the determination of the ecological outlook of those who have testified before Congress with respect to dominance vs. harmony. The first table contains the numerical results for the overall (includes all testimony in the sample) outlook toward this first element of deep ecological thought. The means of the scores for the dominance versus harmony show an overall mix of shallow and deep ecological perspectives. The means range from 3.43 to 2.88 with only a 0.018 standard of deviation among the six chronological categories. These scores illustrate not only the overall continuity of testimony but also a decidedly mixed outlook on ecological issues. There is a slight deep ecological tendency, but not enough, as expressed by the means, to indicate a definitive influence one way or the other. However, the very fact that dominance is counterbalanced by harmony shows a move away from strict stewardship and the Pinchot school of conservationism.

It is significant that the median score for each time segment was either a three or a four. A three indicates a mixed outlook and a four indicates a deep ecological outlook. These findings support the above conclusion of a slight deep ecological lean. One interesting finding is that the first six months of the 104th Congress had the highest statistical mean indicating the highest degree of deep ecological testimony. It is more important, however, that the majority of those testifying reject the notion of human dominance over the land. As seen in Chapter 2, this move away from human dominion over the land is significant, for the prevailing school of environmental thought has long asserted human control and stewardship over the land. The mode indicates which ecological leaning had the highest frequency. From January 1994 to June 1995, a plurality of all individuals testifying before various congressional committees shared a deep ecological attitude regarding dominance versus harmony. Perhaps more than any other statistic, this illustrates the roots of deep ecological thought and provides tentative support for the influence of deep ecology on environmental politics.

Table 7.1
Overall Statistical Chart for Dominance (1) vs. Harmony (5)

	July- Dec '93	Jan- June '94	July- Dec '94	Jan- June '95	July- Dec '95	Jan- June '96
Number	25	64	15	53	21	22
Mean	2.88	3.02	3.20	3.43	2.90	3.00
Median	3	3	4	4	3	3
Mode	3	4	4	4	3	2,3,4
Deviation	1.84	1.86	1.74	1.17	0.69	1.33

Table 7.2
Environment Statistical Chart for Dominance (1) vs. Harmony (5)

	July- Dec '93	Jan- June '94	July- Dec '94	Jan- June '95	July- Dec '95	Jan- June '96
Number	17	32	9	30	16	15
Mean	2.94	3.625	3.44	3.67	2.75	3.00
Median	3	4	4	4	3	3
Mode	2	4	4	4	3	3
Deviation	2.18	1.27	1.78	0.85	0.47	1.29

The standard deviation for all time periods was relatively low, though the 0.69 for the time period of July through December 1995 was substantially lower than the score for any other six-month span. This low score indicates a relative low amount of variance in the type of testimony. The second table concerning dominance versus harmony isolated only those instances where the main subject pertained to environmental matters. Table 7.2 illustrates the data from these findings.

While the overall average of means for the first group of data was 3.07, the average of the means for just testimony concerning the environment was 3.24. Although this 5 percent increase in averages is to be expected, the much higher standard of deviations (0.152 compared to 0.018) is significant. The means for each of the six time spans varied much more for the environmental-specific scores than it did for the overall scores. This variance does not have any direct bearing on the outcome of this study, but it is worth noting. The actual means and medians do, however, have some bearing

Figure 7.1

Comparison of Means for Dominance vs. Harmony

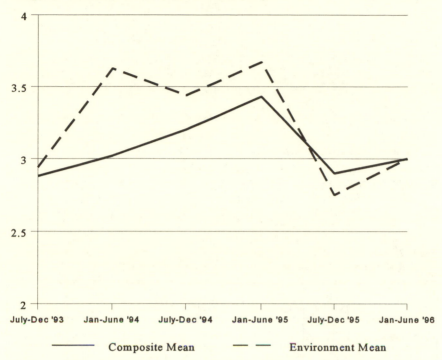

on measuring the effect of deep ecology on environmental politics. Both the means and medians for the environmental testimony illustrate a mix of deep and shallow ecological perspectives, with a definite leaning toward the former between January of 1994 and June of 1995. A score in the 3.6 to 3.7 range highlights a definite penetration of deep ecological ideas into Congressional testimony. Additionally, the overall median during this time period was a four, indicating that a plurality of all individuals testifying shared a deep ecological outlook.[4]

Just as the standard deviation for the time span of July through December of 1995 showed a relatively low variance for the overall numbers, so too did the environment-specific numbers exhibit a relatively low variance during that time period. This is a sharp contrast with the relatively high variance for the July through December 1993 grouping. Overall, both groups of data illustrate a non-domination of nature perspective on the part of those testifying before Congress. This harmonious outlook is perhaps the key element of deep ecological thought. The accompanying graph (Figure 7.1) illustrates the progression of the means. The numerical value of the means

---

[4]It should also be noted, however, that the plurality of testimony made during the first time period had a strong shallow ecological bias.

hovers, for the most part, between 3.00 and 3.5, indicating a slight lean towards deep ecology. But the graph also shows a gradual swing of the ecological paradigm toward deep ecology, which culminates during the first six months of the 104th Congress. After this "peak," there is a noticeable swing away from deep ecology and toward a more centrist or even shallow ecological perspective on the part of those testifying before the new, Republican-controlled Congress. But this should not discount the hiatus that occurs during the first six months. Unfortunately, there is no sure way to determine whether this finding is the result of a time lag or of a Republican-induced deep ecological influence.

Extrinsic vs. Intrinsic Worth. Another element central to deep ecological thought centers on intrinsic versus extrinsic worth of species. Shallow ecologists view species as resources for human consumption whether that be for medicine or for food. Their worth is determined extrinsically. Deep ecologists, however, assign intrinsic worth to all species as well as to the nonliving components of ecosystems. Table 7.3 traces the overall findings for the ecological outlook of those who have testified before the U.S. Congress during the three-year span from July 1993 to June 1996.

Table 7.3
Overall Statistical Chart for Resource (1) vs. Intrinsic Worth (5)

	July–Dec '93	Jan–June '94	July–Dec '94	Jan–June '95	July–Dec '95	Jan–June '96
Number	23	55	11	48	19	19
Mean	1.61	1.73	2.09	1.625	1.68	1.63
Median	1	1	2	1	1	1
Mode	1	1	2	1	1	1
Deviation	1.25	0.91	1.29	0.71	1.23	0.69

The most striking observation from the findings shown in Table 7.3 is the decidedly shallow outlook when compared to the previous findings on dominance versus harmony. The highest mean occurred during the time span of July through December 1994. Yet even that number (2.09) indicated a very shallow ecological outlook on the part of those testifying. The rest of the means ranged from 1.61 to 1.73, an extremely low variance. Additionally, all but one of the median scores was a one, indicating a superficial ecological outlook when it came to the extrinsic (resource) versus intrinsic worth of species. Even the standard of deviation was relatively low for all time spans. The implications of this finding are two-fold. First, it confirms the earlier findings in Chapter 5. The prevailing attitude in each piece of legislation examined in that chapter illustrated a shallow ecological leaning toward the extrinsic versus intrinsic worth of species. Very rarely were species or ecosystems given worth other than that which is derived from external value. The second implication of this finding is that it indicates that the expansion of our moral framework to include all living beings is still far away. Deep ecologists feel that this extension of values to all living beings, is crucial not only to the protection of the environment but also to the preservation of all life, including human.

Table 7.4
Environment Statistical Chart for Resource (1) vs. Intrinsic Worth (5)

	July- Dec '93	Jan- June '94	July- Dec '94	Jan- June '95	July- Dec '95	Jan- June '96
Number	14	32	9	29	16	13
Mean	2.00	2.09	2.33	1.86	1.625	1.77
Median	1.5	2	2	2	1	2
Mode	1	1	2	1,2	1	2
Deviation	1.69	1.06	1.25	0.91	1.05	0.74

While the statistical means for the environment-specific testimony (Table 7.4) leaned slightly more deep (but not deep ecological) in their outlook, there is even one occasion when the environment-specific mean was lower than that of the overall. This occurred during the July through December 1993 time span. While the plurality of the testimony was still superficial, only once was the median score a one. This difference indicates a less shallow outlook on the part of those who dealt with environmental topics in their testimony. Another difference between the two groups of data centered around the average and variance of the means for each of the six time periods. The means ranged from 1.625 (July–Dec. 1995) to 2.33 (July–Dec. 1994), with an overall average of 1.98, indicating a shallow ecological perspective. These results should not be surprising, as the mainstream outlook toward the worth of species is derived from extrinsic instead of intrinsic value. The review of legislation concurred with this finding. Recall that laws such as the Clean Air Act and the Wilderness Act concerned themselves almost solely with human health and welfare. Although the Clean Water Act and the Endangered Species Act provided limited intrinsic worth to species, the overarching ecological attitude was still one of extrinsic worth. Figure 7.2 illustrates the comparison and progression of means.

The progression of means through the six time spans (of six months each) shows no statistically relevant pattern. There is slight fluctuation, with both means peaking in the final six months of the 103rd Congress and dropping slightly thereafter. With a one equating with the lowest possible score on the ordinal ecological scale, the graph helps to put into perspective just how shallow and even superficial the ecological outlook was for those who testified before Congress during the three-year time span. Not only does this provide clues into the overall ecological outlook of the "experts" called upon to testify, but it also provides insight into the ecological perspectives of the legislators who have asked these individuals to testify. Although there is a

Figure 7.2
Comparison of Means for Resource vs. Intrinsic Worth

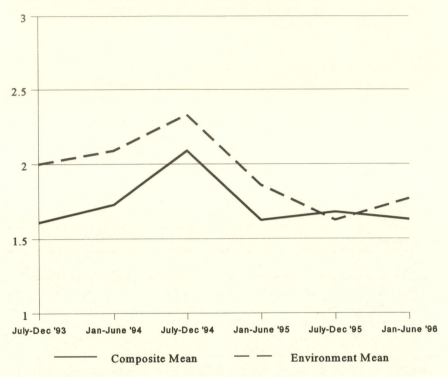

lot of crossover between deep and shallow ecological beliefs in terms of the other four tenets chosen for this study, the debate between extrinsic versus intrinsic worth is one that is clearly in the main of the overall debate and differences among the deep and shallow ecologists. Only on ten occasions during the entire three-year time span did an individual subscribe to either a deep (4) or very deep (5) ecological outlook. This equates to less than 6 percent of all testimony, a clear indication of the lack of a deep ecological influence in terms of intrinsic versus extrinsic worth of species. (It also probably reflects the general majority sentiment within the environmental community; that is, deep ecology is still on the periphery.)

Economic Growth vs. Simple Needs. While the scores were very low for the previous category, they were even lower (on a deep ecological scale) for the question of economic growth versus simple needs/doing with enough. This observation should come as no surprise, as economic growth has become the lifeblood of many politicians who seek election and reelection. To oppose economic growth in politics today is to seal one's own political coffin. Economic growth has been at the forefront of numerous presidential campaigns. In 1992, then-governor Clinton stated the situation in very simple terms: "It's the economy, stupid!" Some believe that this slogan alone led to the defeat of President Bush. Table 7.5 reveals the overall statistical findings for this third tenet of deep ecology, economic growth versus simple needs/doing with enough. Not only are these the lowest scores (in deep ecological terms) for any of the tenets observed in this study, but they also exhibit the lowest degree of variance of any ecological category. The average of the means is 1.525 with a variance of only plus or minus .085. Even the standard deviations for the individual six-month periods are all incredibly low. This indicates a very high degree of homogeneity among those testifying. Perhaps even more telling is the finding that every six-month time span had both a median and a mode of one. The majority of all testimony for the three-year period subscribed to a superficial outlook on the environment in terms of economic growth. Not only is growth supported, but it is also put at the very top of the value hierarchy. Perhaps these firm roots of pro-economic growth account for the vast array of deep ecological literature that denounces growth, consumerism, and materialism.

Table 7.5
Overall Statistical Chart for Economic Growth (1) vs. Simple Needs/Doing with Enough (5)

	July-Dec '93	Jan-June '94	July-Dec '94	Jan-June '95	July-Dec '95	Jan-June '96
Number	31	57	17	66	20	18
Mean	1.52	1.61	1.53	1.45	1.55	1.44
Median	1	1	1	1	1	1
Mode	1	1	1	1	1	1
Deviation	.86	.71	.89	.56	1.00	.73

Table 7.6
Environmental Statistical Chart for Economic Growth (1) vs. Simple Needs/Doing with Enough (5)

	July-Dec '93	Jan-June '94	July-Dec '94	Jan-June '95	July-Dec '95	Jan-June '96
Number	16	29	8	28	8	9
Mean	1.94	1.97	2.125	1.75	2.125	1.67
Median	1.5	2	2	2	1.5	1
Mode	1	2	1	1	1	1
Deviation	1.26	0.75	1.27	0.86	1.84	1.25

Figure 7.3
Comparison of Means for Growth vs. Simple Needs

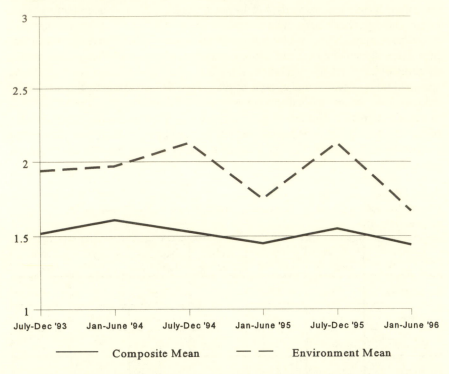

The means were slightly higher for environment-specific testimony, as shown in Table 7.6. The average of these means was 1.898 with a range from 1.67 (Jan.–June 1996) to 2.125 (July–Dec. 1994 and 1995). Thus the variance is substantially greater than it was for all testimony as quantified in the overall scores. Another difference between the two sets of data is that only once is the median a one (Jan.–June 1996). However, the plurality of all time periods (except one) represented a superficial point of view on the part of the individuals testifying. Overall, both sets of findings illustrate a very shallow, if not superficial, ecological perspective when it came to economic growth versus simple needs/doing with enough. Additional support for this conclusion can be found in the fact that only nine pieces of testimony over the entire three-year time span subscribed to a deep or very deep ecological perspective with respect to economic growth. In percentage terms, only about 4 percent of all testimony tipped the scale toward a deep ecological outlook. The struggle to defeat economic growth and development is extremely important in the shallow/deep divide. While shallow ecologists support the notion that economic growth and environmental protection can go hand-in-hand, deep ecologists find it perhaps the single most difficult obstacle to overcome. As these findings illustrate, overcoming the economic growth mindset is a difficult, if not impossible task, indeed. This has caused some deep ecologists to support what I term the "environmental crisis theory." It states that an environmental holocaust must occur before society can ever change. The logic states that in order to preserve the environment, humans must suffer through an environmental calamity that has the ability to severely disrupt all facets of life. Only in the aftermath of such a disaster, some deep ecologists feel, will humans realize that real change is needed. This real change will take the form of a deep ecological ethic that shuns economic growth and development as well as the other tenets that make up current shallow environmentalism.

The relative stability of the scores is in contrast to the difference in scores found in the observations for high technology and centralization versus appropriate technology and decentralization (as will be seen later). While the environmental means do vary somewhat, they all hover just below the shallow ecology mark. There is no discernible progression of means, indicating that both the 103rd and 104th Congress valued economic growth equally. Additionally, it is quite doubtful that had this study looked prior to 1993, the numbers would be much different in terms of support for economic growth over "doing with enough." In Figure 7.3, the two peaks of the line representing the environment mean seem to correlate with a smaller number of cases (only eight in each instance), and thus are probably less reliable than the other data collected. Nevertheless, the data are representational and confirm popular hypotheses about economic growth and environmental protection.

Abundant vs. Limited Resources. Unlike the two previous groups of findings, the data from the overall statistical table for ample resources versus "Earth supplies" limited is quite revealing in terms of a quantifiable and distinct progression. Table 7.7 illustrates a very large degree of variance among the means for each of the six time spans. For example, the mean for July through December 1993 is 2.29. This represents a fairly shallow ecological outlook. On the other hand, the mean for January through June of 1996 is 3.36, which represents a mixed ecological perspective with some deep ecological leanings. It is quite interesting that the median for each of the three time periods during the Republican-controlled 104th Congress was a four, representing a deep ecological outlook. On further examination, however, it should not be unexpected, for conservatives and radical environmentalists share a similar type of fiscal outlook with respect to the availability of resources.

Another interesting finding from the above chart can be found in the modes, which were either a one or a four. While this contains little statistical relevancy except for the fact that four of the six time periods were dominated by instances of deep ecological congressional testimony, it is quite peculiar. There is an entire point increase from the first time period to the last, which is significant in terms of this four-point ordinal scale. This trend is promising for deep ecologists. Unlike the two previous sets of charts, the standard deviation for each time group is relatively high. Yet even the standard of deviations show some variance, ranging from 2.45 to 1.17. It is significant that the time period from January to June of 1996, which had the highest score on the ecological scale, also had the lowest standard of deviation, representing a somewhat higher uniformity among the instances of congressional testimony.

Table 7.7
Overall Statistical Chart for Ample Resources (1) vs. "Earth Supplies" Limited (5)

	July-Dec '93	Jan-June '94	July-Dec '94	Jan-June '95	July-Dec '95	Jan-June '96
Number	24	50	12	32	18	14
Mean	2.29	3.00	2.42	3.06	3.28	3.36
Median	2	3	2	4	4	4
Mode	1	4	1	4	4	4
Deviation	2.13	1.59	2.45	1.80	2.12	1.17

Table 7.8
Environmental Statistical Chart for Ample Resources (1) vs.
"Earth Supplies" Limited (5)

	July-Dec '93	Jan-June '94	July-Dec '94	Jan-June '95	July-Dec '95	Jan-June '96
Number	17	30	7	22	15	11
Mean	2.53	3.37	3.00	3.27	3.33	3.55
Median	2	4	3	4	4	4
Mode	1	4	2,3,5	4	4	4
Deviation	2.39	1.41	2.33	1.54	2.33	1.07

Table 7.8 provides the environment-specific corollary to Table 7.7. It shows a similar progression of means from a 2.53 during the July through December 1993 time span to a 3.55 during the January through June of 1996 time period. The means for the environment-specific testimony were higher than those for the overall scores. These differences ranged greatly, from a 2 percent increase for the July through December of 1995 time span to a 24 percent increase for the July through December of 1994 time period.

All but two of the time groupings had a four for a median score, representing a deep ecological outlook with respect to the availability of resources. The standard of deviation was also relatively high, with deviations ranging from 1.07 to 2.39. This merely illustrates a high degree of diversity among those testifying, but a more significant finding is that a plurality of the pieces of testimony from January of 1994 through June of 1994 and then again from January of 1995 through June of 1996 were deep ecological in outlook (as determined by the ecological numerical scale). Barring alternative causalities (discussed later), this is a sign of a growing deep ecological

Figure 7.4
Comparison of Means for Abundant vs. Limited Resources

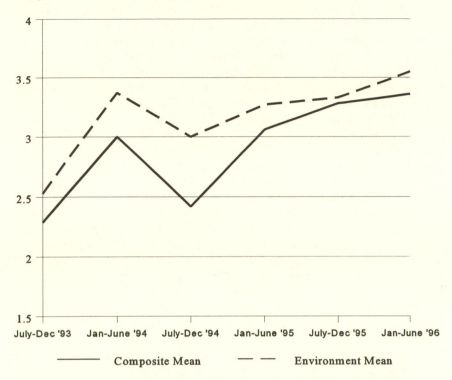

influence on this environmental tenet and should be regarded as an indicator of at least limited penetration of deep ecological ideas into environmental politics.

Figure 7.4 illustrates the progression of ecological perspective from July of 1993 to June of 1996. Starting on the shallow side of the ecological fulcrum, there is a pronounced swing toward the deep ecological side of the balance. This progression is shown by both the overall and the environment mean. It is somewhat of an anomaly that this progression occurs during the shift in control over Congress. The deep ecological optimist would claim that this trend is a sign of growing deep ecological influence despite a relatively hostile Congress. The pessimist would turn his or her attention to possible alternative causalities. One of the main planks of conservatism is fiscal conservatism. Translated, that equates to the belief that resources are limited. This could help to explain the trend exhibited by the graph. Unlike the two previous deep ecological indicators, there is considerable crossover in outlook toward resources between deep and shallow ecology. Many shallow ecologists also hold that the "Earth's supplies" are limited and therefore in need of protection. Since the individual legislators are the ones who issue invitations and summons, the choice of individuals to testify before Congress provides insight into their thinking.

The view that there are not ample resources can be found in many pieces of environmental legislation. Recall that in Chapter 5, virtually all of the legislation reviewed focused upon the fact that the Earth's resources are dwindling and in need of protection. This need for protection, however, was seldom based on deep ecological principles, but rather on anthropocentric needs of a bulging human population. While the results above indicate at least a moderate, if not strong, deep ecological influence on environmental politics, there could easily be an alternative cause—namely the greening of politics in general. Though not applicable to this study, this trend alone is significant and does lend credence to the hypothesis that environmental issues are having a greater influence on politics now.

High Technology and Centralization vs. Appropriate Technology and Decentralization. The last tenet of deep ecology that this study examined was actually a combination of the deep ecological desire for non-dominating technology and decentralization.[5] As with the previous set of data, there is a discernible trend. This trend, however, goes from a slightly deep ecological leaning to a very strong shallow ecological score. The means for the overall score, as shown in Table 7.9, range from a 3.16 (July–Dec. 1993) to a 2.09 (Jan.–June 1996). The trend progresses in an unusual manner if one considers the 104th Congress. The Republican-controlled Congress pushed for many decentralizing initiatives in an attempt to give more power to state and local governments. Although this does not constitute a deep ecological perspective, one would expect it to perhaps skew the results of the study in the opposite manner from that which the trend illustrates. Relative to the other test survey results, the standard deviation of the scores for each time period was about average. Both the median and mode of the July through December 1993 time span, was a four, which represented a definite deep ecological outlook. Again, this is further indication of some level of deep ecological influence on environmental politics. But as the remainder of the data indicates, this influence is short-lived.

By the time period of January through June of 1996, the median and mode had dropped to a two, representing a decidedly shallow ecological outlook. Overall, the trend points toward high technological solutions that are centralized in nature. The reason for this trend is difficult to ascertain, though a few hypotheses do exist to explain the swing toward shallow ecology. First, the rise of anti-technological groups and movements has begun to spark a backlash from individuals favoring technological solutions. The methods of such anti-tech groups and individuals has decreased sympathy for the movement. Another possible explanation is the increased deep ecological activism that supports federal solutions to environmental problems. Because the push for decentralization of federal programs has happened prior to the adoption of deep ecological perspectives on the part of state and local governments, many deep ecologists have become wary of the very decentralization that characterized some of its early thought. The current move toward devolution to state and local decision makers is

---

[5]Although much of the deep ecological literature favors a decentralized approach (bioregionalism), many deep ecological activists continue to support and push for federal solutions to environmental problems.

both a curse and a blessing for deep ecologists. It seems that deep ecologists would have greater influence at the local level, but as explained previously, the federal government offers protection, albeit limited, from special local interests that attempt to overrun ecological concerns.

Table 7.9
Overall Statistical Chart for High Tech/Centralization (1) vs.
Appropriate Tech/Local (5)

	July- Dec '93	Jan- June '94	July- Dec '94	Jan- June '95	July- Dec '95	Jan- June '96
Number	25	60	15	52	17	23
Mean	3.16	2.62	2.67	2.67	2.41	2.09
Median	4	2	2	3	2.5	2
Mode	4	2	4	2	1,4	2
Deviation	1.81	1.35	1.95	1.51	1.54	1.36

Table 7.10
Environmental Statistical Chart for High Tech/Centralization (1) vs.
Appropriate Tech/Local (5)

	July- Dec '93	Jan- June '94	July- Dec '94	Jan- June '95	July- Dec '95	Jan- June '96
Number	16	31	8	26	15	15
Mean	3.44	3.10	3.125	2.92	2.60	2.47
Median	4	3	3.5	3	3	2
Mode	4	4	4	2	2,3,4	2
Deviation	1.60	1.49	1.84	0.95	1.26	1.55

The trend expressed by the data of the overall chart can also be found in the environment-specific chart as noted in Table 7.10. The individual time span means are greater than those of the overall means. The percent increases range from 8 percent (July–Dec. 1995) to 18 percent (Jan.–June 1994 and Jan.–June 1996). This increase is expected in some respects, though not in others. Those discussing environmental matters are more likely to push for appropriate technology. On the other hand, one of the primary subjects of discussion of non-environmental topics was the move toward greater local control and jurisdiction. The means range from a high of 3.44, occurring

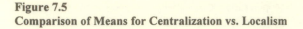

Figure 7.5
Comparison of Means for Centralization vs. Localism

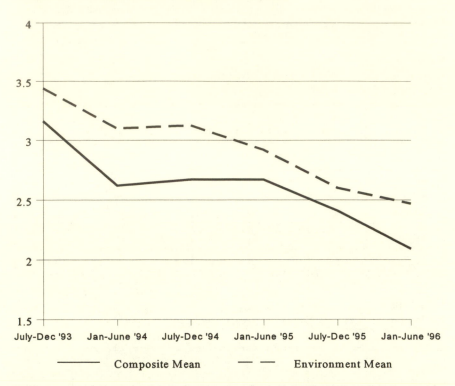

during the July through December 1993 time span, to a low of 2.47, occurring during January through June 1996. This virtual one-point drop is extremely significant on this four-point scale of ecological outlook. The 3.44 represents a definite lean toward deep ecology whereas the 2.47 correlates with a shallow ecological leaning.

The higher ecological scores (means) on the environment-specific pieces of testimony also correlate with higher medians. Only once is the median less than three (which represents a very mixed ecological outlook on the part of those testifying). Another sign of a less shallow ecological outlook is found in the examination of the modes, which shows that there were more instances of a deep ecological outlook (as opposed to any of the other four ecological categories) than any other ecological outlook by those testifying for the time period from July 1993 to December 1994. This changes significantly, however, with the advent of the 104th Congress. Testimony presented before the Congress was dominated (for at least the first 1½ years) by individuals sharing a shallow ecological perspective. Figure 7.5, which compares the progression of the means, makes the trend very noticeable. Additionally, both the overall and environment-specific lines are similar in their downward progression. This downward progression indicates a loss of deep ecological influence concerning appropriate technology and local control.[6]

Figure 7.6
Overall Ecological Scores: Distribution of Shallow and Deep Ecological Testimony

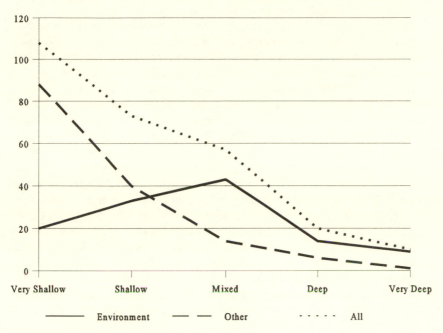

Combining the Tenets

The five different sets of data illustrate the different ecological outlooks of those testifying before Congress according to the five basic tenets of deep ecology. The data indicate that only one of the five deep ecological principles, the belief that the "Earth's supplies are limited," is gaining popularity in the testimony before Congress. Likewise, the data tend to support the conclusion that only one of the five deep ecological beliefs, the support of non-dominating technology and decentralized policy making,

---

[6]This downward progression also provides some insight into the correlation between testimony and legislative action. From January of 1995 to June of 1996, one of the primary concerns of the Congress was decreasing federal control over policies and programs in favor of greater state and local authority. The trend toward favoring federal control, as illustrated by the data, may indicate a backlash on the part of those testifying. The main problem with this line of reasoning is that it fails to take into consideration the variable of appropriate technology versus high technological solutions. To confirm the aforementioned hypothesis, the local versus federal variable would need to be separated from the issue of technology.

is falling out of favor. The schism between harmony and dominance appears to have peaked and then stabilized at a very mixed ecological viewpoint. As for the last two elements of deep ecology, "doing with enough" and the intrinsic worth of species, they have yet to surface in any force in congressional testimony. By separating out each of these elements of deep ecology, it is possible to see how testimony can incorporate some deep ecological perspectives while rejecting others.

However, it is possible to look at the data in a more holistic manner. By classifying each instance of testimony based on the sum of its parts it is possible to assign each individual piece of testimony one overall score on the ecological scale. These scores help to evaluate the overall effect of deep ecology, though they are not as telling since there is considerable mixing of both shallow and deep ecological principles in many environment-specific testimonials. Figure 7.6 gives a graphical account of this holistic data. The 119 scorable[7] pieces of environment-specific testimony broke down as follows: 20 superficial, 33 shallow, 43 mixed, 14 deep, and 9 very deep. The plurality of the group was mixed, with 53 on the shallow side of the midpoint and 23 on the deep side. While this does show a preference for a shallow ecological outlook, the environment-specific pieces of testimony do represent a relative equilibrium when contrasted with either the non-environment or overall scores. An objective observer would hope that all viewpoints would be represented in testimony before Congress. After all, decision makers should be exposed to all sides of an issue. The findings in this study indicate that Congress is being exposed to both deep and shallow ecological testimony on environmentally related subjects. Though there is a preponderance of shallow ecological testimony, it is not as skewed as one might expect. The very fact that Congress is being exposed to deep ecological ideas and attitudes is a measure of the ecophilosophy's influence on environmental politics.

Table 7.11
Overall Ecological Scores, Number

Ecological Classification	Environment	Non-environment	All
Superficial	20	88	108
Shallow	33	40	73
Mixed	43	14	57
Deep	14	6	20
Very Deep	9	1	10

[7]If a particular piece of testimony recorded a "Not Applicable" for all five ecological categories, it was not scored. All other testimony was scored based on the mean average of the individual scores for each ecological category.

Of the 149 scored pieces of non-environment testimony, 128 were either superficial or shallow (88 and 40, respectively). Only 14 were mixed and a minute number, 7, embodied a deep ecological outlook (6 deep, 1 very deep). When both sets of data are combined, the results are much like those of the non-environment testimony. Table 7.11 provides the total for each of three breakdowns of the data.

Table 7.12 illustrates the same data as before, but in percentages. The apparent equilibrium found previously among the data for the environment-specific legislation is now less noticeable. Additionally, it is significant that 59 percent, a strong majority, of all non–environment-specific testimony (that still incorporates the term "environment") was superficial in its overall ecological outlook whereas only 5 percent fell on the deep ecological side of the midpoint.

Table 7.12
Overall Ecological Scores, Percentages

Ecological Classification	Environment	Non-Environment	All
Superficial	.17	.59	.40
Shallow	.28	.27	.27
Mixed	.36	.09	.21
Deep	.12	.04	.07
Very Deep	.08	.01	.04

Figure 7.7 shows the disparity between environment-specific testimony and other testimony in the ecological outlook of the individual or organization testifying. The primary difference between the three sets of data is that the environment-specific has a relatively normal distribution of ecological viewpoints whereas the other two sets are extremely skewed toward the shallow (even superficial) ecological outlook. The conclusions drawn from this holistic evidence as opposed to that from the breakdown evidence cited previously are quite different. Whereas this evidence illustrates the absence of almost any deep ecological influence, the previous data from each of the five tenets suggested that some planks of the deep ecological platform have penetrated environmental politics whereas others have yet to win favor in the political arena.

Figure 7.7
Overall Ecological Scores: Percentages of Shallow and Deep Ecological Testimony

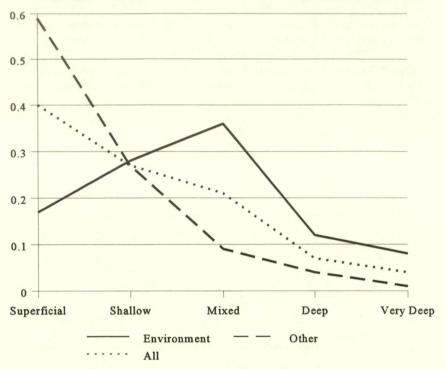

Table 7.13
Composite Scores by Date

Time Period	Overall	Environment-Specific
July - Dec '93	2.12	2.59
Jan - June '94	2.21	2.86
July - Dec '94	2.01	2.72
Jan - June '95	2.16	2.68
July - Dec '95	2.13	2.60
Jan - June '96	2.02	2.39

The final way to measure the ecological leaning of congressional testimony is by the composite score for each time period. This aids in the measurement of progression of influence. Table 7.13 provides the overall composite as well as environmental-specific scores by date. The accompanying graph (Figure 7.8) gives an ill-

Figure 7.8
Progression of Composite Scores

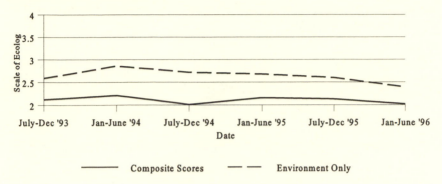

—————— Composite Scores   — — Environment Only

ustrative view of the progression of ecological outlook on the part of those who have testified in the past three years. Before I comment on the trend (or lack thereof) of the composite scores, the differences in the overall composite and environmental composite scores deserves some attention. The environmental scores were between 18 and 35 percent higher than the overall scores. This frequently correlated with approximately ½ point on the ecological scale, which is quite significant on a four-point scale. To classify the scores as a group, the environmental scores, for the most part, were well within the "mixed" range. The overall composite scores, on the other hand, were firmly rooted within the shallow ecological range.

The graphical representation of these scores is more significant for what it fails to show than for what it actually illustrates. Figure 7.8 shows no discernible progression during the three-year time span from July 1993 to June 1996. Both the overall composite and the environmental composite scores support the conclusion that little has actually changed in the overall ecological outlook of those testifying before Congress. However, if one recalls the initial study of each of the five individual tenets, this aforementioned conclusion is not entirely correct. While the trends of three of the five individual element scores exemplified a similar trend to that of the composite scores, two tenets showed a distinctive trend. It just so happens that the trend in favor of high-tech solutions and centralized control offset (ecologically speaking) the opposite trend in favor of limited resources. So while the overall trend appears stable, it is only apparent because of the equalization of two offsetting trends.

One of the reasons for the selection of the three-year time period from July of 1993 to June of 1996 is that it allowed for an analysis of the 1994 election in which the Republican party gained control of both the U.S. Senate and House of Representatives. Some may ask whether one and a half years is a long enough time span to fully measure the effects. Writing in the *American Political Science Review*, Courtney Brown notes that "a great deal can happen quickly with regard to the environment when small changes occur in pollution and policy rates and when the political parties differ in their environmental policies."[8] The data presented here support the conclusion that while the election led to some minor changes in certain elements of environmental testimony, for the most part, testimony before the U.S. Congress continues to have a shallow ecological leaning.

---

[8]Courtney Brown, "Politics and the Environment: Nonlinear Instabilities Dominate," *American Political Science Review* 88, no. 2 (June, 1994): 301.

8

Deep Ecology and the Legal System

INTRODUCTION

This chapter examines the relationship between deep ecology and the legal system in America. It traces the progression of environmental law over the last twenty-five years while exploring contemporary legal writing on the subject of deep ecology and the law. The courts have become a major battleground in the struggle to save the environment. They have become an indispensable medium for environmental action. The sheer amount of environmental litigation has made many law makers ponder incorporating restrictions to citizen suits in new environmental legislation. This would be a major setback to the deep ecology movement. According to Arne Naess, "the general attitude among politicians has been that if a major type of interference in the ecosystem cannot be *proven* to be bad then it is justifiable to continue with business as usual."[1] The manner in which deep ecologists attempt to prove an action to be bad is through the court system. More than any other country, lawyers in the United States have been able to mobilize laws against unecological decisions.[2]

This chapter examines how lawyers and environmental advocates utilize the law to protect wildlife and nature. It also surveys fifty different law review articles that mention the term "deep ecology" to explore contemporary legal thinking on the subject of deep ecology. The final sections of the chapter attempt to explain the rationale behind deep ecology's limited impact on environmental law and how deep ecology would interact with the legal system in a deep ecological world.

The creation of law evolved from the institutionalization and codification of society-accepted norms and values. These norms and values help to guide policy makers in the creation of law and partly explain why citizens obey the law. Environmental

---

[1]Arne Naess and David Rothenberg, *Ecology, Community and Lifestyle: Outline of an Ecosophy* (New York: Cambridge University Press, 1989): 211.
[2]Ibid., p. 146.

law is different than most other law, however, in one key aspect. While other areas of law are products of external values rooted in accepted norms, environmental law is a product of values not rooted in the realm of human customs. Thus it is difficult to integrate into the American legal system. For example, the Constitution "is not a source of environmental rights and duties because the values that environmentalism promotes are not exclusively those of the Enlightenment."[3] Furthermore, there is a natural tension between deep ecology and the ideals on which the legal system is based. The legal system is a top-down, centralized system of governance. While it allows individual access to redress grievances, it is an essentially paternal system. Deep ecology, on the other hand, argues for bottom-up change. It is essentially decentralized and attempts to raise the consciousness level of each individual.

This apparent incompatibility between the legal system and deep ecology is reflected in the "dearth of viable, practical, or theoretical writing in the legal literature about future generations or deep ecology."[4] Deep ecology challenges the current anthropocentric values and ideology of the legal culture. It requires a change in both policy and perspective to a biocentric model. While some deep ecological theorists feel this is possible through incremental change, others feel it requires nothing less than revolution.

VALUES AND THE LAW

The difficulty in any change in the legal system lies in the fundamental linkage between societal values and the law. Laws are supposed to be the formal institutionalization of current societal values and norms. The legal system is in a state of continuous flux, attempting to either "catch up" or "wait for" changes in societal norms. However, it is difficult for even society to agree on certain overarching norms. Frequently, this tension in value systems translates into conflict, not only in society but also, and especially, in the legal system. This is particularly true for environmental law. It "graphically illustrates how competing societal values battle against one another in the statehouses, courthouses and marketplaces of the nation. Environmental protection pits the well-established societal norm of modernization, in a word, 'progress,' against an emerging societal value that supports conservation of the earth's natural resources, including air and water."[5] The situation is even more complicated, for this "emerging societal value that supports conservation," entails many different and competing values ranging from "thoughtful stewardship" to "radical environmentalism." An examination

---

[3]Edwin McCullough, "Through the Eye of a Needle: The Earth's Hard Passage back to Health," *University of Oregon Journal of Environmental Law and Litigation* 10 (1995): 389.

[4]Ibid., p. 416.

[5]Beverly McQueary Smith, "The Viability of Citizens' Suits Under the Clean Water Act After *Gwaltney of Smithfield v. Chesapeake Bay Foundation,*" *Case Western Reserve Law Review* 40 (1990): 1.

of case law illustrates what happens when these differing societal values clash in the courtroom.

EARLY EXAMPLES OF DEEP ECOLOGICAL IDEAS IN THE COURTS

As deep ecology gains greater popular following, many legal scholars are beginning to take notice. Though a body of literature has recently developed that argues for legal rights of animals, plants, and other natural objects, the law has not always neglected such issues. In fact, legal rights for animals was a basic tenet of early English thought; "it is only since humans have had the power to alter natural processes and resources unilaterally that the rights of nonhumans have even been an issue."[6] Before deep ecology became a familiar concept, two environmental writers, law professor Earl Finbar Murphy and conservation biologist David W. Ehrenfeld, independently arrived at the same notion that nonhuman life has value independent of that assigned to it by humans.[7] Law professor Earl E. Murphy wrote in 1977 that the courts had always had a relationship with nature. He explained:

At no time, even in periods of emphasis upon intense exploitation of nature, has the law been silent as to environmental protection. Someone interested in finding such legal purposes can find them at any age if he [sic] searches deeply enough. It may be in manorial custom, municipal ordinances, state statutes, or court decisions concerning nuisance; but the concern of the legal system for the environment, as formally expressed, has always existed.[8]

This relationship between the legal system and nature came to a watershed in 1973 with a landmark Supreme Court case concerning the rights of nonhuman entities. It was the first time that the idea of legal standing for nonhuman life-forms was debated (and almost prevailed).

LEGAL STANDING FOR THE ENVIRONMENT

Sierra Club v. Morton/Should Trees Have Standing?

In the early 1970s, the Sierra Club sued under the Administrative Procedure Act challenging the issuance of commercial development permits for a ski resort on Storm Mountain in the Sequoia National Forest.[9] The area was a national game refuge and the Sierra Club pursued legal litigation to prevent the development of this wild

---

[6]William M. Flevares, "Ecosystems, Economics, and Ethics: Protecting Biological Diversity at Home and Abroad," *Southern California Law Review* 65 (May, 1992): 2039.

[7]Edwin R. McCullough, "Through the Eye of a Needle: The Earth's Hard Passage back to Health," p. 389.

[8]Earl E. Murphy, quoted in Edwin R. McCullough, "Through the Eye of a Needle: The Earth's Hard Passage back to Health," *University of Oregon Journal of Environmental Law and Litigation* 10 (1995): 389.

[9]*Sierra Club v. Morton*, 405 U.S. 727 (1972).

area. It asserted that through its activities, it possessed a special interest in preserving Storm Mountain. They alleged that the proposed development would destroy the scenery and ecological balance of the area in question.[10] The main obstacle to the utilization of the courts for environmental protection concerns the issue of standing. The Sierra Club sued in its "capacity as a membership organization with 'a special interest in the conservation and the sound maintenance of the national parks, game refuges and forests of the country.'"[11] The Sierra Club, however, did not allege that any of its members "would be affected in any of their activities or pastimes [by the development of Storm Mountain]."[12]

The question of legal standing was invoked. Was the party seeking review among the injured? Did the Sierra Club pass the "injury in fact test"? The Court recognized that the Congress had the ability to expand the range of redressable injuries that were subject to citizen standing through legislation.[13] Absent congressional provisions, the injury requirement could be satisfied through shared aesthetic and economic harms. Though the decision explicitly recognized that aesthetic and environmental injuries can satisfy the injury in fact standard, the problem with the Sierra Club's allegation, according to the Court, was that it represented only the interests of the general public.[14] It was unable to demonstrate that any single member of its group suffered concrete and specific harms.[15]

Although the Sierra Club maintained that it represented the interests of the general public, and for this reason should have legal standing to prevent the development, the Club never argued for interests of the mountain. While the case was being heard, Christopher Stone, a legal scholar at the University of Southern California, was grappling with the question of whether inanimate objects should have legal standing of their own. Though he was unable to finish his study in time for use by the Sierra Club lawyers in their oral arguments, he was able to deliver a copy to Supreme Court Justice Douglas for use in the discussion and decision of the case. Stone argued for the extension of legal standing to natural objects. He thought that the Court should look to the harms inflicted upon nature and not the indirect harms caused to any group or to citizens in general. Stone's analysis, *Should Trees Have Standing?*, published as a law review article and then as a book, continues to be a thought-provoking and provocative piece to this day.

---

[10]Ibid., at 734, 735.

[11]Robert B. June, "Citizen Suits: The Structure of Standing Requirements for Citizen Suits and the Scope of Congressional Power," *Environmental Law—Northwestern School of Law of Lewis & Clark College* 24 (Spring, 1994): 761.

[12]*Morton*, 405 U.S. at 734.

[13]Ibid., at 738.

[14]Stanley E. Rice, "Standing on Shaky Ground: The Supreme Court Curbs Standing for Environmental Plaintiffs in *Lujan v. Defenders of Wildlife*," *Saint Louis University Law Review* 38 (Fall, 1993): 199.

[15]*Morton*, 405 U.S. at 736.

In the work, Stone traces the history of legal rights. He argues that each extension of rights to some new entity throughout legal history was a little unthinkable. The legal scholar explains:

We are inclined to suppose the rightlessness of rightless "things" to be a decree of Nature, not a legal convention acting in support of some status quo. It is thus that we defer considering the choices involved in all their moral, social, and economic dimensions. And so the United States Supreme Court could straight-facedly tell us in *Dred Scott* that Blacks had been denied rights of citizenship "as a subordinate and inferior class of beings, who had been subjugated by the dominant race. . . ." In the nineteenth century, the highest court in California explained that Chinese had not the right to testify against white men in criminal matters because they were "a race of people whom nature has marked as inferior, and who are incapable of progress or intellectual development beyond a certain point . . . between whom and ourselves nature has placed an impassable difference."[16]

Similar explanations were made by the Court concerning the justification for the denial of rights to Jews and women. Today, most everyone looks back in disgust at the narrow-mindedness and morally corrupt nature of such statements. Stone borrows from the land ethic advanced by Aldo Leopold. Remember that it was Leopold who made a very similar line of argumentation by tracing the extension of rights to women and blacks. Stone's article explained that he was quite serious about proposing legal rights for the forests, oceans, rivers, and other natural objects in the environment.[17] Such a proposal was considered in the 1970s, as it is today, very radical. But is it really that radical, that far-fetched, or that unwelcomed?

Writing in 1973, Stone argued that the answer to these questions was no. In fact, Stone felt that the legal system was ripe for such a change. He wrote, "[i]n fact, I do not think it would be a misdescription of recent developments in the law to say that we are already on the verge of assigning some such rights, although we have not faced up to what we are doing in those particular terms."[18] In *Morton*, the Supreme Court came close to agreeing with Stone. Due to unusual circumstances, the Supreme Court was only seven justices strong. It decided, with a 4 to 3 majority, against the Sierra Club on the basis that the Sierra Club did not meet the standing requirement. Justice Stewart, writing for the majority, argued that

aesthetic and environmental well-being, like economic well-being, are important ingredients of the quality of life in our society, and the fact that particular environmental interests are shared by the many rather than the few does not make them less deserving of legal protection through the judicial process. But the "injury in fact" test requires more than an injury to a cognizable interest.[19]

---

[16]Christopher D. Stone, *Should Trees Have Standing?: Toward Legal Rights for Natural Objects* (Los Altos, CA: William Kaufman, 1974): 6.

[17]Ibid., p. 9.

[18]Ibid., p. 10.

[19]*Morton*, 405 U.S. at 734–735.

The majority addressed the question of legal standing as it was presented in oral arguments, preferring not to entertain this new question of standing for inanimate objects. The Court ruled that "a mere 'interest in a problem,' no matter how long-standing the interest and no matter how qualified the organization is in evaluating the problem, is not sufficient by itself to render the organization 'adversely affected' or 'aggrieved' within the meaning of the APA."[20] The idea of legal standing for natural objects was, however, addressed in the dissenting opinions of the Court.

Justice Douglas provided one of the most memorable dissents in the field of environmental law. In chambers, Douglas distributed a pre-publication copy of Stone's article and fiercely lobbied his fellow justices. His dedication to environmental protection is very transparent in his dissent. The Supreme Court Justice wrote, "Contemporary public concern for protecting nature's ecological equilibrium should lead to the conferral of standing upon environmental objects to sue for their own preservation."[21] Douglas noted that the law already recognizes standing for some inanimate objects. For example, standing has been conferred upon ships. In *Tucker v. Alexandoff*, the Court stated that "[a] ship is born when she is launched, and lives so long as her identity is preserved. Prior to her launching she is a mere congeries of wood and iron. . . . In the baptism of launching she receives her name, and from the moment her keel touches the water she is transformed. . . . She acquires a personality of her own."[22] Additionally, Douglas illustrated how corporations are inanimate objects that are provided legal standing. Using these examples of accepted legal standing for other inanimate objects, Douglas argues that all natural objects should be awarded similar rights:

So should it be as respects valleys, alpine meadows, rivers, lakes, estuaries, beaches, ridges, groves of trees, swampland, or even air that feels the destructive pressures of modern technology and modern life. The river, for example, is the living symbol of all the life it sustains or nourishes—fish, aquatic insects, water ouzels, otter, fisher, deer, elk, bear, and all other animals, including man, who are dependent on it or who enjoy it for its sight, its sound, or its life. The river as plaintiff speaks for the ecological unit of life that is part of it.[23]

Douglas viewed the courts as an appropriate actor in safeguarding America's wilderness. His opinion was perhaps less concerned with legal precedent (though he did not ignore this subject) and more concerned with how to best protect the environment. He noted, "with all respect, the problem is to make certain that the inanimate objects, which are the very core of America's beauty, have spokesmen before they are destroyed."[24] In *Morton*, the spokesperson was the Sierra Club. According to Douglas, the group should not just have represented its members, but rather represented the actual mountain and game refuge to be developed. In a footnote,

---

[20]Ibid., at 739.

[21]Douglas (dissent), *Morton*, 405 U.S. at 743.

[22]*Tucker v. Alexandoff*, 183 U.S. 424, 438 (1902).

[23]Douglas (dissent), *Morton*, 405 U.S. at 744.

[24]Ibid., at 745.

Douglas explained that "permitting a court to appoint a representative of an inanimate object would not be significantly different from customary judicial appointments of guardians *ad litem*, executors, conservators, reviewers, or counsel for indigents. The values that ride on decisions such as the present one are often not appreciated even by the so-called experts."[25]

The difficulty in protecting wilderness areas, according to Douglas, lies in the different standards upon which standing may be conferred. For example, those who hike the Appalachian Trail, or climb the Guadalupes in West Texas, or even canoe the Quetico Superior in Minnesota have standing to defend such natural areas even if they live thousands of miles away. The harm they would experience from development of these areas is real. However, those who are generally concerned with the well-being of a certain waterway or a tract of forests are denied standing in a court of law. For Douglas, this "is why these environmental issues should be tendered by the inanimate object itself. Then there will be assurances that all of the forms of life which it represents will stand before the court—the pileated woodpecker as well as the coyote and bear, the lemmings as well as the trout in the streams."[26] The deep ecological ideas are transparent in Douglas's dissent. He even quotes Aldo Leopold's land ethic, noting that "'the land ethic simply enlarges the boundaries of the community to include soils, waters, plants, and animals, or collectively, the land.' That, as I see it, is the issue of 'standing' in the present case and controversy."[27] It would be difficult to find a better example of the influence of deep ecology on the legal system than that contained in the words of Justice Douglas. Though Douglas was unable to persuade enough of his colleagues to adopt his "deep ecological" ideas, his words and theories on environmental law continue to pervade and inspire those in the legal profession.

Justice Blackmun, in less explicit terms, supported his fellow Supreme Court Justice. Blackmun asked, in his dissent, "must our law be so rigid and our procedural concepts so inflexible that we render ourselves helpless when the existing methods and the traditional concepts do not quite fit and do not prove to be entirely adequate for new issues?"[28] The Justice exemplified the battle between competing societal values. Like Douglas, Blackmun was concerned with doing what was right, even though current legal theory had perhaps yet to catch up. Like Stone and Douglas, Blackmun argued that extending the right of legal standing to groups such as the Sierra Club to litigate on behalf of natural preserves was not a radical change. For, "it should be no cause for alarm. It is no more progressive than was the decision in *Data Processing* itself. It need only recognize the interest of one who has a provable, sincere, dedicated, and established status. We need not fear that Pandora's box will be opened or that there will be no limit to the number of those who desire to participate in environmental litigation."[29]

---

[25]Ibid., at 750.

[26]Ibid., at 752.

[27]Ibid., at 752.

[28]Blackmun (dissent), *Morton*, 405 U.S. at 755.

[29]Ibid., at 757–758.

Blackmun takes issue with the Court's choice to conclude its opinion with a footnote reference to de Tocqueville. The Supreme Court Justice chose to conclude his dissent with a footnote reference to "the older and particularly pertinent observation and warning of John Donne."[30] The footnote stated:

No man is an Iland, intire of itselfe; every man is a peece of the Continent, a part of the maine; if a Clod bee washed away by the Sea, Europe is the lesse, as well as if a Promontorie were, as well as if a Mannor of thy friends or of thine owne were; any man's death diminishes me, because I am involved in Mankinde; And therefore never send to know for whom the bell tolls; it tolls for thee.[31]

The deep ecological overtones in Blackmun's writing are apparent. The ecological themes of interconnectiveness and biocentrism are illustrated in his arguments.

The case of *Sierra Club v. Morton* continues to serve as perhaps the prime example of the influence of deep ecology on the doctrine of legal standing, if not an example of its influence on the entire legal system. More than any other case examined in this chapter, the influence of deep ecological ideas is transparent.

United States v. Students Challenging Regulatory Agency Procedures

Though the Court did not go as far as Justices Douglas or Blackmun had wished, it did provide other environmental advocacy groups with a clear direction for meeting tests for legal standing. One of the first post-Morton cases was brought by Students Challenging Regulatory Agency Procedures (SCRAP). In the case, a group of law students in Washington, DC, challenged a proposal made by the Interstate Commerce Commission that would increase railroad freight rates for recycled goods. The group claimed that the proposed rates were unreasonably high and would increase the use of natural resources because it would decrease recycling and thus impede the students' enjoyment of these resources.[32] The Court determined that the members of SCRAP had alleged sufficient injury in fact because they "used the forests, streams, mountains, and other resources in the Washington metropolitan area for camping, hiking, fishing, and sightseeing."[33]

Thus unlike the Sierra Club, which claimed standing on behalf of the public, SCRAP was able to clearly show injury on part of its individual members. Additionally, the Court also relaxed the causation component of environmental standing. In another case five years later, the Court granted standing to the Carolina Environmental Study Group, Inc., even though their alleged chain of causation was attenuated and lacked

---

[30]Ibid., at 760.

[31]*Devotions*, XVII, quoted in Blackmun (dissent), *Morton*, 405 U.S. at 760.

[32]*United States v. Students Challenging Regulatory Agency Procedures*, 412 U.S. 675–679 (1973).

[33]Ibid., at 685; See also, Stanley E. Rice, "Standing on Shaky Ground: The Supreme Court Curbs Standing for Environmental Plaintiffs in *Lujan v. Defenders of Wildlife*," *Saint Louis University Law Review* 38 (Fall, 1993): 199.

a proximate relationship between the claimed harm and the allegedly illegal statute.[34] Though environmentalists were able to gain greater access to the courts, standing continued to be construed under an anthropocentric framework. Groups interested in preserving wildlife areas had to first show how their members, not the natural objects, were injured. The courts only listened to cases where a human suffered direct harm regardless of the severity of the harm to the environment.

From 1970 to the present day, the standing doctrine in environmental litigation has undergone significant change. Prior to 1970, environmental organizations were virtually excluded from the legal system. Yet by the mid to late 1970s, "the standing hurdle had been transformed from 'a significant doctrinal barrier to a nettlesome technicality.'"[35] The removal of this barrier allowed environmental groups and concerned citizens the ability to challenge federal agency action. Environmental plaintiffs reaped the benefits of relaxed standing requirements during the 1970s and 1980s, even as new standing limitations increasingly denied access to other litigants.[36] This relative open-door invitation for litigation, however, has recently begun to close. Recent environmental decisions by the Supreme Court have reinstituted a more stringent standing analysis.

Lujan v. National Wildlife Federation

A new era of environmental litigation was ushered in with *Lujan v. National Wildlife Federation*.[37] The case marked the beginning of the end of liberalized standing for environmental organizations. The National Wildlife Federation (NWF), a large non-governmental environmental organization, challenged a Bureau of Land Management (BLM) decision that reclassified certain federal lands "under the 'land withdrawal review program' of the Federal Land Policy and Management Act of 1976 (FLPMA)."[38] This decision would open these lands to mineral exploitation and development. The members of the NWF sought review of the BLM's actions because they alleged that the actions in question violated certain safeguarding statutes, including the procedural mandates of the FLPMA, which require agencies to develop public land use plans and provide environmental impact reports of proposed actions. The group alleged that the recreational use and aesthetic enjoyment of the lands shared by its members were adversely affected.[39]

---

[34]See Stanley E. Rice, "Standing on Shaky Ground: The Supreme Court Curbs Standing for Environmental Plaintiffs in *Lujan v. Defenders of Wildlife*," p. 199; See also *Duke Power Co. v. Carolina Environmental Study Group, Inc.*, 438 U.S. 59 (1978).

[35]Stanley E. Rice, "Standing on Shaky Ground: The Supreme Court Curbs Standing for Environmental Plaintiffs in *Lujan v. Defenders of Wildlife*," p. 199.

[36]Ibid., p. 211.

[37]*Lujan v. National Wildlife Federation*, 497 U.S. 877 (1990).

[38]Stanley E. Rice, "Standing on Shaky Ground: The Supreme Court Curbs Standing for Environmental Plaintiffs in *Lujan v. Defenders of Wildlife*," p. 211.

[39]Ibid., pp. 211–212; *Wildlife Federation*, 497 U.S. at 879.

The Court never addressed the actual merits of the case, ruling instead on the issue of standing. It reversed a decision by the DC Circuit Court of Appeals that upheld a preliminary injunction preventing additional reclassifications.[40] The Court held that the NWF members failed to allege specific facts illustrating actual injury and did not sufficiently show that any such injuries stemmed from the agency action in question. Additionally, the Court also rejected NWF's claim of organizational injury, citing its failure to demonstrate injury or causation.[41] According to Stanley Rice, "the Wildlife Federation decision requires plaintiffs to plead injury with such specificity that standing appears to be possible only when organizations establish a 'direct connection between [their] members' use of [a particular area] and the location where the action of the third party will occur.'"[42] The decision paved the way for an even more limiting interpretation of the standing doctrine for environmental litigants. It was a significant setback for deep ecologists attempting to seek environmental protection through the courts. Though the NWF did not specifically limit standing for citizen suits provisions (a popular measure whereby environmental advocates are able to bring suit through specifically outlined congressional legislative provisions), it set the stage for another important case, *Lujan v. Defenders of Wildlife*, which would take this next step forward (or backward from a deep ecological viewpoint).

Lujan v. Defenders of Wildlife

The case of *Lujan v. Defenders of Wildlife*[43] (hereinafter *Defenders*) ensured that plaintiffs attempting to sue via congressional grants of standing will be subject "to a restrictive interpretation of the standing doctrine."[44] Section 7 of the Endangered Species Act (ESA) requires that federal agencies consult with the Secretary of the Interior whenever their actions may adversely affect a protected species. The underlying dispute in *Defenders* occurred when the Secretary reversed a previously issued regulation that stated that this consultation provision applied to U.S.-funded projects in foreign countries. The Defenders of Wildlife sued under the citizen suit provision of the ESA. The suit alleged that certain overseas projects funded by U.S. agencies threatened their interests in observing endangered species in those areas.[45] Instead of addressing the merits of this underlying dispute, the Court focused on the issue of standing. It ruled that the Defenders did not have standing to bring the claim because its members failed to demonstrate injury as required by article 3 of the Constitution. The narrow

---

[40]*National Wildlife Federation v. Burford*, 835 F.2d 305 (DC Cir. 1987).

[41]*Wildlife Federation*, 497 U.S. at 887, 898–99.

[42]Stanley E. Rice, "Standing on Shaky Ground: The Supreme Court Curbs Standing for Environmental Plaintiffs in *Lujan v. Defenders of Wildlife*," p. 212.

[43]112 S. Ct. 2130 (1992).

[44]Stanley E. Rice, "Standing on Shaky Ground: The Supreme Court Curbs Standing for Environmental Plaintiffs in *Lujan v. Defenders of Wildlife*," pp. 199–200.

[45]Ibid., p. 200.

interpretation of injury was furthered by the fact that the Court rejected the plaintiff's procedural standing based on the citizen suit provision of the ESA.[46]

The Court thus established a standard for standing that threatens to quell the ability of environmental plaintiffs to sue government agencies even when in accordance with congressional grants of standing. Article 3 of the Constitution has been interpreted by the court to mean that a plaintiff must meet three specific tests to demonstrate standing. First, the alleged injury (actual or threatened) must be a result of the defendant's alleged unlawful conduct. Second, the plaintiff must show causation, or that the injury is in fact traceable to the action in question. Finally, the plaintiff must illustrate redressability, or that the injury will likely be redressed by a favorable outcome.

It is important to note that the doctrine of legal standing applies only to human plaintiffs. Thus, it begs for an anthropocentric value system; for it looks only to harms incurred by humans and completely ignores those caused to the ecosystem or wildlife area in question. Just as values help to form our laws, our laws help to mold our values. Currently, the doctrine of legal standing requires that environmental plaintiffs think (and perhaps act) in a shallow ecological manner. This does not mean that deep ecologists have not attempted to abide by the shallow ecological rules of standing to advance deeper goals. The Defenders of Wildlife is an animal rights organization that seeks "to preserve, enhance and protect the natural abundance and diversity of wildlife including the integrity of natural wildlife ecosystems."[47] The motives behind the case brought forth by this organization appear to at least have some deep ecological overtones. When deep ecologists attempt to operate within their value framework, they are quickly excluded from the legal process. When a group called Citizens to End Animal Suffering and Exploitation, Inc., attempted to sue on behalf of dolphins under the Marine Mammal Protection Act, the Court held that such inanimate objects lacked standing in a court of law.[48] Prior to *Defenders* and *National Wildlife*, environmental groups were able to gain access to the legal system without meeting a strict standard of standing. With this door now closing, the need for specific anthropocentric harms is even greater. Though the courts may be making it more difficult for environmental groups to bring suit, they are beginning to recognize the intrinsic worth of species.

---

[46]Ibid., p. 201; See also *Lujan v. Defenders of Wildlife*, 112 S. Ct. 2137–2146 (1992).

[47]*Brief for the Respondents*, quoted in Stanley E. Rice, "Standing on Shaky Ground: The Supreme Court Curbs Standing for Environmental Plaintiffs in *Lujan v. Defenders of Wildlife*," p. 214.

[48]*Citizens to End Animal Suffering and Exploitation, Inc. v. New England Aquarium*, 836 F. Supp. 45 (D. Mass. 1993).

INTRINSIC WORTH

Tennessee Valley Authority v. Hill

A famous case in 1978, *Tennessee Valley Authority v. Hill*, illustrated both the incalculable nature of species and the teeth of the ESA.[49] The case revolved around the little-known endangered snail darter, a three-inch member of the perch family. The Tennessee Valley Authority (TVA) spent $100 million to build the Tellico Dam in order to flood a stretch of the Little Tennessee River. Just as the dam gates were about to be closed, it was discovered that the area to be flooded by the dam was the only known habitat of the snail darter. The Administrator of the Environmental Protection Agency (EPA), who had previously designated the fish as an endangered species, concluded that if the dam gates were closed, the only known habitat of the snail darter would be destroyed. Thus the Administrator ordered the closure of the dam and shortly thereafter the TVA brought suit to overturn the Administrator's decision.[50]

The case was eventually heard by the U.S. Supreme Court. The TVA argued that the snail darter had no known use, economic or otherwise. The Attorney General actually brought a pickled snail darter to the oral arguments to illustrate just how small it was. Unfortunately for TVA, the Congress failed to place a minimum size requirement in the ESA. A majority of the Court not only upheld a lower court's decision to enjoin operations of the dam project,[51] but it also stated that "Congress viewed the value of endangered species as 'incalculable.'"[52] Chief Justice Burger wrote in the opinion of the court:

It may seem curious to some that the survival of a relatively small number of three-inch fish among all the countless millions of species extant would require the permanent halting of a virtually completed dam for which Congress has expended more than $100 million. The paradox is not minimized by the fact that Congress continued to appropriate large sums of public money for the project, even after congressional Appropriations Committees were apprised of its apparent impact upon the survival of the snail darter. We conclude, however, that the explicit provisions of the Endangered Species Act require precisely that result.[53]

The decision, however, would only temporarily save the snail darter. The notion that a little fish could prevent a $100 million dam was preposterous to many laypeople and law makers alike. Senator Howard Baker of Tennessee described the darter as "the bane of my existence, the nemesis of my golden years, the bold perverter of the

---

[49]*Tennessee Valley Authority v. Hill*, 437 U.S. 153 (1978).

[50]James P. Karp, "Aldo Leopold's Land Ethic: Is an Ecological Conscience Evolving in Land Development Law?" *Environmental Law—Northwestern School of Law of Lewis & Clark* 19 (Summer, 1989): 747–748.

[51]Ibid., p. 748.

[52]*Tennessee Valley Authority v. Hill*, at 187.

[53]Ibid., at 172.

Endangered of the Endangered Species Act."⁵⁴ The snail darter became the centerpiece for lobbying against the ESA. In the end, both the TVA and the darter lost. The TVA lost the suit, and when the darter turned up in South Chickamauga Creek, 60 miles away, Senator Baker was finally able to push through an ESA exemption to finish Tellico Dam.

The snail darter case was an important case for deep ecologists who wanted strict enforcement of the ESA. Though an exemption was passed, the Court's (and the EPA's) persistence in its enforcement served as an important moral victory for deep ecologists concerned with the preservation of biodiversity, no matter the economic ramifications. The ESA is one of the most deep ecological laws ever construed by the federal government. Unfortunately, it was the snail darter that perhaps undermined the popular support of the act.

Fish and Wildlife Coordination Act

An interesting case study that examines the influence of deep ecology on both the courts and the Congress is the Fish and Wildlife Coordination Act.⁵⁵ The act "requires governmental agencies, including the U.S. Army Corps of Engineers, to consult with the Fish and Wildlife Service, the National Marine Fisheries Service and state fish and wildlife agencies about the effects of a proposed water project on fish and wildlife."⁵⁶ Unlike the ESA, the law does not demand that environmental and ecological values prevail over economic or development values. It only asks for the careful consideration of environmental factors. Thus, the battle between environmental and economic values found its way into the legal system on a number of occasions.

Sierra Club v. Alexander. In *Sierra Club v. Alexander*, the Court held that the Fish and Wildlife Coordination Act does not require the decisions of the U.S. Army Corps of Engineers to always correspond with the views of the Fish and Wildlife Service.⁵⁷ The Court stated that the Service's views shall be given serious consideration but that the ultimate decision shall be based on the careful weighing of all the factors that are deemed relevant in each particular case. The Court chose not to take a deep ecological stance, preferring instead the dominant, anthropocentric, social paradigm. Consequently, the act failed to abate the destruction of fish and wildlife. Unfortunately

---

⁵⁴Howard Baker, quoted in John Fleischman, "Counting Darters, Endangered Fish Species," *Audubon* 98, no. 4 (July, 1996): 84.

⁵⁵Fish and Wildlife Coordination Act, 16 U.S.C. 661 (1994).

⁵⁶Edwin McCullough, "Through the Eye of a Needle: The Earth's Hard Passage back to Health," p. 425.

⁵⁷*Sierra Club v. Alexander*, 484 F. Supp. 455 (N.D.N.Y.); affirmed without opinion, 633 F.2d 206 (2d Cir. 1980).

for the deep ecologists, environmental values are frequently subordinated to economic ones when they are left to the discretion of individual agencies.[58]

Northwest Resource Information Center, Inc. v. Northwest Power Planning Council. The failure of the Fish and Wildlife Coordination Act was traced by the Court of Appeals for the Ninth Circuit in *Northwest Resource Information Center, Inc. v. Northwest Power Planning Council (Northwest Resource)*:

In the wake of devastating losses of salmon and steelhead in the mid-1970s, Congress enacted the Fish and Wildlife Coordination Act of 1976. 16 U.S.C. 661–666c. The Coordination Act provided that fish and wildlife have "equal consideration" in the planning and development of hydropower project. In 1978, however, Federal fishery agencies considered invoking the protection of the Endangered Species Act ('ESA'), 16 U.S.C. 1531–44, for Snake River runs. Despite the mandate of the Coordination Act, it was not until the threat of action under the ESA that the depletion of anadromous fish in the Columbia River Basin was considered to be more than merely an issue that would resolve itself over time. Also in 1978, Congress was preparing to revise Northwest electric policies in light of forecasts predicting serious power shortages during critical water years expected in the 1980's. Recognizing the tremendous, detrimental impact of dams on the fish runs, Congress acknowledged "that no longer [should] fish and wildlife be given a secondary status." 126 Cong. Rec. H10,681 (1980) (Statement of Rep. Dingell). In 1980, Congress enacted the Northwest Power Act ("NPA" or "Act").[59]

The failure of the Coordination Act to protect fish and wildlife was rectified with the Northwest Power Act. The case at hand, *Northwest Resource*, was initiated by companies purchasing power from the Bonneville Power Administration. The companies challenged the Pacific Northwest Electric Power and Conservation Planning Council's final amendments to the Columbia River Basin and Wildlife Program. They argued that the Council violated the NPA because they failed to conduct a critical cost-benefit analysis for each measure in the program.[60]

The Court of Appeals decision illustrated the principle of deep ecology that it is impossible to place monetary or economic values on fish and wildlife. The Court stated:

Finally, engaging in a critical cost-benefit analysis of each program measure intended to project, mitigate, and enhance fish and wildlife would work against such efforts. Cost-benefit analysis "measures only the magnitude of costs and benefits; it does not assess the distribution, or equity, of the resulting gains and losses." In other words, non-economic values the Program seeks to further, such as equity, ecology, conservation, and culture, would be ignored. In addition, the application of cost-benefit analysis to the NPA's fish and wildlife provisions would eviscerate another design of the Act; to allow knowledge that is less than scientific uncertainty be a basis

---

[58]Edwin McCullough, "Through the Eye of a Needle: The Earth's Hard Passage back to Health," p. 425.

[59]*Northwest Resource Information Center, Inc. v. Northwest Power Planning Council,* 35 F.3d 1371, 1377 (9th Cir. 1994).

[60]Edwin McCullough, "Through the Eye of a Needle: The Earth's Hard Passage back to Health," p. 426.

for sound decision-making, thereby shifting the burden of proof to those challenging fishery managers' recommendations. We reject the [intervenor's] contention that a critical cost-benefit analysis of each program measure is required.[61]

The Court recognized that traditional anthropocentric models of species valuation do not work to protect the environment for the environment's sake. Deep ecologists point to the example of the Fish and Wildlife Coordination Act as proof that environmental protection must go beyond the anthropocentric framework if it is to succeed in protecting native species. The act also illustrates how the doctrine of intrinsic worth is penetrating all three branches of the federal government. While this does not necessarily indicate a deep ecological influence, it does indicate a move away from traditional anthropocentric and shallow ecological thinking.

ECOLOGY

Another basic tenet of deep ecology, and ecology in general, is that everything is interconnected. This basic principle of ecology notes that all living things are connected in an intricate web of life. Environmentalists point to these relationships in order to block certain activities that may disrupt even a small part of an ecosystem; for even small alterations in the ecosystem can cause a ripple that affects every life form. This principle of interconnectiveness was advanced by Aldo Leopold and others, and now has found its way into the legal system. For example, a Vermont statute requires that builders obtain a state permit before they may develop the land. The state will not issue a permit if it will destroy or significantly jeopardize necessary wildlife habitat. The law requires the decision maker to weigh the economic, social, cultural, and recreational public benefits from the development versus the economic, environmental, or recreational loss to the public from the destruction or alteration of the habitat. One Vermont court found that a proposed development would interfere with the wintering areas for deer and ruled that the land was "necessary wildlife habitat," even though the deer is hardly an endangered species.[62] The court thus recognized the connection between habitat preservation and both deer and human welfare. Additionally, the court acknowledged the fact that deer and humans share the same land and that both uses of the land need to be considered.

United States v. Riverside Bayview Homes

In *United States v. Riverside Bayview Homes*, the Supreme Court recognized the link between wetlands and water quality. Section 404 of the Clean Water Act requires landowners to obtain a permit from the Army Corps of Engineers before

---

[61]*Northwest Resource Information Center, Inc. v. Northwest Power Planning Council*, at 1394–1395.

[62]James P. Karp, "Aldo Leopold's Land Ethic: Is an Ecological Conscience Evolving in Land Development Law?" *Environmental Law—Northwestern School of Law of Lewis & Clark* 19 (Summer, 1989): 755.

engaging in dredging or filling in waters covered by the law. The Corps' Administrator had interpreted the law to include wetlands. In the case at hand, the Supreme Court ruled that waters covered by the act included wetlands because they served to slow the flow of surface runoff and prevent flooding and erosion.[63] While this still represented an anthropocentric outlook, the Court did note that wetlands "serve significant natural biological functions, including food chain production, general habitat, and nesting, spawning, rearing and resting sites for aquatic . . . species."[64] The Court thus recognized what Leopold and other ecologists have long noted: the interconnectiveness of waterways, wetlands, plants, and animals. The logical extension of the Court's observations is a substantiation of the idea that humans are part of, and not separate from, the ecosystem. The influence of deep ecology in this case is very apparent.[65]

Just v. Marinette County

Just v. Marinette County[66] is a case that many deep ecologists would point to as embodying the principles of the eco-philosophy. The case arose from a challenge to a Wisconsin shoreland zoning ordinance that required landowners to receive a permit before filling or grading in a wetland area. When a group of landowners were prevented from filling their land because of the lack of a permit, they brought suit contending that the shoreland zoning ordinance amounted to a regulatory taking.[67] The Wisconsin Supreme Court posed the question: "Is ownership of a parcel of land so absolute that man can change its nature to suit any of his purposes?"[68] The court's answer would please many deep ecologists. It stated, "An owner of land has no absolute and unlimited right to change the essential natural character of his land so as to use it for a purpose for which it was unsuited in its natural state and which injures the rights of others."[69] Furthermore, the court noted that "the changing of wetlands and

---

[63]Ibid., p. 749.

[64]*United States v. Riverside Bayview Homes*, 474 U.S. 134–135 (1985), quoting 33 C.F.R. at 320.4(b)(2)(I) (1985).

[65]Additionally, this acknowledgment of interconnectiveness has been recognized by the EPA. In 1988, the EPA vetoed the granting of a permit by the Corps of Engineers under the same section of the Clean Water Act. The Agency blocked the permit to fill a wetland because the site provided "a valuable wildlife habitat for a variety of amphibians, reptiles, birds and mammals." The economic costs or benefits of these species was never an issue; thus the decision combined two tenets of deep ecology: interconnectiveness and intrinsic worth. See James P. Karp, "Aldo Leopold's Land Ethic: Is an Ecological Conscience Evolving in Land Development Law?" p. 750, quoting from *Current Developments,* 19 Environmental Reporter (BNA) 41 (May 13, 1988).

[66]*Just v. Marinette County*, 56 Wis. 2d 7, 201 N.W.2d 761 (1972).

[67]James P. Karp, "Aldo Leopold's Land Ethic: Is an Ecological Conscience Evolving in Land Development Law?" p. 750.

[68]*Just v. Marinette County*, at 17, 201 N.W.2d at 768.

[69]Ibid.

swamps to the damage of the general public by upsetting the natural environment and the natural relationship is not a reasonable use of that land."[70] The language of the court reflects a deep ecological influence. Though the court did not embrace biocentrism by emphasizing the effects of environmental degradation on the quality of human life, it did recognize at least limited rights for the land as well as the interconnectiveness between the health of the land and that of the welfare of general public.

Usdin v. State

In *Usdin v. State*, the New Jersey Superior Court did not exhibit as much of a deep ecological influence as the Wisconsin Court in *Marinette County*, but it did illustrate a growing concern for environmental protection in the legal system.[71] The court found:

We are continually being made aware that our vital natural resources, our whole ecology and quality of human life, may no longer be considered limitless or indestructible. . . . No longer are we able to afford the luxury of squandering nature or indiscriminate over-development, without consequential regard, and masquerading as free and private enterprise. Perhaps it is trite, but nevertheless true: rights and responsibilities must go hand in hand. While all forms of development adversely affect the environment to the extent that they add to demands already being made, the right to use land should be carefully measured against the environment's capacity to tolerate such a use and the extent of harm which the proposed use would impose upon the established and proper use of neighboring lands. I must conclude that with a proper balancing of ecology at stake. . . . A private landowner has no right to misuse his own land to the severe detriment of another; how can he be heard to complain when a governmental entity acts to insure this result, even if development is strictured or he is required to maintain the natural state?[72]

The observations of the court indicate a limited, but nonetheless important, deep ecological influence. The court noted that humans have certain responsibilities toward the environment, indicating that the environment has certain rights of its own that humans must respect. Additionally, the court acknowledged the linkages between development and ecosystem health. However, the fundamental value framework under which the court operated was still anthropocentric.

---

[70]Ibid.

[71]James P. Karp, "Aldo Leopold's Land Ethic: Is an Ecological Conscience Evolving in Land Development Law?" p. 751.

[72]*Usdin v. State*, 173 N.J. Super. 311, 329–330, 414 A.2d 280, 289 (1981).

A. E. Nettleton Co. v. Diamond

In *A. E. Nettleton Co. v. Diamond*, the New York Court of Appeals upheld a state statute that made it unlawful to import the skins and hides of endangered species.[73] The court chose not to emphasize the human element of species protection, i.e., the aesthetic or scientific value of endangered species. Rather, the court stated that "protection of the animals listed in the Mason Act is necessary not only for their natural beauty and for the purpose of biological study, but for the key role they play in the maintenance of the life cycle."[74] The New York decision is consistent with both Aldo Leopold's land ethic and the deep ecology philosophy. It emphasizes the value of a fully functioning ecosystem, with all of the cogs in the wheel. Additionally, the court seems to acknowledge that humans are part of the ecosystem, another basic tenet of deep ecology.

All four of these cases dealing with interconnectiveness illustrate a deep ecological influence on the courts. Though most of the language continues to fall within an anthropocentric framework, each case recognized the interconnectiveness of all life within an ecosystem.

SHIFTING THE BURDEN

Deep ecologists seek to preserve as much of the natural wilderness as possible. They think that humans should have an ethical obligation to respect the natural integrity of the land as well as the right for all life to flourish. In the courtroom, these moral beliefs translate into a shift in the burden of proof. It requires that those who wish to pollute or change the physical or biological nature of the land have the burden to prove that they in fact are not culpable. This shift in the burden of proof is significant because it is better able to safeguard nature and promote a land ethic.

Landers v. East Texas Salt Water Disposal Co.

Landers v. East Texas Salt Water Disposal Co. is a frequently cited toxic tort case in which it was impossible to determine causation with multiple defendants. East Texas Salt Water Disposal Co. owned a pipeline that conveyed salt water near the plaintiff's land. When the pipe broke, thousands of barrels of salt water flowed onto the plaintiff's land and into his pond, killing all of the fish. At the same time, brine and salt water escaped from a different source, an oil well pipeline, and it also flowed into the plaintiff's pond. Prior to this case, the law "did not recognize any claim for damages for loss of use and enjoyment of land where there were multiple

---

[73]James P. Karp, "Aldo Leopold's Land Ethic: Is an Ecological Conscience Evolving in Land Development Law?" p. 753.

[74]*A. E. Nettleton Co. v. Diamond*, 27 N.Y.2d 182, 194, 264 N.E.2d 118, 124, 315 N.Y.S.2d 625, 633 (1970).

defendants and it could not be determined which one caused the harm."[75] The court in *Landers*, however, refused to adopt a state common law that "effectively relieves the two defendants of the consequences of their wrong, and requires the innocent plaintiff to suffer injuries without recompense."[76] The court chose to hold each defendant liable for the full amount of damages unless they apportioned the damages between them. The case effectively shifted the burden of causation from the plaintiff to the defendant, ensuring that those who pollute either pay for damages or prove alternative causality.

Attorney General v. Thomas Solvent Co.

A Michigan case, *Attorney General v. Thomas Solvent Co.*, established that the burden rests with the party seeking to pollute. The Attorney General for the state of Michigan filed a lawsuit to prevent the threat of harm to public health resulting from contaminants found in the soil at the Thomas Solvent Company. A number of toxic industrial chemicals had been stored by the defendant in fifty-five-gallon drums. Additionally, the defendant kept cleaning solvents in underground tanks. When the chemicals and solvents downstream from Thomas Solvent Co. were found to match those in the aforementioned storage tanks, the Attorney General sought an immediate injunction to stop the contamination. The Attorney General also sought to remove the contaminants from the groundwater to prevent the contamination of adjacent unpolluted property and wells.[77] The court ordered the defendant to install a well to purge groundwater.

When the defendant appealed the preliminary injunction on the basis that it granted relief beyond that required to preserve the status quo, the court answered that "the object of a preliminary injunction is to preserve the status quo, which is the last, actual, peaceable, non-contested status which preceded the pending controversy, so that upon the final hearing the rights of the parties may be determined without injury to either."[78] Furthermore, the court held:

The status quo ante is an unpolluted environment. It is clear that the status quo in this case is the maintenance of uncontaminated groundwater and soil. Defendant's proposed solution would not prevent the contaminants defendant has already poured into the ground from flowing into neighboring properties. Therefore, to preserve the status quo, it was appropriate to require

---

[75]James M. Olson, "Shifting the Burden of Proof: How the Common Law Can Safeguard Nature and Promote an Earth Ethic," *Environmental Law—Northwestern School of Law of Lewis & Clark College* 20 (Winter, 1990): 909–910.

[76]*Landers v. East Texas Salt Water Disposal Co.*, 151 Tex. 251, 248 S.W.2d 734 (1952).

[77]James M. Olson, "Shifting the Burden of Proof: How the Common Law Can Safeguard Nature and Promote an Earth Ethic," p. 913.

[78]*Attorney General v. Thomas Solvent Co.*, 146 Mich. App. 55, 380 N.W.2d 58 (1985).

defendant to install groundwater purge wells and monitoring wells and to treat all purged groundwater with a granular activated carbon filtration system.[79]

The court assigned a very high value on an unpolluted environment and placed the burden of proof on the defendant. It established a precedent whereby when hazardous waste is discovered, the burden of proof can be transferred to the defendants. Although this does not indicate a clear deep ecological influence, the shifting of the burden of proof is regarded by many deep ecologists as the first step toward a much greater deep ecological influence on the legal system.

LIMITATIONS TO DEEP ECOLOGY AND THE LAW

The previous survey of case law indicates a modest, yet limited influence of deep ecology on the courts. Despite the headway made on such issues as interconnectiveness and incalculable economic costs, lawyers have been largely unsuccessful in creating rights for the environment. A. Dan Tarlock observes that "[a]ppeals for new legal rights usually rest on an appeal to a sympathetic tradition, but there was little basis in western civilization to which advocates of the environment could appeal."[80] He outlines four reasons why the effort to create new legal rights for nature has failed. First, rights for the environment do not conform with the paradigm of constitutional rights. Second, common-law theories lack both an ethical and a scientific consensus to specify consistent outcomes in advance of controversy. Third, the attribution of rights to non-human entities lack an adequate philosophical basis according to the current dominant social paradigm. Finally, Tarlock notes that welfare economics prescribed that each controversy should have a different outcome.[81]

While Tarlock does not explicitly state it, the primary reason for the lack of greater deep ecological influence is that the American legal system and environmental laws are grounded in anthropocentric thought. Even in the cases that exhibited a deep ecological influence, the anthropocentric overtones were apparent. The courts have recognized certain nonconsumptive values in nature such as wilderness recreation, aesthetics, and intact ecosystems, but according to Scott W. Hardt, "federal environmental laws recognize value in nature, but that value has consistently been defined in relation to human benefits, and there has been no legal recognition that the environment has value for its own sake."[82] It is not until this anthropocentric mindset changes that deep ecology will be able to make greater headway into the legal system.

---

[79]Ibid., at 63-64, 380 N.W.2d at 58.

[80]A. Dan Tarlock, "Earth and Other Ethics: The Institutional Issues," *Tennessee Law Review* 56 (Fall, 1988): 53.

[81]Ibid.

[82]Scott W. Hardt, "Federal Land Management in the Twenty-First Century: From Wise Use to Wise Stewardship," *The Harvard Environmental Law Review* 18 (Summer, 1994): 345.

PROSPECTS FOR A DEEP ECOLOGICAL INFLUENCE

Though deep ecology has had limited success in influencing the law, many legal scholars have given thought to how the courts would operate within a deep ecological framework. Edwin R. McCullough concludes that the wisdom offered by deep ecologists and by such individuals as Aldo Leopold "encourages an immediate and radical change of equalizing non-economic values and economic values and protecting non-human life. Unfortunately, there are no indications of such change in the law in the near future."[83] Despite such glum prospects (from a deep ecological perspective), many theorists feel that the principles of deep ecology can offer important tools for improving environmental law.

The solution, according to some, is to adopt an environmental ethic that will dominate all legal decision making. Environmental law inherently possesses an ethical dimension. The moral relationship between human activity and ecosystem health is beginning to be acknowledged in current legal, economic, and logical thought.[84] However, advocates for reform of environmental law note that ontological, not just ethical, changes are needed to confer deep ecological principles on the legal system. To embrace nonhuman entities within the courts "requires a step beyond ethics, one that is more onto-logical than ethical. . . . Legal scholars, lawyers and judges must begin to ask a fundamental question: Are legal doctrines, principles and rules ontologically true to the natural order of things independent of human thought?"[85] Such probing reveals major flaws in the current legal system; for how can environmental degradation and ecosystem destruction conform with the natural order of things? This question lies at the heart of environmental law. It asks whether the current shallow ecological framework, on which the legal system is based, is an appropriate paradigm for environmental law. Deep ecologists hope to steer environmental law to ensure that human activity maintains, rather than disrupts, the natural order of things.

Two different approaches to environmental law have surfaced with respect to deep ecology. The first attempts to assign legal rights to nonhuman entities. This approach was discussed in the review of Christopher Stone's *Should Trees Have Standing?* It would allow concerned citizens to bring suit on behalf of the environment. Genuinely interested parties could then act as guardians for environmental objects. Under such a system, "when a friend of a natural object perceives it to be endangered, he [or she] can apply to a court for the creation of a guardianship."[86] According to its advocates, the benefits to such a "deep ecological" legal system help to economize

---

[83]Edwin R. McCullough, "Through the Eye of a Needle: The Earth's Hard Passage back to Health," p. 389.

[84]James M. Olson, "Shifting the Burden of Proof: How the Common Law Can Safeguard Nature and Promote an Earth Ethic," *Environmental Law—Northwestern School of Law of Lewis & Clark College* 20 (Winter 1990): 892.

[85]Ibid., p. 893.

[86]Christopher Stone, quoted in David Hoch, "Stone and Douglas Revisited: Deep Ecology and the Case for Constructive Standing," *Journal of Environmental Law and Litigation* 3 (1988): 139.

the legal process while ensuring that the environmental object is not "sold-out" in negotiation among private litigants. Currently, environmentalists can sue only for environmental costs associated with human welfare. If a stream is polluted, then those downstream may sue for health, recreational, or aesthetic harms caused by the pollution. Any monetary reparation is based on human costs. Under the legal-rights-for-nature approach, a concerned citizen may act as a representative for the river, much like a parent may act on behalf of a child or mentally challenged individual. The river would be able to sue for harms to its health independent of any associated human costs. If found liable, the defendant would pay damages to the river in the form of a trust fund set up for environmental clean-up and restoration. (It may be possible to even extend such a system so that a person could sue the river if it should flood and be able to receive reparations for damages from the trust fund. Admittedly, this is taking the theory of legal rights to an extreme.)

Christopher Stone and others have introduced the notion of legal considerateness to complement legal rights for nature. Legal considerateness includes not only rights, but also obligations of others toward the legally considerate object. While it may not be practical to suggest that a tree may make out a will, it is practical to suggest that people have legal obligations not to cut down the tree. Thus the tree is given legal consideration without actually possessing legal rights.[87] This may be the only way to incorporate legal rights for nature because the prospects for the establishment of legal standing for natural objects do not appear promising (which has led some to speculate that such a change may only be possible through legislative statutes).[88]

Some criticize this approach (besides the obvious practical difficulties) because it rests on a rights-based framework that is still human centered. Instead, these legal scholars promote stewardship, responsibility, and trust independent of a lawsuit context.[89] One of the major obstacles to such a system is the restrictions common law places on proving cause. Problems such as global air and water pollution lie beyond the scope of the courts because of the difficulties in establishing and proving causal links between the specific actions of particular people and the specified environmental degradation. One solution proposed by James Olson and others is to shift the burden of proof with respect to the effects of toxic and hazardous chemicals released into the water, air, and land. The courts have already begun to adopt a limited application of this concept. *Landers v. East Texas Salt Water Disposal Co.* and especially *Attorney General v. Thomas Solvent Co.* illustrate how the courts can shift the burden of proof with respect to the release of toxic materials. Some now suggest that the courts undertake a more systematic and widespread effort to utilize the burden of proof to preserve the natural state of the environment. Instead of a revolutionary change, the practical implications associated with a shift in the burden of proof, which

---

[87]David Hoch, "Stone and Douglas Revisited: Deep Ecology and the Case for Constructive Standing," *Journal of Environmental Law and Litigation* 3 (1988): 133–134.

[88]Ibid., p. 142.

[89]Ibid.

would work within the prevailing legal paradigm, may be able to better realize the goals of deep ecology.[90]

One manner to incorporate elements of both approaches is through the public trust doctrine. The public trust doctrine is a legal principle that those advocating legal reform cite as providing an axiom that expresses the ethical duty and ontological reality of environmental protection in the courts. In *National Audubon Society v. Superior Court*, the California Supreme Court ruled that the public trust doctrine can be utilized to require the city and the state to reconsider their decisions concerning the allocation of water in order to protect the people's heritage in local waterways.[91] The court determined that the doctrine could be expanded beyond the mere protection of navigation, commerce, and fishing. The public trust doctrine should be flexible to meet the changing needs of the public.[92] The court noted the importance of "the preservation of those lands in their natural state, so that they may serve as ecological units for scientific study, as open space, and as environments which provide food and habitat for birds and marine life, and which favorably affect the scenery and climate of the area."[93] Though the reasons advanced by the court are both anthropocentric and ecocentric, it would be difficult to find a deep ecologist who did not agree with the court's language in this case.

The Wisconsin case, *Just v. Marinette County*, discussed previously, is also an example of the application of the public trust doctrine. Recall that the court upheld the legitimacy of a Wisconsin shoreline zoning ordinance. The court applied the public trust doctrine, finding that the ordinance preserved the original integrity of the environment and natural resources. Thus the court affirmed "the California Supreme Court's conclusion that the legitimacy of human activities with land can only be ascertained in an ecological context."[94]

The examples of the use of the public trust doctrine are unique, however, to the states. The federal courts have been less willing to apply the doctrine to environmental cases. In one federal case, the judge concluded that "the inevitable trade-off between economic and ecological values presents a subject-matter which is inherently political, and which is far too serious to relegate to the ad hoc process of 'government by lawsuit' in the midst of a statutory vacuum."[95] The judge decided that the Congress, not the courts, was the appropriate medium for resolving questions of environmental

---

[90]Ibid.

[91]*National Audubon Society v. Superior Court*, 33 Cal. 3d 419, 658 P.2d 709, 189 California Reporter. 346, cert. denied, 464 U.S. 977 (1983).

[92]James P. Karp, "Aldo Leopold's Land Ethic: Is an Ecological Conscience Evolving in Land Development Law?" *Environmental Law—Northwestern School of Law of Lewis & Clark* 19 (Summer, 1989): 754–755.

[93]*National Audubon Society v. Superior Court*, at 434-35, 658 P.2d at 719, 189 California Reporter at 356 (quoting Marks v. Whitney, 6 Cal. 3d 251, 259-60, 491 P.2d 374, 380, 98 California Reporter. 790, 796 [1971]).

[94]James P. Karp, "Aldo Leopold's Land Ethic: Is an Ecological Conscience Evolving in Land Development Law?" p. 755.

[95]*Tanner v. Armco Steel*, 340 F. Supp. 532, 534 (S.D. Tex. 1972).

policy. The relationship between the courts and the Congress is an intricate one beyond the scope of this book. However, it is worth noting that the separation of powers causes problems for deep ecologists wanting to influence policy, for if either power is unsympathetic to deep ecological principles, then it may circumvent the other. The reason that many deep ecological advocates have approached the courts for help is that they have traditionally been more open to citizen concerns. Additionally, the vague nature of many environmental statutes allows courts sympathetic to deep ecology the ability to inject such an influence into the operation and enforcement of an environmental statute, regardless of the original intent of the legislators. These differing approaches to incorporating deep ecology into the legal system have received limited, but growing, attention in both theory and practice. A review of current legal scholarship illustrates this point.

SURVEY OF LAW REVIEW ARTICLES

A search of the Lexis database of law review articles yielded fifty-two different articles in which "deep ecology" was referenced. Thirty-three different law reviews were represented in the sample. The dates of the articles ranged from 1986 to 1996. Most journals carried only one article mentioning "deep ecology," with only two publishing more than two articles on the subject. *Environmental Law* of the Northwestern School of Law of Lewis and Clark College carried the most articles of any journal, with ten since 1989. The content of these articles helped provide the background research for this chapter as well as helped to shed light on legal scholarship and deep ecology.

The vast majority of the articles (thirty of fifty-two) lacked any bias toward the subject; usually due to the fact that the term was mentioned only in passing. The other twenty-two articles had an almost perfect distribution between pro (seven), mixed (seven), and con (eight). Though it would not be prudent to make sweeping conclusions based on the small number of articles in this study, the data do seem to indicate a lack of any explicit bias for or against deep ecology in the world of legal scholarship. Each article delved into the subject of deep ecology to a different degree. For example, twenty of the articles defined the philosophy of deep ecology while thirty included an actual discussion of deep ecology. However, only twelve of the fifty-two articles that mentioned "deep ecology" actually discussed the relationship between deep ecology and the legal system. Instead, most (thirty-four of fifty-two) preferred to concentrate on the broader topic of environmental ethics. The survey of the articles does indicate that deep ecology, and especially Leopold's land ethic, is beginning to gain widespread notice in the legal field. At the very least (given the limitations of Lexis), an average of one article every 1½ months has been published since 1993 in a U.S. law review. Though every article does not discuss the relationship between deep ecology and the law in an in-depth manner, the ecophilosophy is gaining exposure in legal circles. This exposure is destined to at least have some influence on the legal system. Whether this influence is positive or negative is yet to be determined.

CONCLUSION

Deep ecology, on the whole, has yet to penetrate the legal system. Though some courts have begun to recognize certain principles of deep ecology, they have yet to embrace the moral and ethical component of the ecophilosophy. Deep ecology requires a revolutionary moral adjustment in the law, and since the law changes only in small increments, it is very difficult to achieve such a dramatic change through the legal process.[96] Deep ecology requires a complete reorientation of the mind and the heart. The prospects for such a change are doubtful in the legal system:

Although legal scholars shout "revolutions" and "paradigm shifts" aplenty, few legal changes really involve the type of moral readjustment, the type of human humility, for which Leopold [and the deep ecologists who followed him] sounded the call. Law bookshelves are filled with masses of human wisdom and examples of one precedent after another, but few of the volumes discuss changes of heart. The law moves in small steps, not lengthy jumps. When a lengthy jump is needed, the case reporters provide little help. Guidance on real social change, therefore, is best derived from sources and authors outside the law.[97]

However, according to Gary D. Meryers, "[w]hile the deep ecology philosophy may not have gained sufficient popular acceptance to mandate adoption into our legal system, the lessons it teaches ought to be studied seriously by policy makers and elected officials as we move into the twenty-first century."[98]

Deep ecologists, of course, contend that their perspectives can and should play an important role in the development of environmental law. They think that there is already a greater awareness, both culturally and philosophically, of the moral claims of the animals and that the law is lagging behind the times. David Hoch notes, "Law is essentially a reactive and conservative force whose purpose is to preserve a way of life. Because the law reflects societal values, sweeping cultural changes are not articulated in the law until they are established in society. . . . The very contemplation [of legal rights for natural objects] increases societal awareness, thereby encourages society to grant these rights."[99] Deep ecology will have an influence in the legal system only as far as it is able to influence societal values. But it is the mere contemplation of legal rights that may be able to influence societal values. Thus it is when humans begin to think of the environment not just in human terms, both inside and outside

---

[96]William M. Flevares, "Ecosystems, Economics, and Ethics: Protecting Biological Diversity at Home and Abroad," *Southern California Law Review* 65 (May, 1992): 2039.

[97]Eric T. Freyfogle, "The Railroad and the Holocaust," *University of Illinois Law Review* (1986): 301.

[98]Gary D. Meryers, "Old-Growth Forests, the Owl, and Yew: Environmental Ethics Versus Traditional Dispute Resolution Under the Endangered Species Act and Other Public Lands and Resources Laws," *Boston College University Environmental Affairs Law Review* 18 (Summer, 1991): 662.

[99]David Hoch, "Stone and Douglas Revisited: Deep Ecology and the Case for Constructive Standing," p. 148.

of the courtroom, that it is reasonable to surmise that its influence on the legal system (and society) will be great.

An alternative consequence of this paradigm shift is that the legal system will become meaningless. Deep ecology promotes decentralization and the building of intimate relationships between humans and the land. The deep ecologist Paul Shepard observed that the law "may yield remedial effects . . . [and] do some . . . piecemeal good. But [it] cannot even describe, much less solve the problem."[100] The legal system, and government in general, may actually hinder, more than help, this transformation to deep ecology and a land ethic; for it places additional barriers between people and the environment. Formal institutions have the effect of stifling awareness on the part of the individual citizen. Deep ecology is essentially a grass-roots movement that empowers private citizens to make responsible and ethical land use decisions at the local level. If the law is indeed a reflection of social development, then the legal system of a society that values deep ecology would perhaps no longer involve itself in environmental matters, for land use decisions would be made by private citizens who value ecological sustainability. Whether deep ecology will be able to penetrate the legal system and lead to revolutionary changes remains to be seem. James P. Karp notes that "there is significant evidence that progress is being made toward a land ethic. The ideal has not yet been reached, but neither has progress toward it been glacial. Steady progress comes from every area of the law and from each of the two essential conclusions drawn from Leopold's ethic."[101] The coming years should reveal just how far society and the courts will embrace the principles of deep ecology.

---

[100]Paul Shepard, quoted in David Hoch, "Stone and Douglas Revisited: Deep Ecology and the Case for Constructive Standing," pp. 152–153.

[101]James P. Karp, "Aldo Leopold's Land Ethic: Is an Ecological Conscience Evolving in Land Development Law?" p. 737.

III

Deep Ecology and the Media

In the name of "deep ecology," many environmentalists have taken a sharp turn to the ultra-left, ushering in a mood of extremism and intolerance. As a clear signal of this new agenda, in 1990 Greenpeace called for a "grassroots revolution against pragmatism and compromise."

—Alan W. Bock, *The Orange County Register*

[Deep ecology] thinks little of individual lives, whether human or non-human. It advocates "bioregional organization" (i.e., running human life in accordance with "natural constraints"), a sense of rootedness, and a ritualization of life which includes the recovery or recreation of primal rituals. The open totalitarianism here barely needs pointing out; what does need pointing out is how undeep it is.

—Alexander Volokh, *Reason*

[We cannot] just clean up the mess and manage it better. . . . We need to be infused with the idea of deep ecology—meaning we share this planet with a lot of other things and we need to look at how we can live in harmony with them.

—Marla Donato, *Chicago Tribune*

9

Media and Politics

Part III examines the relationship between the media, deep ecology, and politics. The media has played (and will play in the foreseeable future) an important role in the framing of issues for public policy discourse. It is not uncommon for executive and legislative departments to constantly monitor CNN broadcasts for the latest-breaking news as well as circulate a folder of important clippings every morning from that day's newspapers. But the influence of the media is not just felt at the federal level. Regional papers help to influence regional policy makers, and as it has been discussed before, virtually all electoral politics are local in nature. Nevertheless, the media also assumes an even more important role: the education of the mass public. This is why the treatment by the media of deep ecological ideas and concepts is so important in any measurement of the effects of this ecophilosophy.

LINKS BETWEEN THE MEDIA AND POLITICS

The political scientist James Q. Wilson observes that "politicians have become increasingly dependent on the media."[1] The next chapter analyzes over fifteen years of media coverage of deep ecology. The literature search yielded over 400 articles in a variety of media sources. One trend that seems almost certain is that as politicians become increasingly dependent on the media, the media has increasingly covered deep ecological ideas. This symbiosis between government and the fourth estate equates to a useful indicator of the effect of deep ecological beliefs. The relationship between politics and the media may be best summarized by Wilson:

---

[1]James Q. Wilson, *American Government: Institutions and Policies* (fifth edition) (Lexington, MA: D. C. Heath and Company, 1992): 239.

The relationship between journalism and politics is a two-way street: though politicians take advantage as best they can of the media of communication available to them, these media in turn attempt to use politics and politicians as a way of both entertaining and informing their audiences. The mass media, whatever their disclaimers, are not simply a mirror held up to reality or a messenger that carries the news. There is inevitably a process of selection, of editing, and of emphasis, and this process reflects, to some degree, the way in which the media are organized, the kinds of audiences they seek to serve, and the preferences and opinions of the members of the media.[2]

One of the more prevalent complaints from deep ecologists is that the news media, and particularly the national news media, is biased against the deep ecological cause. When Theodore Kaczynski was identified as the prime suspect for the Unabomb killings, ABC News reported alleged ties between Kaczynski and the deep ecological group, Earth First! It was virtually implied that the radical group had supplied the names and targets for certain timber-related bombings. Such implications and negative publicity are taken very seriously by the deep ecologists; for they are aware that "cultural politics are centralised through the mass media, especially TV."[3]

With the advent of the Internet, deep ecologists have just recently been able to spread their message in a relative cheap, yet far-reaching manner. Many of the primary reference materials in this study were obtained through such electronic media, and over the long run, these alternative mechanisms may be able to displace the importance of the traditional news media. It is the nature of politics to respond to changes in how communications are carried on. After all, politics themselves are essentially a form of communication.[4] Yet, due to the newness of the Internet and to still limited popularity, at least for now, the traditional news media is the primary source of information. The media does not just inform, it also performs the roles of gatekeeper, scorekeeper, and watchdog, of the federal, state, and local governments.[5]

Because of the great power of the media, it is frequently the subject of much political discourse concerning party or issue bias. Politicians charge that coverage is either too liberal or too conservative,[6] too pro or anti a certain issue, or too critical or uncritical of a particular candidate for office. Whatever the bias may be, and the next chapter will closely examine this bias as concerning deep ecological issues, one thing is certain: the media has an enormous influence on the public. One study in

---

[2]Ibid., p. 245.

[3]Arne Naess and David Rothenberg, *Ecology, Community and Lifestyle: Outline of an Ecosophy* (New York: Cambridge University Press, 1989): 145.

[4]Wilson, *American Government: Institutions and Policies*, p. 240.

[5]Ibid., p. 247.

[6]Although many of the complaints concerning bias come from the conservative spectrum on the political pendulum, charges of conservative bias do in fact exist, especially in local areas where certain regional newspapers and telecasts are extremely conservative in their reporting.

North Carolina found that the issues that "citizens believed to be important politically were very similar to the issues that newspapers and television newscasts had featured."[7]

Basically defined, the news media is in the business of reporting, editorializing, and organizing information for the mass public and the policy makers. Media takes the form of newsprint, television and radio broadcasts, popular magazines, scholarly journals, and virtually any other means by which news is conveyed to an audience.[8] One of the more interesting aspects of the news media is the great diversity it possesses. Though the national news media receives the most attention from social scientists, this study includes both local and international, both popular and scholarly, and both conservative and liberal media sources.

If one were to base the effectiveness of the media in conveying deep ecological thoughts on the number of people who hold such beliefs, the results would indicate an apparent inadequacy in the media. Mark McBeth comments in *Spectrum: The Journal of State Government* that the vast majority of people exhibit a rather shallow utilitarian view of environmental protection. Respondents to his study "support environmental protection only if benefits outweigh costs. [They] seem to view the environment as an economic asset to be protected for the economic benefit of humans."[9] This evidence alone, however, does not provide a clear explanation of the treatment of deep ecological ideas and events by the media. For what if the media has performed a superior job in conveying the deep ecologist's message and, contrary to the predictions of these radical environmentalists, the public just does not agree?

While one may conclude that since most voters hold a shallow, rather than deep, ecological view of environmental matters, they would elect politicians with similar positions. This is true to an extent, for those officials who ignore public opinion and devise policies to the contrary will eventually suffer at the polls. But this is largely a non sequitur; for the purposes of this study the "major effects of the media, however, probably have much less to do with how people vote in an election and much more to do with how politics are conducted."[10] One empirical example of how media-influenced public opinion has affected environmental politics is described by Ronald Cheek:

The origins of the EPA can be traced to the environmental movement. By 1969, public opinion concerning environmental issues had become sufficiently solidified to bring about the adoption of a national statement of policy on the environment. This national statement was driven primarily by the media's exposure of environmental issues. As a result of the widespread belief that

---

[7]Wilson, *American Government: Institutions and Policies*, p. 253.

[8]Though the term is defined relatively broad in scope, this study does not enlarge the definition to the point that all media, such as lectures and leaflets, are included in analysis.

[9]Mark K. McBeth, "The Environment v. the Economy: Attitudes of State Rural Development Officials," *Spectrum: The Journal of State Government* 69, no. 1 (Winter, 1996): 17–25.

[10]Wilson, *American Government: Institutions and Policies*, p. 252.

industry was not always responding to its social responsibilities, environmental social issues became public policy through legislation and regulations regarding environmental protection.[11]

So while pubic opinion is a variable of some use in determining the effects of deep ecology on environmental politics, the manner in which the news media frames and discusses issues related to this ecophilosophy is even more important. For better or worse, everyone believes that the media has a profound effect on politics.[12] Thus, determining how the media conveys deep ecological ideas is one indicator, though indirect, of the influence that deep ecology has on environmental politics.

---

[11]Ronald G. Cheek, et al. "Environmental Apocalypse Now: Environmental Protection Agency Policies as Threats to the Environment," *Industrial Management* 37, no. 3 (May, 1995): 6.

[12]Wilson, *American Government: Institutions and Policies*, p. 252.

10

Media Coverage of Deep Ecology

With the term "deep ecology" occurring in over 200 different news media publications, there can be no doubt that the philosophy has been the subject of at least occasional coverage in the past few years. The ecophilosophy has found its way into national and regional newspapers, scientific and popular magazines, foreign papers and international news wires, and television and radio broadcasts. This chapter takes a look at the rhetoric of the media and its treatment of deep ecology with the goal of orienting the reader to the varying perspectives in the news media. A statistical analysis (Chapter 11) will later provide a breakdown of the coverage of deep ecological issues according to the differing types of media.

As with any relatively unfamiliar concept or idea, "deep ecology" has not always been used correctly in the news media. In April of 1987 the *Los Angeles Times* defined deep ecology as "a discipline that concerns itself with 'the radical separation between humans and nature.'"[1] Deep ecology actually concerns itself with the interconnectiveness between humans and nature and criticizes those who attempt to draw any type of separation between the two. The *New York Times*, in 1988, included the term as part of a quiz to test reader knowledge of "multi-cultural literacy." The quiz was more of a sarcastic attempt at humor than an honest attempt to inform the public.[2] Since that time, both national newspapers have either defined the term correctly or mentioned it in passing (with the possible assumption that the reader already knew the meaning of "deep ecology"). But even as late as June of 1993, the term was still being misused in major regional newspapers. The *Chicago Tribune* made a very

---

[1]Kathleen Hendrix, "A New Global Vision Called Ecofeminism; Activists Trace Separation of People, Nature to Men's Domination of Environment," *Los Angeles Times,* 2 April 1987, sec. C, p. 1.

[2]"Book Review Desk: Christmas Books; What's Inanna? Modem? Ska? A Quiz for the Winter Solstice," *New York Times*, 4 December 1988, sec. 7, p. 12, col. 1.

confusing, if not factually incorrect, reference to deep ecology in an article appearing on June 24, 1993.[3] The paper carried an article showcasing new, sustainable forms of architecture designed to ultimately help U.S. competitiveness and propel the economy. Although there was a "deep ecology dimension," the overall goal of the sustainable development movement is human-centered and thus not fully compatible with deep ecology.

NEGATIVE REPORTING

Besides the misuse of the term itself, deep ecologists are most often concerned with the negative media coverage that they claim hampers the movement. This study of 372 articles about deep ecology substantiated claims that the plurality of all media stories are indeed unfavorable toward the deep ecology philosophy. One glaring example of such reporting is Alan W. Bock's expression of opinion in the *Orange County Register* that deep ecology poses a threat to the new pragmatism of environmentalism. He wrote, "This broad-based vision is challenged by a new philosophy of radical environmentalism. In the name of 'deep ecology,' many environmentalists have taken a sharp turn to the ultra-left, ushering in a mood of extremism and intolerance. As a clear signal of this new agenda, in 1990 Greenpeace called for a 'grassroots revolution against pragmatism and compromise.'"[4] It is interesting how many people clump together all so-called radical environmentalists. Many deep ecologists would take issue with Greenpeace being described as a deep ecological organization. Bock's use of the words "intolerance" and "extremism" are not uncommon in media descriptions of deep ecology. Moving from local papers to international news magazines, the *Economist* made a very critical comment in passing, describing deep ecology as a less peaceable and violent movement. It cited the group Earth First! for disabling logging machinery.[5]

The environmental news wire *Greenwire* carried an article about U.S. environmentalist Douglas Tompkins, who had purchased 270,000 hectares of land in Chile to create a nature reserve in Palena. The article basically recounted a statement of a Chilean official, who explained the government's impression of deep ecology. The official stated that "the Deep Ecology movement promotes abortion rights, population control and 'maintaining uninhabited areas,' which he claims are 'totally incompatible with Chilean legislation.'"[6] This article illustrates that deep ecology is viewed as a threat not just in the United States but also in countries around the world.

---

[3]Casey Bukro, "Critics Unable to Crack Glass Energy Hogs," *Chicago Tribune*, 24 June 1993, zone N, p. 1.

[4]Alan Bock, "Are We at an Environmental Crossroads?," *Orange County Register*, 21 April 1996, Editorial, sec. G, p. 1.

[5]"A Bad Press for Machines. Cranks and Proud of It," *The Economist* (January 20, 1996): 86.

[6] "Chile: Deputy Calls for Probe into Park, Deep Ecology," *Greenwire* (April 27, 1995).

One of the most negative articles was published in *Reason* magazine. Alexander Volokh reviewed the book *The Green Crusade: Rethinking the Roots of Environmentalism*. The book itself was very anti–deep ecology and Volokh expressed the views of the author very well. Environmentalists such as Arne Naess and Paul Shepard are singled out as deep ecologists who are self-professed unmakers of civilization. The article explains that deep ecology rejects anthropocentrism in favor of biocentrism or biospherical egalitarianism. Thus, according to the author, the ecophilosophy "thinks little of individual lives, whether human or non-human. It advocates 'bioregional organization' (i.e., running human life in accordance with 'natural constraints'), a sense of rootedness, and a ritualization of life which includes the recovery or recreation of primal rituals. The open totalitarianism here barely needs pointing out; what does need pointing out is how undeep it is."[7] Volokh explains that deep ecologists want a return to the hunter-gatherer life-style in which humans live in small, isolated communities. He scoffs at the idea that this will produce a less warlike society absent a global policing authority or a universal moral principle. The reviewer concludes, "They reject rationality and look forward to a new being that might overcome the limitations of logos. As Rubin puts it, 'if there were a deep ecology that persisted in asking why and how, it would show the shallowness of those who have appropriated that name.'"[8]

In October of 1994, the *National Review* carried a review of the book, *Higher Superstition: The Academic Left and Its Quarrels with Science*. The reviewer, Stanley Rothman, thought it necessary to offer a critical side comment indicting deep ecology; although it would be difficult to imagine any article in the *National Review* not being critical toward deep ecology.[9] The Reason Foundation, which publishes *Reason* magazine, wins the award for the most negativity. Author Gregory Benford quotes a member of the "eco-warrior group Earth First!" saying "Looks like a sea of shit, or a disease."[10] According to Benford, deep ecologists bring a message enshrined in the hard-core environmental movement. Interestingly enough, Benford claims that this message is "one the media has preached for decades."[11] The article is very appropriate for this book as it describes the powerful environmental lobby that influences public policy. But the article also states:

To see the future, look to the fringes. The environmentalists are a powerful lobby, but they also have a wing that will, if you get in their way, spike your tree, slip sand into your backhoe's gas tank, or sink your tuna boat. This wing includes the Earth Firsters, but there are hundreds

---

[7]Alexander Volokh, review of *The Green Crusade: Rethinking the Roots of Environmentalism*, *Reason* 26, no. 10 (March, 1995): 59.

[8]Ibid.

[9]Stanley Rothman, review of *Higher Superstition: The Academic Left and Its Quarrels with Science*, *National Review* 46, no. 19 (October 10, 1994): 70.

[10]Gregory Benford, "The Designer Plague," *Reason* 25, no. 8 (January, 1994): 36.

[11]Ibid.

of others in lesser camps such as the Animal Liberation Front, the Hunt Saboteurs who disrupt big-game sport, Albion Nation, and assorted Deep Ecologists.[12]

According to Benford, these groups are not policy pragmatists with whom one can make compromises or agreements. Rather, "their views occasionally surface anonymously, as when 'Miss Ann Thropy' welcomed AIDS in *Earth First! Journal* as 'a necessary solution.'"[13] Benford cites a letter published in the *Los Angeles Times* by David Graber, a National Park Service research biologist, who wrote,

Human happiness, and certainly human fecundity, are not as important as a wild and healthy planet.... We have become a plague upon ourselves and upon the Earth. It is cosmically unlikely that the developed world will choose to end its orgy of fossil-energy consumption, and the Third World its suicidal consumption of landscape. Until such time as *Homo sapiens* should decide to rejoin nature, some of us can only hope for the right virus to come along.[14]

Benford continues to criticize the deep ecological movement, claiming that ecotage has resulted in damages of $25 million a year in the United States. Though the first rule of ecotage according to Edward Abbey is to honor all life and not to hurt anyone, Benford claims that Earth First!ers deliberately attempt to kill desert bikers and loggers. While the author of this highly negative article contends that the media has adopted the Earth First! platform, it is ironic that the plurality of all articles examined had more in common with this one than with those placing the movement in a favorable light.

Another article worth examining, if only briefly, discussed the relationship between deep ecology and Christianity. John B. Cobbs wrote, in the periodical *Second Opinion*, that Christian stewardship requires an anthropocentric framework.[15] This support for stewardship is echoed in an article by Harold Gilliam of the *San Francisco Chronicle*, who wrote, "Even stewardship is a bad word among some devotees of deep ecology who identify it with tyranny. Stewardship or human management should not extend to wilderness areas, but that leaves 99 percent of the Earth subject to human intervention, and the attempt should be to make our intervention benign. That's what stewardship is all about."[16] While this does not take an overly critical stance toward deep ecology, it nevertheless advocates a shallow, rather than a deep, ecological approach to environmental policy making.

---

[12]Ibid.

[13]Ibid.

[14]Ibid.

[15]John B. Cobbs, "Biblical Responsibility for the Ecological Crisis," *Second Opinion* 18, no. 2 (October, 1992): 10.

[16]Harold Gilliam, "The Greening of the Spirit," *San Francisco Chronicle*, 22 December 1991, sec. Z1, p. 13.

POSITIVE REPORTING

The purpose of this review of media stories is not to provide the reader with an all-encompassing account of media coverage. Rather, it is to illustrate the different perspectives found in the news about deep ecology. While the above articles were representative of the various "negative" articles about deep ecology, what follows is a representative grouping of positive ones. Rita Henley Jensen, a New York legal affairs writer, wrote an article in the *ABA Journal* about a group of lawyers who have adopted a deep ecological life-style. The article focused on William R. Miller, a partner in a rather large law firm. Miller and his co-workers are studying the principles of deep ecology and bioregionalism, which Jensen describe as the precepts "of the burgeoning simplicity movement, a cultural phenomenon that started in the Northwest but is spreading nationwide."[17] The similarities between this article in a professional journal and an article in the *Earth First! Journal*[18] are striking. Just as Haugen in the *Earth First! Journal* described the trap of the "American dream," so too does Jensen in this article. She argues that many lawyers get caught up in this American dream "even if it means they become prisoners of their cellular phones, e-mail and laptop computers, and eventually lose control of their lives."[19] The intent of the article was to show that there is an alternative to the traditional American dream and that alternative embraces deep ecological ideas. Compared to most articles, this article was very much pro–deep ecology and is representative of about 10 percent of all articles on the subject of deep ecology.[20]

To illustrate how deep ecology has both penetrated the mainstream and gained international exposure, one need look no further than the magazine *Foreign Affairs*. The November/December 1995 issued carried an article that asked, "Has deep ecology gone too far?"[21] With such a question in its title, the logical answer, according to most people, would be yes. But the article takes an extremely balanced stance toward the issue. While Donald Worster, the author of the article, reviews an extremely anti–deep ecology book, the review concludes on the side of the deep ecologists. Though it is significant that the article would favor deep ecology, it is perhaps more significant that the article was carried by *Foreign Affairs* magazine in the first place. It shows the pervasiveness and spread of deep ecology to a variety of media sources.

---

[17]Rita Henley Jensen, "Recycling the American Dream: Many People Talk About Simplifying Their Lives. These Lawyers Are Not Only Doing It, They Are Making It Part of Their Practices," *ABA Journal* 82 (April, 1996): 68.

[18]Tim Haugen, "The Wild Ranch Manifesto," *Earth First! Journal: The Radical Environmental Journal*. Available from gopher.ige.aoc.org:70/00/orgs/ef.journal/4; INTERNET.

[19]Jensen, "Recycling the American Dream: Many People Talk About Simplifying Their Lives. These Lawyers Are Not Only Doing It, They Are Making It Part of Their Practices," p. 68.

[20]This is not to say that only 10 percent of all articles are positive, but rather that only about 10 percent are so favorable to deep ecology and its ideals.

[21]Donald Worster, "The Rights of Nature; Has Deep Ecology Gone Too Far?" *Foreign Affairs* (November/December, 1995): 111.

It is difficult to classify book reviews, for at what point do they stop espousing the attitudes of the author and begin with the reviewer's own commentary? In the previous example, the reviewer took a very critical stance toward the content and message of the book, one that ultimately favored deep ecology. One of the more interesting book reviews found in the study was published in *The Progressive*, perhaps a more likely source for carrying an article on deep ecology. It too reviewed an anti–deep ecology book but did not conclude in favor of deep ecology. Rather it took a balanced approach, discussing the merits of the author's ideas while providing thoughtful criticism.[22]

Though two of the previous articles were found in professional journals, the majority of articles on deep ecology are found in everyday newspapers and popular magazines. One such example of an article is found in the October 1, 1995 edition of the *Virginian-Pilot*. It would be difficult to find a deep ecologist who would not agree with the message advanced by Tom Robotham: America's love affair with nature is destroying it. Robotham argues that much of our "environmentalism" is decidedly shallow, for programs such as recycling do not require much self-sacrifice, yet they are frequently singled out as environmental success stories. One example the author uses to illustrate how America's love affair with nature is destroying it is the ever-growing popularity of all-terrain utility vehicles. Robotham observes, "Ironically, these sleek machines reflect our hunger for wilderness adventure—and we buy them thinking that they'll somehow help us get back to nature. What we seem to have missed is that they use more fossil fuel than Cadillacs."[23] America's love of national parks is another example the author discusses. Robotham states that America's zeal to frolic with trees, rivers, and mountains is taking an alarming toll on these preserves. Such attitudes do not reflect a deep ecological awareness. The article concludes that it is time to rethink our attitudes toward nature, for "'how we image a thing, true or false, affects our conduct toward it.'"[24]

The Progressive, in its May, 1994 edition, featured an interview with the environmentalist David R. Brower.[25] Needless to say, the interview was very pro–deep ecology, as Brower is one of the inspirational forces behind the movement. Brower described the need for wholeness, the ability to capture the inter-relatedness of all those fragments that make up the environment. According to Brower, the deep ecology movement attempts to accomplish this goal. The environmentalist makes reference to Arne Naess, who "invented" the deep ecology movement and who explains that *Homo sapiens* "are recent arrivals on this planet, and we should have just a little bit of humility.

[22]James Jay Gould, review of *Green Delusions: An Environmentalist Critique of Radical Environmentalism*, *The Progressive* 57, no. 3 (March, 1993): 39.

[23]Tom Robotham, "America's Love Affair with Nature May Destroy It in the End," *Virginian-Pilot* (Norfolk), 1 October 1995, sec. J, p. 1.

[24]Ibid.

[25]David Kupfer, "David Ross Brower; Environmentalist; Interview," *The Progressive* 58, no. 5 (May, 1994): 36.

That seems to be one of our great shortages. We're heavy on hubris."[26] It is interesting that not once was a radical environmentalist asked to testify before Congress, yet magazines continue to feature interviews of deep ecologists.[27]

Writing for the *Chicago Tribune*, Marla Donato discussed the need for an infusion of deep ecology into the environmental movement. The article argues that people need to move away from the idea that the Earth is an endless supply of resources for human needs and wants. It explains that we cannot "just clean up the mess and manage it better. . . . We need to be infused with the idea of deep ecology—meaning we share this planet with a lot of other things and we need to look at how we can live in harmony with them."[28] Such rhetoric is clearly identifiable with the deep ecology movement and fits into that 10 percent of positive articles discussed previously.

Though each of the above articles took a favorable stance toward deep ecology, none was more thorough and complete than Kirkpatrick Sale's article in *The Nation* on May 14, 1988.[29] At a time when few media sources were even covering deep ecology, *The Nation*, a magazine that fits into the "popular news magazine category," carried a 4,000-plus-word article on deep ecology and its critics. Sale systematically discussed each of the main criticisms of the movement, taking careful pains to answer each of them from a deep ecological viewpoint. Sale begins by addressing criticism from Murray Bookchin and the social ecologists. He traces the history of social ecology's discontent with the ecophilosophy as well as some of the more fierce diatribes found in the news media against deep ecology. Sale asks the question, why does deep ecology arouse so much passion? He proceeds to answer the question after providing a detailed definition of the movement, discussing its roots and history since Arne Naess originated the term. The answer Sale finds deserves repeating:

Now, it is easy enough to see why all of this might be upsetting to those in the politic and mainstream and to traditional socialists as much as diehard capitalists. Taken in the broad, it represents a fundamental challenge not only to the typical American technological way of life but to much of what constitutes Western civilization itself.[30]

Sale examines the three major criticisms of deep ecology and attempts to defend the philosophy before each of them. He ultimately concludes that environmentalists should work together, for diversity in thought, as diversity in nature, is beneficial. This article, as well as those showcased above, is meant to provide the reader with an idea of the type of positive media coverage deep ecology has received. Attention is now turned to a more focused examination of media coverage beginning with a

---

[26]Ibid.

[27]See also, Dean Kuipers, "Eco Warriors; Environmental Activists," *Playboy* 40, no. 4 (April, 1993): 74.

[28]Marla Donato, "Walking Lightly on the Earth: Some Solutions to the World's Woes Could Be Right in Your Own Backyard," *Chicago Tribune*, 21 March 1990, p. 9.

[29]Kirkpatrick Sale, "The Cutting Edge: Deep Ecology and Its Critics," *The Nation* 246, no. 19 (May 14, 1988): 670.

[30]Ibid.

look at how the media covered the alleged links between deep ecology and the Unabomber.

CASE STUDY: DEEP ECOLOGY AND THE UNABOMBER

Both the *Washington Post* and *USA Today*, two major U.S. newspapers, carried articles concerning deep ecology and the Unabomber. For fifteen years, the man known as the Unabomber successfully evaded the law and sent mail bombs to certain individuals involved in technological progress. The link between radical environmentalism and the Unabomber was originally made in an *ABC News* story that claimed Theodore Kaczinski (the person eventually caught for the bombings) had attended a local Earth First! meeting in which he was supplied with the name and address of a future target. A letter written by Alan Caruba published in *USA Today* stated:

The Unabomber should more correctly be called the "Ecobomber." He's a serial killer who has found justification for his psychopathic behavior in the core values of the environmentalist movement. He represents a branch of environmentalism called "deep ecology," which advocates the active destruction of civilization. Those who have died or been maimed by the Unabomber have been, in effect, the victims of the growing desperation of a hard-core environmentalist. Publishing his manifesto will not deter him from killing.[31]

This published letter was a fierce attack against deep ecology and radical environmentalism.

The *Washington Post*, six days later, published an article by Joel Achenbach, which allowed an Earth First!er to distance the group and the deep ecological movement from the Unabomber.[32] Likewise, an Associated Press report published in *The Record* and the *Rocky Mountain News* asserted that the Unabomber was not a deep ecologist.[33] Overall the media coverage of the alleged link between the Unabomber and deep ecology was fair and non-biased. Though deep ecologists were upset at the media for making the assertion that there might be a link, the openness of major media sources to publish the opinions of Earth First!ers is significant.[34]

---

[31]Alan Caruba, "Letters to the Editor," *USA Today*, 14 July 1995, sec. A, p. 6.

[32]Joel Achenbach, "The Hunt For Unabom; in the Bay Area, Fear and Suspicion Creep in Like the Fog," *Washington Post*, 20 July 1995, sec. C, p. 1.

[33]Richard Cole, "Activists: He's Not One of Us; No Support for Unabomber," *The Record*, 9 July 1995, sec. N, p. 9.

[34]Based on research and reading, this author believes that the link between deep ecology and the Unabomber is very tenuous, if not nonexistent. Although the Unabomber embraced an anti-technology stance, also endorsed by deep ecologists, the current available evidence does not indicate the Unabomber targeted individuals because of their shallow ecological perspectives. Additionally, while a small number of radical environmentalists advocate harming humans, the great majority of deep ecologists shun any sort of action that endangers human life.

A LOOK AT THE DIFFERENT MEDIA SOURCES

Scientific Magazines

Though deep ecology is a social philosophy, it does after all have its roots in the science of ecology. Thus it should come as no surprise that the term is found with increasing frequency in scientific journals and periodicals. A book review in the *New Scientist*, provided a brief, but favorable description of deep ecology.[35] The journal *BioScience* is also known to carry articles mentioning the term "deep ecology," though, like the preceding example, they are mostly book reviews.[36] While deep ecology is finding its way into scientific magazines, the articles that provide in-depth analysis of the philosophy are few and far between.

Popular News Magazines

Just as deep ecology has found its way into regional and national newspapers, so too has it entered into the realm of the popular news magazines.[37] It has received both positive and negative coverage in such media sources. For example, an article in the May 22, 1995 edition of *Newsweek* defined the philosophy in a favorable way, describing it as "a philosophy advocating that human activity have the least possible impact on nature."[38] This favorable treatment of the environmental perspective is in sharp contrast with reporting found five years prior in another popular newsmagazine, *U.S. News & World Report*. Though the article was fair to deep ecology, it criticized Earth First! The author of the article attempted to trace the roots of radical environmentalism and concluded:

Such extremist views spring out of a broader philosophy, called Deep Ecology, and its core tenet of "biocentrism"—a belief that the human species is just an ordinary member of the biological community and that every species has some degree of ethical standing. Earth Firsters [*sic*] take this philosophy to its extreme, however, and as a result they have a truly radical vision of the future. Most members claim to abhor modern industrial society, which they maintain has brought the world to the brink of ecological collapse, and they look forward to living in a world of scattered hunter-gatherer tribes. "Back to the Pleistocene" is a rallying cry for many.[39]

---

[35]Brendan Hill, review of *The Biophilia Hypothesis, New Scientist* 141, no. 1941 (January 29, 1994): 44.

[36]For an example, see: Bryan G. Norton, review of *Beginning Again: People and Nature in the New Millennium, BioScience* 44, no. 1 (January, 1994): 37.

[37]Contextually defined in this case as the "big three": *Newsweek, Time,* and *U.S. News & World Report.*

[38]David Schrieberg, "Firestorm in Paradise," *Newsweek* (May 22, 1995): 66.

[39]Betsy Carpenter, " Redwood Radicals," *U.S. News & World Report* 109, no. 11 (September 17, 1990): 50.

Perhaps one of the most insightful articles found in popular newsmagazines was an article by Jennifer Foote in *Newsweek*.[40] The article discusses the different types of tactics radical environmentalists employ, making it clear that many refuse to break laws or take part in ecotage. Foote quotes a government scientist, who is also a member of Earth First!, who says that "illegal action is not necessary to be an active contributor to the movement."[41] The author describes the unifying principles of radical environmentalism, claiming that the philosophy of biocentrism unifies radical environmentalists. Groups such as Earth First!, the Wolf Action Network, the Rain Forest Network, Virginians for Wilderness, Preserve Appalachian Wilderness, and numerous other small groups throughout the country endorse the idea of ecocentrism. Foote states, "Though still considered an eccentric and impractical theory by some mainstream environmentalists, the concept of 'deep ecology' is finding increasing grass-roots support."[42] The article concludes with a discussion of the need for a diverse environmental movement. It explains how the radicals need the mainstream and vice-versa. Overall, the article takes a balanced approach, citing a wide range of sources. While these three examples are not entirely representative, they do give an idea of the media coverage of deep ecology in popular newsmagazines. Because of the limited number of articles in such sources, it is difficult to quantify or even discern noticeable trends. On the other hand, major U.S. newspapers have carried numerous articles on deep ecology over the last fifteen years. Attention is now turned to them.

Major U.S. Newspapers

This section examines four major U.S. newspapers: the *Washington Post*, the *Christian Science Monitor*, the *New York Times*, and the *Los Angeles Times*. The differences between these four newspapers as well as the apparent trends in coverage are very interesting and revealing. Insight gained from the following analysis is important in tracing the overall trend in media coverage and political popularity.

Washington Post. There have been eight articles in the *Washington Post* that mentioned the term "deep ecology." Of these eight, two were positive, three were mixed, and two were negative (one was not applicable). These numbers, however, are quite deceptive. Not a single negative article appeared in the newspaper prior to 1996 and no positive article has been published since 1995. Though the two negative articles published in 1996 were not feature stories, they did make negative side comments. One was a *Washington Post Magazine* story[43] and the other was an article on the Hubble telescope and space exploration. The latter grouped the ideas of deep

---

[40]Jennifer Foote, "Trying to Take Back the Planet," *Newsweek* (February 5, 1990): 24.

[41]Ibid.

[42]Ibid.

[43]Bill Heavy, "Bill and Molly's Excellent Adventure; He Forgot the Cooking Oil. He Brought the Wrong Map. Was This Any Way to Impress a 9-Year-Old?" *Washington Post*, 17 March 1996, p. W27.

ecology, Earth First!, and the Unabomber together for their anti-technological ideas.[44] Surprisingly, these are the only two articles to appear in the *Post* that took a negative position towards deep ecology.

It is interesting that the above article groups deep ecology with the Unabomber, when six months earlier the *Post* carried a story that allowed an Earth First!er to distance the group from the Unabomber.[45] Another favorable mention, but one made in passing, appeared on the *Post* editorial page on Memorial Day, 1993.[46] A short but favorable article appeared in 1991 in which the concept of deep ecology was described. It was described as a philosophy that "challenges the idea that humans have a special right to dominate nature, to alter or use up Earth's resources."[47] Though it is probably unwise to comment on a trend based on only eight articles, there is a noticeable progression in the *Post*'s coverage.

From April 22, 1990 until March 20, 1991, the three articles appearing in the newspaper were balanced, not taking a pro or con position toward deep ecology. These articles included a very lengthy exposé on David Foreman[48] and a feature article on Earth First![49] As substantive reporting on deep ecology goes, these were probably the most accurate and informational articles to appear in the *Post* in the last fifteen years. Since 1991, in-depth reporting on deep ecology in the *Post* has been dramatically reduced. From October, 1991 until January, 1996, the only references to deep ecology were those that mentioned the philosophy favorably in passing. Since that time, however, the only articles to appear have taken a negative position. Thus the progression over the past six years moves from in-depth reporting, to favorable mentions, to negative asides.

Christian Science Monitor. The *Christian Science Monitor* (*CSM*) is the second of the four major U.S. newspapers examined here, and it is the paper with the second lowest number of articles mentioning the term "deep ecology." It exhibits a trend similar to the *Washington Post*, in that there is a definite trend away from reporting the philosophy in a positive manner. One main difference, however, is that half of the ten articles appearing in the *CSM* mentioned the term "deep ecology" in passing and without any substance by which a determination could be made. There was not a single negative article about deep ecology until 1996 when Brad Knickerbocker reviewed E. O. Wilson's book *The Diversity of Life*. The indirect attack against deep

---

[44]Charles Paul Freund, "Hubble's Eye on Infinity; What We See in Space May Not Be the Scientist's View," *Washington Post*, 21 January 1996, sec. C, p. 5.

[45]Achenbach, "The Hunt for Unabom; in the Bay Area, Fear and Suspicion Creep in like the Fog," p. 1.

[46]Norman Lear, "A Call for Spiritual Renewal," *Washington Post*, 30 May 1993, sec. C, p. 7.

[47]Beth Joselow, "Urban Growth," *Washington Post*, 20 October 1991, p. W11.

[48]See, John Lancaster, "The Green Guerrilla; 'Redneck' Eco-Activist Dave Foreman, Throwing a Monkey Wrench into the System," *Washington Post*, 20 March 1991, sec. B, p. 1.

[49]See, Thomas Goltz, "Earth First Meeting Reflects Gap Between Radicals, Mainstream," *Washington Post*, 19 July 1990, sec. A, p. 3.

ecology takes place when Knickerbocker explains that a strength of Wilson's book is that it avoids the deep ecological rhetoric of Gaia theory and the belief that the earth is one huge organism.[50]

Between April 1, 1992 and March 24, 1996, there is not single article, book review, or editorial that discusses deep ecology (other than mentioning the term in passing). In fact, there are only two articles between 1987 and 1996 that offer any insight into the ecophilosophy. One of these provides a short definition of the term, stating that deep ecology "sees man as a part of nature rather than Biblically directed to dominate the Earth."[51] The other article was a book review of Christopher Manes' *Green Rage*.[52] In 1987, the *CSM* published a letter to the editor defending deep ecology. The letter concerned the meaning of deep ecology; it stated:

The meaning of deep ecology needs to be looked at. The forest community is just as important as any human community. And by portraying the "radical environmentalists" as the villains who are injuring people and equipment, perhaps the message is missed. The logging establishment needs to understand that there may be something wrong with its procedures. If ecological wisdom is not heeded, then the monkey-wrenching will continue.[53]

Another article appeared in January of 1987 that also placed the philosophy in a favorable light;[54] however, as with the *Washington Post*, it seems deep ecology has recently fallen out of favor with the *CSM*. Whereas some of the earlier articles were either pro–deep ecology or covered the subject objectively and indepth, articles in the past couple of years are decidedly negative.

New York Times. Since 1980, the *New York Times* has published thirteen articles that mentioned the term "deep ecology." Like the *Post*, most of the articles (ten) did more than just mention the term in passing. The first article appeared in November of 1985, and though the piece, entitled "New Leaders and a New Era for Environmentalists," included some favorable references, it did not focus on deep ecology.[55] More importantly, it is the only article on deep ecology in the *Times* to ever portray the environmental movement as a whole in a favorable light. Since 1985, five articles have taken a neutral point of view while four articles have been negative. The most

---

[50]Brad Knickerbocker, "Ringing a Biodiversity Alarm," *Christian Science Monitor*, 22 October 1992, p. 11.

[51]Brad Knickerbocker, "Indians Fight for Religious Freedom," *Christian Science Monitor*, 1 April 1992, p. 14.

[52]On a personal note, I highly recommend this book for those who wish to learn more about the thoughts and tactics of radical environmentalists. Manes writes under the pseudonym Miss Ann Thropy in the *Earth First! Journal*.

[53]Letters to the Editor, "The Meaning of Ecology," *Christian Science Monitor*, 24 August 1987, p. 13.

[54]See Donald L. Rheem, "Behind the 'Redwood Curtain,'" *Christian Science Monitor*, 13 January 1987, p. 16.

[55]Philip Shadbecoff, "New Leaders and a New Era for Environmentalists," *New York Times*, 29 November 1985, sec. D, p. 2d, col. 1.

recent article (at the time of this writing), published in January of 1996, was a book review that merely repeated the author of the book's opinion that deep ecology is both irrational and antidemocratic.[56] The last full year reviewed by this study, 1995, yielded one negative, one mixed, and one not-applicable article on deep ecology.

The mixed article provided a brief description of deep ecology, stating that it placed equal worth and value on a tree as on human life.[57] The negative article was a book review that described deep ecology as antidemocratic. A lot of the negative criticism found in the *Times* is part of book reviews.[58] In 1989 and 1990, six articles appeared in the *Times*, four of which were mixed and two negative. The high number of articles in 1990 is consistent with later findings that found 1990 to have the highest ratio of deep ecological articles to the overall number of articles on the environment.

Perhaps the most complete story about deep ecology appeared in the November 4, 1990 edition of the *New York Times*.[59] Trip Gabriel, who writes frequently about the environment, provided an indepth feature article on deep ecology and radical environmentalism. Gabriel concentrated on the group Earth First! He explained that both their tactics and beliefs are different from those of mainstream environmental organizations. The author elaborated that deep ecology holds "that a man has the same rights as a mouse. Human beings are not meant to exert dominion over the earth; all species have equal title to the earth's bounty."[60] While Gabriel is careful to allow Earth First! to defend its views, he does interject his own, frequently negative opinion. The combination of views produced a balanced article:

Though the theory has a certain noble simplicity, Earth Firsters [*sic*] have used it to arrive at some truly revolutionary conclusions. Our current technological culture is unethical, they say, since it permits humans to prosper while driving other species toward extinction. To protect the rights of trees and wolves—and to save the human species—we must be prepared to give up such planet-destroying extravagances as cars, televisions, planes and computers. A Luddite phobia of technology runs deep through Earth First, whose members have even opposed the University of Arizona's development of a telescope on a fragile desert mountain.[61]

Gabriel claims that few Earth First!ers actually practice deep ecology. The author explains the different focus of mainstream groups and deep ecologists, drawing on the differences between anthro- and ecocentrism. The primary issues for deep ecologists are overconsumption and overpopulation. This leads the author to highlight some of the more extreme deep ecological policy proposals such as closing the borders and refusing to send aid to Ethiopia and allowing the people to starve to restore Nature's

---

[56]"Earth Day '95," *New York Times*, 23 April 1995, sec. 7, p. 19, col. 1.

[57]Jon Bowermaster, "Take This Park and Love It," *New York Times*, 3 September 1995, sec. 6, p. 24, col. 1.

[58]See *New York Times*, 25 November 1990, sec. 7, p. 13, col. 1, Book Review Desk.

[59]Trip Gabriel, "If a Tree Falls in the Forest, They Hear It," *New York Times*, 4 November 1990, sec. 6, p. 34, col. 1.

[60]Ibid.

[61]Ibid.

balance. Perhaps the most infamous statement Gabriel reprints is the one concerning the worthiness of AIDS as Nature's way of fighting back. In all fairness, he does allow Dave Foreman to refute charges that he is an eco-fascist. Foreman states in the article, "People are going to die. It's not because I want them to. It's because they've overshot the carrying capacity of the planet. I really think there is going to be a major ecological collapse. There's going to be a concomitant die-off of the human population. The next 20 years aren't going to be very pleasant."[62] Thus it is ultimately up to the public to decide for themselves whether such eco-fascism is a form of totalitarianism or prophecy.

Gabriel's article is the only feature story on deep ecology that covers the subject in an indepth and objective manner. Other articles appearing during 1990 included a book review of James Gorman's *Spare That Tree or Else*, and an article about Earth First! and Redwood Summer, which mentioned deep ecology only as a seminar subject.[63] Of the two articles appearing in 1989, one was mixed and one was negative. The mixed article provided a definition of deep and shallow ecology. It stated that the difference between shallow environmentalists and deep ecologists was that "the shallows say, 'Clean up our mess, and everything will be fine.' The deeps say, 'How can we live in more harmony with our planet?'"[64] The other article appearing that year was a negative one written by Jim Robbins entitled "Saboteurs for a Better Environment."[65] The article depended heavily on an interview with Murray Bookchin,[66] who describes Earth First! members as eco-fascists, repeating many of their aforementioned extreme population-related policy proposals. He concludes that Earth First! rhetoric "could lead to racism or cultural chauvinism. It's evil stuff no matter how well intentioned they may be."[67]

It is interesting to observe the trend in *Times* coverage. The first article that mentioned deep ecology was published in 1985. It placed the philosophy in a favorable light. Since that time, no other article has done so; instead, articles have oscillated between those that are neutral and those that are decidedly negative. During 1989 and 1990, deep ecology received extensive coverage in the newspaper, including a couple of feature articles on the philosophy and the group Earth First! Between 1990 and 1995, however, coverage was minimal, with only one article on the subject, and that article only mentioned the term in passing. Between April 1995 and January 1996, the *New York Times* did carry four articles generally to the detriment of deep

------

[62]Ibid.

[63]Katherine Bishop, "Militant Environmentalists Planning Summer Protests to Save Redwoods," *New York Times*, 19 June 1990, sec. A, p. 18, col. 1.

[64]Kirk Johnson, "In Schools, New Emphasis on Environment," *New York Times*, 21 November 1989, sec. B, p. 1, col. 2.

[65]Jim Robbins, "Saboteurs for a Better Environment," *New York Times*, 9 July 1989, sec. 4, p. 6, col. 1.

[66]See Chapter 1 for a summary of Bookchin's primary criticisms of deep ecology. Bookchin founded and runs the Institute for Social Ecology.

[67]Robbins, "Saboteurs for a Better Environment," p. 6

ecology, since two of them were negative, one was mixed, and one mentioned the term only in passing. While the *Times* cannot be said to be representative of all media sources, the trend exhibited is similar to those in the *Washington Post* and the *Christian Science Monitor*.

Los Angeles Times. The last of the major four U.S. newspapers examined here is the *Los Angeles Times* (*LAT*). Deep ecology is found in more articles in this newspaper than in the *Washington Post* and *New York Times* combined. Between 1985 and 1995 (no articles in 1996) the *LAT* carried twenty-two articles that mentioned the term "deep ecology." Of these twenty-two, there was an equal number of positive, mixed, and negative articles (three apiece). The *LAT* had, by far, the most amount of "mention only" references, recording thirteen "not-applicables." Of the eight most recent articles, since May 1992, six were classified as not-applicables and two were positive. The implications of this finding will be discussed later.

Peter Carlin wrote an article for the February 5, 1995 edition of the *LAT* magazine, which featured companies that attempt to stress social values such as environmentalism as much as the bottom line. Though the article was not pro–deep ecology, it did mention it in a favorable light.[68] The other article that made positive mention of deep ecology was a brief review of a book by Bill Devall. The article did not take a position either way, but was classified as a positive reference because it described the ideas of Devall and deep ecology without criticism or comment.[69]

The *LAT* has not published a negative article about deep ecology since 1991 when, oddly enough, an article from the Entertainment Desk reviewed a play that poked fun at deep ecologists.[70] Just the fact that deep ecology has found its way into the West Coast theater indicates a growing awareness of the philosophy. Unfortunately for the deep ecologists, this growing awareness is being met with skepticism and criticism. An article five days prior to this play report reviewed Dave Foreman's book, *Earth Angel: Confessions of an Eco-Warrior*.[71] The review, however, did not make any judgments on deep ecology, mentioning the term only in passing.

Although 1990 was the biggest year for the *New York Times* for reporting about deep ecology, not one article was carried by the *LAT* that year. One negative article appeared in each of the years 1989 and 1988. The first was an article on "Ecology's Family Feud," compliments of Murray Bookchin. Bob Sipchen of the *LAT* quoted Bookchin's harsh criticism of deep ecology without allowing for a response by a deep

---

[68]Peter Carlin, "Pure Profit: For Small Companies That Stress Social Values as Much as the Bottom Line, Growing Up Hasn't Been an Easy Task," *Los Angeles Times*, 5 February 1995, Magazine, p. 12.

[69]Susan Salter, "In Brief: Environment," *Los Angeles Times*, 5 September 1993, p. 5, Book Review Desk.

[70]Robert Koehler, "Stage Beat: Andi Matheny Acts Up at West Coast Ensemble," *Los Angeles Times*, 15 March 1991, part F, p. 21, col. 1.

[71]Page Stegner, *Los Angeles Times*, 10 March 1991, Book Review, p. 1.

ecologist.[72] The other negative article was also by Bob Sipchen in which he dismissed the philosophy of deep ecology in a book review of Holmes Rolston's *Rules for the Ethical Exploitation of Nature: Environmental Ethics Duties to and Values in the Natural World*.[73] All three of the negative articles in the *LAT* were not overly biased or critical to the philosophy when compared to those found in other papers. Likewise, the positive articles were not directly supportive of the ecophilosophy. For example, another article by Sipchen featured Gary Snyder's path to deep ecology but was more concerned with the poet Gary Snyder than with the ideas and values of deep ecology.[74]

Yet to be examined thus far are the mixed articles that have appeared in the *LAT*, with the last one published in February of 1989. Two were book reviews by Alex Raksin in which the concept of deep ecology was defined and explained.[75] The only feature article that extensively reported about deep ecology was one by Ann Japenga in 1985 about the group Earth First! It covered the arrest of prominent Earth First!ers and stated that the group pledged that radical tactics would continue until policies were changed.[76] The lack of in-depth reporting in the *LAT* is both surprising and expected. It is surprising because deep ecology has its firmest roots in the West and a substantial number of local protests and actions take place there. It is expected because the publicity already given to such actions has made people fairly aware of such groups as Earth First! and so there is less of a need for in-depth feature stories.

Both the *Washington Post* and the *New York Times* had a relatively low number of articles classified as not-applicable, for on most occasions when the term "deep ecology" was used, some degree of information was provided as to its meaning. The *LAT*, however, had numerous articles classified as non-applicable. It would mention the term in passing as if it assumed the readers were familiar enough with the philosophy to understand. Most uses of the term included titles of lectures, the Foundation for Deep Ecology, and as part of book reviews. Three articles do, however, warrant special attention. The first was an article about John Muir and the environmental legacy

[72]Bob Sipchen, "Ecology's Family Feud: Murray Bookchin Turns Up Volume on a Noisy Debate," *Los Angeles Times*, 27 March 1989, part 5, p. 1, col. 2.

[73]Bob Sipchen, review of *Rules for the Ethical Exploitation of Nature: Environmental Ethics Duties to and Values in the Natural World*, *Los Angeles Times*, 21 February 1988, Book Review, p. 6.

[74]Bob Sipchen, "Gary Snyder's Path of the Deep Ecology Movement," *Los Angeles Times*, 28 November 1986, part 5, p. 1.

[75]See, Alex Raksin, "Nonfiction in Brief," *Los Angeles Times*, 26 February 1989, Book Review, p. 4.; and, Alex Raksin, "Now in Paperback," *Los Angeles Times*, 30 March 1986, Book Review, p. 10.

[76]Ann Japenga, "Earth First! A Voice Vying for the Wilderness: Group Says Radical Tactics Will Continue Despite Arrests," *Los Angeles Times*, 5 September 1985, part 5, p. 1, col. 3.

he has left. The article discussed the debate among various sects of the environmental movement over which can claim Muir as their founder.[77]

Another article was a feature story on radical environmentalism that discussed both the rhetoric and the tactics of radical environmentalism. The article, however, made only passing reference to deep ecology.[78] The final article to make a passing reference was one on ecofeminism. It provided a brief definition of deep ecology by describing it as "a discipline that concerns itself with 'the radical separation between humans and nature.'"[79] This reference was discussed earlier in the chapter, and again can be classified as an incorrect definition of the philosophy.

Overall, the high frequency of mentions and the low frequency of explanations do indicate a greater awareness of deep ecology in the western United States. Though it may be imprudent to make such a conclusion based on merely a comparison of major newspapers, additional evidence (see Chapter 11) will bear out the validity of such a conclusion. The mere fact that deep ecology is found in titles of lectures and seminars as well as the fact that the term is frequently referred to simply in passing indicates a higher level of awareness on the part of either the *LAT* readership or its staff (or perhaps both).

CONCLUSION

The purpose of this chapter was to examine the various forms, media, and types of news coverage on deep ecology. The examples of negative and positive articles illustrated the wide range of coverage in the media. Both sides of the spectrum were represented. The examples of news coverage of deep ecology and the Unabomber were provided to show how coverage can differ over a specific incident or event. Deep ecology has found its way into many different types of news media: popular and professional journals, regional and national newspapers, and news wires and news broadcasts. The comparison of the major U.S. newspapers served to highlight trends in the national news media with respect to coverage of deep ecology. Chapter 11 will help to quantify such trends as well as explore larger trends in media coverage as a whole.

---

[77]Bob Sipchen, "The Muir Mystique: After 150 Years, the Naturalist Has Become Patron Saint to All Environmental Factions, but His Legacy Is Still in Dispute," *Los Angeles Times*, 20 April 1988, part 5, p. 1, col. 2.

[78]Mark A. Stein, "From Rhetoric to 'Ecotage': Environmental 'Fanatics' Try to Keep Things Wild," *Los Angeles Times*, 29 November 1987, part 1, p. 1, col. 1.

[79]Kathleen Hendrix, "A New Global Vision Called Ecofeminism: Activists Trace Separation of People, Nature to Men's Domination of the Environment," *Los Angeles Times*, 2 April 1987, part 5, p. 1, col. 1.

11

The Media and Deep Ecology:
A Closer Look

Chapter 10 provided an overview of media coverage of deep ecology, but it did not provide quantified data to help answer the central question of this book: what effect has deep ecology had on environmental politics? This chapter, by contrast, examines trends in all media coverage through a detailed and comprehensive measurement of deep ecology and the media. It attempts to compute and ascertain certain trends in media reporting. Additionally, it provides a comparison of those results found while analyzing congressional testimony and those found in this chapter in order to answer questions concerning the relationship between the media and the political process. Finally, the chapter looks at how deep ecologists view the media and the ironic relationship that has formed between the two entities. This chapter will hopefully provide a window into the political process and allow further discussion of the role of deep ecology in environmental politics.

SURVEY METHOD

This chapter attempts to identify the treatment of deep ecological issues by various forms of news media. The initial collection of data consisted of a review of all articles and transcripts contained in the Nexis database in which the term "deep ecology" or some variant thereof occurred.[1] This search yielded over 400 articles, 372 of which were unique.[2] Each article was then examined for its approach toward "deep ecology."

---

[1]Forms include "deep ecology," "deep ecological," and "deep ecologist."

[2]On some occasions, the same article appeared in multiple media forms. While these were recorded as just one article for the overall tally, when articles were broken up according to region, each newspaper or media form in which the article appeared was recorded separately.

An ordinal scale was used to further classify each article based on a simple three-pronged range of Positive (1), Mixed (2), and Negative (3). Additionally, a "Not Applicable" was assigned to articles that mentioned the term only in passing or had no real substantive material by which to classify them. Along with recording the date and rating of each article, the publication and publication type were noted as well as any extraneous information that pertained to the literature review. The data were then compiled and sorted to help resolve the question of the treatment of deep ecological issues by the media.

FINDINGS

Of the 372 different articles, 91 were negative, 76 mixed, 69 positive, and 136 unscorable. These initial findings yielded a 1.32 ratio of negative to positive treatment by the media. On the surface, this general ratio indicates a fair and balanced reporting of deep ecology with a slight leaning toward the negative. The fact, though, that negative articles possessed a plurality of all those that were scorable indicates at least a partially negative bias in overall media coverage.

The distribution of the articles is also of some interest.[3] The type of media with the most references to the term "deep ecology" was magazines, with major papers coming in a close second. Magazines, with 169 entries, and major papers (as defined by Nexis), with 159 entries, overshadowed all other forms of media (regional papers—31, wire services—14 and newsletters—4). Of the sources that had an attached geographical reference, Western news sources had the greatest number of articles about deep ecology with 56 different articles. Figures for other geographical places included, Southeast—27, Northeast—36, and Midwest—16. Additionally, 40 of the articles reviewed were from non-U.S. news media. Although these data give the reader an idea of the distribution of deep ecological articles, they do not illustrate the full picture of the relationship between deep ecology and the media.

One telling statistic is the number of articles each year about deep ecology. Without a firm reference point for comparison, however, it is difficult to rely on the mere number of articles per year when one takes into consideration that the Nexis library has constantly expanded over the last fifteen years (and especially in the past five). Viewing the number of deep ecological articles as a percentage of all articles about the environment does, however, allow for a reference point for comparison. Table 11.1 breaks down the number of deep ecological articles by yearly increments and notes how those figures relate to the total number of articles about the environment. The table does suggest a progressive trend toward greater media coverage of deep

---

[3]This distribution of articles, however, is not based solely on the occurrence of the term "deep ecology," or some form thereof, because of the restrictions that a Nexis search places upon the media forms at the researcher's disposal.

ecological ideas, events, and concepts. Excluding the year 1990, there was a greater number of articles on deep ecology each year from 1980 till the present.[4] Some will state that this increase in number is due merely to the fact that the Nexis library has expanded, causing this apparent trend. But if one considers these numbers in relation to the total number of environmental articles, the same increasing trend is also apparent. Figure 11.1 illustrates this trend. This trend indicates that deep ecology is receiving greater media coverage. But this media coverage varies drastically according to the type and region of publication.

Table 11.1
Breakdown of Frequency of Deep Ecological Articles by Percentage of Total Environmental Articles

Year	Number	Percentage N/A	Percentage of Total Environmental Articles (×1000)
1996[a]	28	.29	[b]
1995	87	.34	.18
1994	55	.44	.13
1993	49	.41	.15
1992	36	.42	.12
1991	28	.36	.12
1990	48	.29	.23
1989	13	.31	.08
1988	12	.50	.11
1980-87	15	.33	.04

[a]Statistics reflect only January through June of 1996.
[b]This number is based only upon articles on the environment from January through June of 1996.

Table 11.2 breaks down the ratios of negative to positive according to both publication type and region. These results are quite interesting. In the Northeast, papers are almost twice as likely to report negatively as opposed to positively toward deep ecology, whereas Midwest and regional papers are twice as likely to report positively

---

[4]This also excludes the year 1996 as complete information is still lacking to provide a final verdict. Collectively, the time period of 1980 to 1987 had more articles than either 1989 or 1988, but it should be noted that the figure for the former time period consists of seven separate years. The reason for this grouping was due to the fact that there were so few articles for each individual year between 1980 and 1987.

Figure 11.1
Percentage of Deep Ecological Mentions to All Environmental Articles

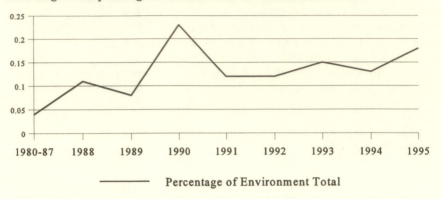

—————— Percentage of Environment Total

Table 11.2
Ratio of Negative to Positive Articles

Northeast Papers:	1.71	Southeast Papers:	1.14
Non-U.S. Papers:	1.5	West Papers:	0.8
Magazines:	1.45	All Regional Papers:	0.5
Overall Average:	1.32	Midwest Papers:	0.5
All Major Papers:	1.26		

Table 11.3
Percentage Negative of All Articles

Northwest Papers	.33
Southeast Papers	.30
Magazine	.28
Overall Average	.24
Non-U.S. Papers	.23
All Major Papers	.21
Regional Papers	.16
West Papers	.14
Midwest Papers	.13

Table 11.4
Percentage Negative of Those Scored

Non-U.S. Papers	.45
Southeast Papers	.44
Northeast Papers	.44
Overall Average	.39
Magazines	.39
All Major Papers	.37
West Papers	.30
Regional Papers	.29
Midwest Papers	.22

toward this ecosphilosphy. It should be noted that geographical papers consist of both major and regional papers; for example, the *Los Angeles Times*, although a national paper in scope, is also counted in the "West Papers" category. Magazines were slightly more critical in their coverage than all major papers. It is also significant that non-U.S. papers were 1½ times more likely to criticize deep ecology than to condone it.

Another manner in which to view the ratio of characteristics of various forms of news media is through the negative percentage of all articles (Table 11.3). One out of every three articles in Northeast papers containing the term "deep ecology" was negative. By comparison, only about one out of eight articles in Midwest papers was negative in its reporting of deep ecology. The overall average for percent negative of all articles was roughly one out of every four. These tables include those articles that mention deep ecology only in passing. For a better indicator of percent negative, Table 11.4 lists the percent negative of just those articles that were scored.

Nearly half of all references in non-U.S. papers to the term "deep ecology" did so in a negative fashion. Although this study is primarily concerned with the effect of deep ecology on American politics and policy, one should consider all forms of media that penetrate into this country. After all, how many times are decisions made here based on the experiences and toils of foreign governments?

A full 44 percent of articles in both Southeast and Northeast papers took a negative position toward deep ecology. The overall average as well as the percentage negative for magazines and major newspapers were in the high thirties. Again, the regional newspapers as a whole took a less critical approach toward deep ecology than their national brethren. The comparatively low number of negative articles in Western and Midwestern papers is perhaps indicative of the deep ecological movement as

Table 11.5
Percentage Positive of All Articles

Regional Papers	.32
Southeast Papers	.26
Midwest Papers	.25
Magazine	.20
Northeast Papers	.19
Overall Average	.19
West Papers	.18
All Major Papers	.17
Non-U.S. Papers	.15

Table 11.6
Percentage Positive of Those Scored

Regional Papers	.59
Midwest Papers	.44
Southeast Papers	.39
West Papers	.37
Non-U.S. Papers	.30
All Major Papers	.30
Overall Average	.29
Magazines	.27
Northeast Papers	.26

a whole. The most active Earth First! chapters are in these regions and most rally cries of the deep ecological movement concern forests and wilderness in the West and Midwest.

Some may think it redundant to consider the percentage positive according to the various types of publications. However, this task is not redundant when one considers that the additional variable of "mixed" is included as well as taking into full account those articles that make only passing reference to deep ecology. Almost one out of every three articles about deep ecology in regional papers took a positive approach toward deep ecology (Table 11.5). On the other hand, national or major papers took such an approach only 17 percent of the time, or roughly one out of six times. This is a major finding of the study. The regional news media is consistently more positive and less negative toward deep ecology than national newspapers. As noted in the previous chapter, the national news media holds the most influence in federal policy making. But since all electoral politics are local, one must wonder if the local media assert themselves in this category.

Unfortunately for the deep ecologists, not all regions are equally favorable to deep ecology. Only 18 percent of articles mentioning deep ecology in Western papers takes a favorable stance. Coupled with the low percentage of negative articles in Western papers, the factors indicate either that papers in this region contain a lot of balanced and mixed articles about deep ecology or that the term is used frequently in news discourse. The next set of data will help to resolve this question. These figures, percentage positive of all articles, provide some insight as to how various publications treat the subject, but an even better indicator is the percentage positive of only those articles that were applicable (scorable) to this study. Table 11.6 provides such data.

Table 11.6 helps to resolve the above dilemma concerning Western papers. Although the clear majority of all articles mentioning deep ecology in Western papers fell into the category of either mixed or not applicable, a full 37 percent of all scorable articles were positive and 30 percent were negative. The most interesting observation from the above figures concerns the treatment of deep ecology by regional papers. Well over half (59%) of those articles that discussed deep ecology, besides merely mentioning the term, were positive. For comparison, the percentage positive for major papers was only 30 percent, nearly half of the regional percentage. This provides further evidence to support the conclusion that regional newspapers possess a kinder and more sympathetic disposition toward deep ecology than do the national newspapers. Forty-four percent of articles about deep ecology in Midwestern papers were generally receptive toward deep ecological ideas. Southeastern and Western newspapers were not far behind at 39 and 37 percent, respectively. However, magazines and Northeast papers were positive toward deep ecology in only one out of four of their articles about this ecophilosophy.

The distribution of articles by region also provides insight as to the regional popularity of deep ecological thoughts.[5] Western newspapers ran as many stories on deep ecology as the Southeast (or Northeast) and the Midwest combined.[6] There were fifty-six articles in newspapers published in Western United States. For comparison, the Northeast finished a distant second with thirty-six articles. The Southeast and Midwest carried twenty-seven and sixteen articles, respectively, on the subject of deep ecology. These results were not entirely unpredictable. The majority of deep ecological activism takes place in the West and, as shown here, is reflected in the news reporting. It is odd, however, that only sixteen articles appeared in the Midwest region, while over twice that number appeared in the Northeast. As mentioned previously, when Midwestern papers did run articles about deep ecology, they were relatively more positive than those in the Northeast region.

Table 11.7
Percentage of "Mentioned Only"

West Papers:	.52	Overall Average:	.37
Non-U.S. Papers:	.50	Southeast Papers:	.33
Regional Papers:	.45	Magazines:	.27
Midwest Papers:	.44	Northeast Papers:	.25
All Major Papers:	.43		

One way to shed further light on this subject of regional and publication type differences in acceptance of deep ecological ideas is to examine the percentage of "mentioned only" references. When a news medium presents a concept or idea that the editors regard as unfamiliar to their audience, it is quick to summarize or explain such a term. Based on this premise, an analysis of which publication types frequently referred to deep ecology by mentioning the term in passing only provides insight as to the general knowledge of the idea. As Table 11.7 shows, more than 50 percent of all references to deep ecology in Western newspapers were made only in passing without any substantive comments. This figure differs drastically from the 25 percent of the times that this occurred in Northeast papers. It is perhaps expected that magazines would register a much lower figure than either category of newspaper (regional or national) because magazine articles tend to be more in depth and specialized as opposed to newspapers. Furthermore, any given newspaper is likely to publish many more articles in any given week or month than a magazine and thus the likelihood that the term was merely mentioned is increased. The differences in the number of "mentioned-

---

[5]The concept of distribution does not, however, provide as lucid a picture as might be called for by this study. The variation in regional papers, in both quantity and quality, has a bearing on the distribution of articles. Additionally, the number of papers per region is not accounted for in the study.

[6]Twenty-two of the fifty-six articles in western papers were in the *Los Angeles Times*.

only" indicates a differing degree of knowledge among certain regions in the United States as well as among the staffs of the various types of news media.

Of the 372 articles, in excess of 25 percent were book reviews. Of the 101 book reviews, 24 articles were negative, 26 were mixed, and 14 were positive. The remaining 37 registered a not applicable (this included instances when only the title of a book was mentioned). The high percentage of book reviews indicates that the subject of deep ecology is still one dominated by scholarly and academic works rather than popular news coverage. The reviews, however, do provide insight as to the ecological perspective of those reviewing. The fact that a minority of the articles were negative (as opposed to both mixed and positive) does suggest a somewhat optimistic trend for deep ecologists. On the other hand, the number of negative book reviews clearly outnumbered positive ones by a ratio exceeding 5 to 3.

Table 11.8
Breakdown of "Not Applicable" Articles

Book title or review:	.27
Foundation for Deep Ecology:	.18
Lecture/Class Title:	.07
Other:	.49

Table 11.8 provides the breakdown of those articles that were 'not applicable' for evaluation. The Foundation for Deep Ecology was cited on twenty-five occasions during the course of the study. In all but one of these instances, the Foundation was mentioned only in passing. The one occasion in which the author of the article had an opinion of this organization, the review was negative. From a deep ecological viewpoint, one truly promising finding from this study is the mention of the term as part of a class or lecture. "Deep ecology" was used nine times as part of an announcement of a class or lecture. Many deep ecologists believe that the largest impediment to moving away from the shallow ecological mindset is the lack of awareness and education. Education and awareness is key to instilling deep ecological beliefs in the public. Deep ecologists think that the majority of Americans agree with their viewpoints toward the preservation of the environment but are unaware of the vast environmental destruction taking place around them.[7] As discussed in Chapter 3, the group Earth First! justifies its radical actions such as tree sitting as efforts to increase awareness.

---

[7]This is a claim frequently made by Earth First! The group relies on public opinion surveys and their own "intuition" to substantiate such claims. The primary problem with such assertions is that although the public may support environmental protection in principle (as shown through public opinion polls), support diminishes when direct economic and social factors, such as loss of jobs and increased taxes, are taken into consideration.

Figure 11.2
Comparison of Percentages of Article Distribution

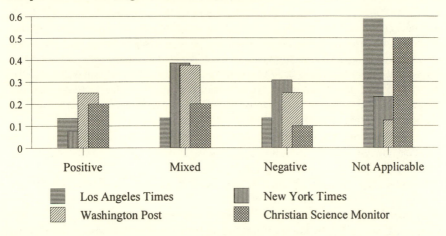

Figure 11.3
Progression of Coverage of Four Major U.S. Newspapers

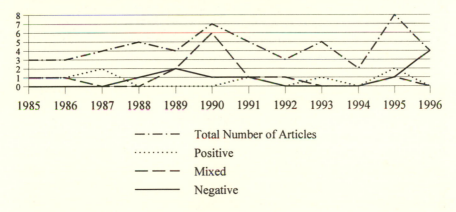

COMPARISON OF MAJOR PAPERS

Chapter 10 examined coverage by four major newspapers. While providing the reader with a feel for the general flavor of reporting, it lacked any discernible patterns in media bias. Figure 11.2 illustrates the percentage of article distribution (positive, mixed, negative, and not applicable) for the *Los Angeles Times*, *New York Times*, *Washington Post*, and *Christian Science Monitor*. Just a quick glance indicates that the distribution of reporting differed substantially between the papers. Perhaps the only two newspapers to share a similar distribution are the *Washington Post* and the *New York Times*. Reporting on deep ecology in both papers was mostly mixed, though each had more negative than positive articles. In both the *Christian Science*

Monitor and the *Los Angeles Times*, the term "deep ecology" appeared primarily in passing or in situations warranting a "not applicable" categorization.

Combining the news coverage in the *New York Times, Washington Post, Los Angeles Times*, and *Christian Science Monitor* creates an interesting set of data to examine. Figure 11.3 illustrates the progression of coverage of the four major U.S. newspapers. Both negative and positive coverage is consistently low. This finding shows that coverage of deep ecology in the major newspapers is absent much negative or positive bias. The data point to two different conclusions. Either there is substantial disinterest in the subject or the coverage on radical environmentalism is very objective, an objectivity that is rarely found in other media sources.

The total number of articles peaked in 1990 and then again in 1995.[8] These "peaks," though, are still fairly low, equating to only two articles in each of the four newspapers. The "total number" line graph illustrates the overall low number of scored articles on deep ecology. This number does exclude articles that mentioned the term in passing, but is more useful for the purposes of this study since it is the effects of deep ecology on environmental politics that we are trying to determine. The media helps with this study because the reporting, whether it be positive, mixed, or negative, can help measure prevailing attitudes toward the ecophilosophy.

The number of negative articles peaked in 1989 and is now again on the rise. In fact, the first half of 1996 alone had more negative articles than any previous full year of the study. The number of positive articles peaked early (in 1987) and has since hovered below two articles per year in the four major newspapers. The number of mixed articles peaked in 1990 but was insignificant in the years before and after. Collectively, these trends indicate first and foremost that there is a relative dearth in coverage of deep ecology in the four major newspapers. Second, coverage of the ecophilosophy is not very consistent, varying year to year. Third, there appears to be an increase in negative reporting as the steep increase in 1995 and 1996 indicates in Figure 11.3. Despite this increase in negative coverage, the progression of coverage illustrates the overall unbiased coverage by the major newspapers.[9] The ratio of negative to positive coverage in the major papers is approximately 5 to 4, which does indicate balanced reporting on behalf of the newspapers.

OVERALL TRENDS IN MEDIA COVERAGE

Thus far, media coverage of deep ecology has been broken down in a number of ways. Both regions and media types have been carefully examined to ascertain differences in coverage and bias toward deep ecology. Table 11.9 provides data on the means, modes, and medians of the media coverage since 1980. It also illustrates the variance and the amount of reporting on deep ecology for each time period. The

---

[8]Please note that the data for 1996 are incomplete, but extrapolating upon the first half of 1996, the total number of articles should approach that of the 1995 total.

[9]Although this is promising for deep ecologists, the relatively low number of articles on which this determination is made casts a doubt over any positive aspect of this trend.

most glaring statistic portrayed on the chart concerns the relative negative means for every time period except two (July–Dec. 1995 and 1980–1987).[10] The highest mean score, equating to the most negative reporting, occurred in 1992, with the time period from January to June, 1996, coming in a close second. The median for both of these time periods was three, meaning that a majority of all coverage in each of these time periods was negative. From 1980 to 1987, the mean score for media coverage was a 1.6, indicating a positive bias in favor of deep ecology. This is very significant, for it illustrates the early "honeymoon" between the ecophilosophy and the media. A plurality of all coverage during these years was positive. Since 1987, media coverage has been decidedly negative.

Table 11.9
Selected Statistical Data from Survey of Media Reporting

Time Period	Mean	Mode	Median	Standard Deviation	Number Scored	Number Total
Jan-June 1996	2.25	3	3	.829	20	28
July-Dec 1995	1.875	1,2	2	.630	32	44
Jan-June 1995	2.12	3	2	.693	25	43
July-Dec 1994	2.14	3	2	.747	14	25
Jan-June 1994	2.06	3	2	.809	17	30
1993	2.10	3	2	.739	29	49
1992	2.38	3	3	.609	32	52
1991	2.17	3	2	.694	18	28
1990	2.12	2	2	.471	34	48
1989	2.0	1,2,3	2	.750	9	13
1988	2.17	3	2.5	.967	6	12
1980-87	1.6	1	1.5	.489	10	15

The modes indicate the predominant bias in the media for any given time period. For example, the mode for the time span from January to June, 1996, registered as a three, indicates a plurality of the media coverage was negative (as opposed to mixed or negative). It should be acknowledged that "not applicables" are not included in these calculations, for many of the modes would be "n/a"s. From 1991 to 1996, the

---

[10]Owing to the extremely low number of articles from 1980 to 1987, the time span was condensed and included as a single line item on the data chart.

plurality of coverage for each time span, excluding the one from July to December, 1995, was negative (three). The only time span to have a plurality of positive coverage, as noted before, was from 1980 to 1987. The medians indicate a more balanced pattern of media coverage. Of the eleven time periods, seven recorded a median of two which indicates mixed reporting. The most negative years for deep ecology, using the three different averages as indicators, were 1992 and the first half of 1996. By contrast, those years most favorable to deep ecology were the time span from 1980 to 1987 and the one from July to December of 1995.

While there appears to be frequent oscillation between negative and positive bias, a trend toward greater negativity does seem apparent. Even more, negative reporting is significantly more frequent than either mixed or positive reporting, sometimes outnumbering the latter two combined. The column for standard deviation indicates the relative variance in reporting, indicating how spread out the data were for each time period. For example, 1988 had a relatively high standard of deviation, indicating that whereas the plurality of all reporting was negative, a fair number of positive articles offset the negative reports.[11] The lowest amount of variance in reporting occurred in 1990, with a majority of mixed articles and only a few negative and positive articles. The standard deviation allows the reader to see the degree of variance for each time period. Overall, the selected data indicate a trend toward increased media coverage.[12] This coverage is somewhat balanced, but is increasingly tilting toward the negative side of the fulcrum.

COMPARISON OF CONGRESSIONAL TESTIMONY AND MEDIA REPORTING

The question that has yet to be addressed concerns how the media's perception of deep ecology influences environmental politics. By comparing and re-computing the numerical data of both congressional testimony and media coverage it is possible to better ascertain this supposed link. Table 11.10 illustrates the "deep ecological scores" both for the media and for congressional testimony from 1993 to 1996.[13] A comparison of the changes (either more negative or more positive) between the six time intervals yields interesting results. From July 1993 to June of 1996, the scores of the congressional testimony changed in the same direction as those of the media except in one instance (from T4 to T5). When media reporting became more or less supportive of deep ecology, so too did those testifying before Congress.

---

[11]Additionally, the low number of articles contributed heavily to the high degree of variance.

[12]Table 11.1 and Figure 11.1, which highlight the number of articles as a percentage of all articles on the environment, are, however, a more reliable indicator of this trend.

[13]The scores are based on a five point scale, with a 5 indicating very deep ecological and a 1 indicating very shallow ecological outlook. The media scores, which were originally based on a three-point scale, were converted using the equation, $X = 7 - 2Y$, where X is the converted score and Y is the original score. The congressional testimony scores were determined through the averaging of the "5 principle" scores evaluated in Chapter 7.

Another interesting correlative relationship is the percent negative and positive of those scored: 67.5 percent of those testifying before Congress in the sample were negative toward deep ecology. This compares to 44.5 percent of those testifying before Congress on actual environmental subjects. The media, on the other hand, recorded an overall average of 39 percent negative. Likewise, only 11.2 percent overall, and 19.3 percent of those testifying on environmentally related subjects, were positive toward the ecophilosophy. This compares to an overall average of 24 percent in the media sample. Finally, the ratio of negative to positive was significantly higher for those who testified before Congress (6.03) than for the overall media (1.32).

Although these comparisons seem to indicate a much more sympathetic media, the differences in scoring and sampling make such a conclusion tenuous at best. The sample for the media was drawn from only articles that mentioned the term "deep ecology." The congressional sample, however, had to be drawn from those individuals who referenced the term "environment" since on only one occasion was deep ecology utilized. The term "deep ecology" was 2½ times more frequently used in the media than in the congressional hearings. Of the 1,217,424 media articles from July 1993 to June 1996 in the Nexis database, deep ecology was mentioned 191 times. On the other hand, of the 16,099 pieces of congressional testimony during the same period, the term surfaced only once. Though this comparison of the media and congressional testimony yields interesting results, it does not concretely illustrate any new linkages between the media and politics.

Table 11.10
Relationship Between Congressional Testimony and Media Reporting

Dates	Congressional Testimony (all)	Congressional Testimony (environment-only)	Media Reporting
July-Dec 1993 (T1)	2.12	2.59	2.80
Jan-June 1994 (T2)	2.21	2.86	2.88
July-Dec 1994 (T3)	2.01	2.72	2.72
Jan-June 1995 (T4)	2.16	2.68	2.76
July-Dec 1995 (T5)	2.13	2.60	3.25
Jan-June 1996 (T6)	2.02	2.39	2.5

DEEP ECOLOGY'S IMPRESSION OF THE MEDIA

To this point, the primary focus of this chapter has been on the media's impression of deep ecology. It has illuminated media biases as well as contributed information as to the interaction between deep ecology and politics in the United States. Although the media may or may not have a particular bias toward deep ecology, there are definite opinions on behalf of the deep ecologists toward media coverage. Their relationship with the media is much like that between them and the government. On one hand, the media is indispensable in broadcasting their messages; on the other hand, deep ecologists frequently feel manipulated by the media.

A content analysis of the *Earth First! Journal* shows many references to the media in the writings of this deep ecological group. The first group of references found in the *Earth First! Journal* concern the role of the media in publicizing deep ecological events. Deep ecologists use the media to publicize their activities and efforts. When individuals act under the auspices of Earth First!, or other deep ecological groups, in an attempt to change government policy or to educate the public during their "radical" actions, they almost always incorporate the media. A media spokesperson is almost always designated, as in the case of when a group of Earth First!ers blockaded themselves in front of the gates of Macmillan-Bloedel's cedar lumber distribution center in Tacoma, Washington.[14] When another group of Earth First!ers took over Office of Surface Mining in Columbus, Ohio, they quickly called the media and gave the media live interviews in an attempt to convey their messages to the general public.[15]

The media is an indispensable ally for broadcasting the feelings and beliefs of deep ecologists and Earth First! Though deep ecologists use the media to highlight their actions, sometimes their message is not always conveyed as they would like, a point that will be discussed in detail later. Due to the radical nature of their actions, deep ecologists frequently risk arrest and bodily harm. Many members of Earth First! and other deep ecological groups have been attacked by angry loggers and others who found themselves the target of deep ecological activities. The media serves as an insurance policy and sometimes as the prime protector of the activists.[16] When the Friends of the Wolf shut down the Alaska Highway outside of Whitehorse in the Yukon Territories, media cameras protected the protestors from bodily harm. At the same time, the media was used to send "a strong message to the Yukon Territorial Government: Stop the aerial wolf kill!"[17]

As mentioned before, the media does not always convey the message that the deep ecologists would prefer. An article in the *Earth First! Journal* aptly describes the situation:

As for media coverage, we knew that it would be tough to break the stranglehold of the industrial masters of the Mobile pulp and paper colony. Still, we were the second story on the NBC

---

[14]Leslie Hemstreet, "MacBlo in Tacoma," *Earth First! Journal: The Radical Environmental Journal*. Available from gopher.ige.aoc.org:70/00/orgs/ef.journal/5; INTERNET.

[15]Whaley Mander, "What Do You Mean You Won't Arrest Us?" *Earth First! Journal: The Radical Environmental Journal*. Available from gopher.ige.aoc.org:70/00/orgs/ef.journal/7; INTERNET.

[16]There are accounts where police officers and local sheriffs stepped aside and watched as Earth First!ers were attacked and hurt.

[17]David Barbarash, "Activists Blockade Yukon Highway," *Earth First! Journal: The Radical Environmental Journal* (Brigid, 1995). Available from http://envirolink.org/orgs/ef/Brigid.html; INTERNET.

affiliate who used our video footage and actually conveyed our message reasonably. The print media was less favorable, although we were highlighted on the front page beneath the *Mobile Press Register* banner with a small photo and caption referring to the article in the Business section. We were particularly angry that their photographer was late and didn't get shots of the banner, and they wouldn't use any of our photos. Obviously, we made some phone calls to the appropriate editors at the newspaper as well as to the local AP feeder who refused to help us at all.[18]

This frustration with the media does not stop deep ecologists from trying to convey their message through the media. Mike Roselle wrote, "We should never doubt for a moment, though, that if our small voice is heard by reasonable people, we can change public perceptions and thereby change political reality. In the electronic fog that now passes for news media, smaller groups cannot ignore the power of words, or the impact of personal actions. Because eventually the truth gets out. It always does."[19] Some, including a few deep ecologists, might characterize this statement as idealistic and naïve, but it is perhaps the only hope deep ecologists have to change society and its relationship with the environment. If the media is the only hope of the deep ecologists, then the situation for them is grim. The results of this study show an increasingly negative media, not to mention the anecdotal evidence found in deep ecological publications accusing the media of being oblivious to anthropogenic environmental destruction such as global warming caused by fossil fuel use. Still, the deep ecologists talk of educating the media.[20]

Though the media may be viewed as a constructive, yet unreliable, tool for the deep ecologists, it is also a tool used by those wishing to derail the movement. In the case of the car bombing of Judi Bari, the media was used as a tool of the Federal Bureau of Investigation (FBI) to indict Bari and other deep ecologists in the eyes of the public. The FBI created the illusion through the media that Bari was a terrorist who was injured by her own bomb.[21] The police also used the media to stage events to discredit deep ecologists. When a group of Earth First! members delivered a press release and a derogatory picture of the proposed Mark O. Hatfield National Forest to Hatfield's office, the police were waiting. The police invited the media to the office

---

[18]Compiled by Katuah Earth First!, Native Forest Network, TAGER, and Broadened Horizons Riverkeepers, "Mission Impossible: The Chips Hit the Fan," *Earth First! Journal: The Radical Environmental Journal* (Brigid, 1996). Available from http://envirolink.org/orgs/ef/Brigid96.html; INTERNET.

[19]Mike Roselle, "A War of Words over Violent Analogies," *Earth First! Journal: The Radical Environmental Journal* (Litha, 1995). Available from http://envirolink.org/orgs/ef/Litha.html; INTERNET.

[20]Rhys Roth, "Global Warming," *Earth First! Journal: The Radical Environmental Journal* (Lughnasadh, 1995). Available from http://envirolink.org/orgs/ef/Lughnasadh.html; INTERNET.

[21]Judi Bari, "The Bombing Story—Part 1: The Set-Up," *Earth First! Journal: The Radical Environmental Journal*. Available from gopher.ige.aoc.org:70/00/orgs/ef.journal/10; INTERNET.

ahead of time, allowing them the best camera angles for recording the arrest of the Earth First!ers by the police officers (at least according to Earth First! accounts).[22]

The media is also used by the timber industry. In the words of Earth First!er Mark Ottenad, "Using simple sound bites easily digested by the media and an uninformed public, the pro-timber industry subsidy crowd offers spurious and superficial reasons for destroying public forests without environmental safeguards or judicial review."[23] But perhaps the most insidious threat posed by the media to deep ecology, and the environmental movement in general, is generated by environmental organizations themselves. According to Karyn Strickler, the major environmental organizations are currently engaged in destructive fighting over media coverage that threatens the entire movement.[24] Thus the media serves as a two-edged sword. On one side, the deep ecologists are able to use the media for both protecting its members and educating the public. On the other side, the media can splinter the environmental movement and destroy the message of the deep ecologists.

CONCLUSION

This chapter offers insight into the relationship between the media and deep ecology. It provided a statistical analysis of over 400 articles that appeared in the last 15 years. Although the survey method was admittedly subjective, the simplicity of the scoring process helped to increase its objectivity.[25] The breakdown of the articles yielded a plurality of those scoring "not applicables." Of those scored, negative articles were most predominant, followed by mixed and positive. Regardless of the bias of the articles, there is a substantial increase in the total number of articles. This observation, though important, is somewhat offset by the minimal increase in the number of articles as a percentage of all articles on the environment.

One of the most interesting findings of this chapter is the drastic regional differences in media bias. For example, Northeast newspapers recorded a 1.71 ratio of negative to positive articles. By contrast, the ratio was only 0.5 for Midwestern newspapers. There were also differences in media types. For example, regional papers reported much differently than major newspapers. The former recorded a 0.5 ratio of negative to positive articles while the latter logged a 1.26 ratio. Of those articles scored in regional papers, 59 percent were positive, compared to only 30 percent

[22]Mike Roselle, "The Man Without a Bioregion: The End of Humor," *Earth First! Journal: The Radical Environmental Journal* (Beltane, 1995). Available from http://envirolink.org/orgs/ef/Beltane.html; INTERNET.

[23]Mark Ottenad, "Salvage: Timber Industry Welfare Is Ecological Disaster," *Earth First! Journal: The Radical Environmental Journal* (Beltane, 1995). Available from http://envirolink.org/orgs/ef/Beltane.html; INTERNET.

[24]Karyn Strickler, "Environmental Politics Ain't for Sissies: Living Up to the Legend," *Earth First! Journal: The Radical Environmental Journal* (Samhain, 1995). Available from http://envirolink.org/orgs/ef/Samhain.html; INTERNET.

[25]Degrees of negativity and positivity were not taken into consideration and thus a substantial amount of subjectivity was avoided.

in all major newspapers and 27 percent for magazines. Another interesting finding was the large number of book reviews on the subject of deep ecology. Over 25 percent of all articles were book reviews, which indicates that the term is still largely used in academic circles. This observation corresponds with the relative dearth of reporting in the four major U.S. newspapers.

The media is used by a plethora of actors, including environmental activists, the government, and the timber industry. Although the activists attempt to use the media to their advantage, the media is frequently employed against the movement. This study confirms deep ecological claims that the media assumes the role of the opponent more than the proponent. There is a discernible trend toward greater negativity in reporting, with a majority of all articles on the subject hurting, rather than helping, the deep ecological movement.

Conclusion: Avoiding the Mine by Trying to Stop the Tanker

In Chapter 4, the analogy of trying to stop an oil tanker in time to avoid a mine was used to illustrate how difficult it is to stop a large object with lots of momentum. The object that deep ecology attempts to stop is the current anthropocentric, dominant social paradigm. The philosophical and intellectual collection of ideas and principles embodied by deep ecology is designed to create environmentally conscious human behavior. However, this is much easier said than done. To accomplish this feat, deep ecology calls for a fundamental change in the current dominant social paradigm. It calls for a biocentric or ecocentric value framework. Quite simply, it attempts to avoid environmental disaster by putting society's engines in full reverse and hoping to stop in time. This book has attempted to illustrate how deep ecology and radical environmentalism have tried to reverse the engines of society and thus craft American environmental policy.

Because deep ecology emphasizes decentralization and personal relationships with nature, those who call themselves deep ecologists do not follow rigid guidelines. Rather they develop their "own" deep ecology. For this reason, it was difficult to measure the influence of deep ecology on environmental politics. However, the basic principles of the ecophilosophy provided sufficient guidance to hypothesize how the government, economy, or legal system would operate in a deep ecological world. The primary focus of this book, though, was less concerned with speculating how such entities would look in a deep ecological world, but rather with measuring how much influence deep ecology has already had.

RECAP OF MAJOR FINDINGS

Many aspects of deep ecology have been examined in this book. Everything from its history to its political involvement has been discussed. The book has provided both an overview of the philosophy as well as original research into the relationship between politics and the ecophilosophy. However, because the book has covered such an array of material, a summary of the major issues is in order.

History of Deep Ecology

Though the term "deep ecology" is only twenty-five years old, its ideas and principles date back thousands of years. Deep ecology has firm roots in the cultural and political history of the United States. The Native Americans exemplified, to an extent, how humans can live within their surroundings. The religious and cultural attachment to the land found in Native American literature and practices illustrates many of the principles of deep ecology. The Anglican peoples who came to America in the last 500 years brought, however, a much more shallow ecological perspective toward the environment. Gradually, the reverence for nature exhibited by the Native Americans would influence the new inhabitants.

Deep ecology received its first interaction with American politics with the writings and actions of Henry David Thoreau. Thoreau was followed by John Muir. Both men combined a concern for environmental protection with political involvement. Their environmental perspectives differed considerably from those of their contemporaries by incorporating many modern-day deep ecological principles. The observations made by these individuals were scientifically studied by George P. Marsh and Aldo Leopold. These scientists laid the foundation for ecological studies. Leopold, however, went further. He proposed a new system of ethics, one that would incorporate the land into the societal ethical framework. The contributions from all four of these American deep ecological pioneers continue to influence environmental politics and policy making to this day.

Their influence is not isolated to only environmental politics, for they serve as forefathers of the deep ecological movement. The deep ecologists "are contemporary heirs of the tradition of Thoreau and Muir. . . . Deep ecology offers some criticism of society and provides at least a 'partial vision of what a just social order might involve.' It also rejects the crude utilitarianism of progressive conservationism."[1] Deep ecologists have also adopted some of the tactics developed by their forerunners. Thoreau's civil disobedience and Muir's hands-on approach are reflected in the daily actions of deep ecologists.

Tactics of Deep Ecology

The tactics employed by deep ecologists are as diverse as the ideas of deep ecologists. A wide array of tactics are employed depending on the situation and the radical-ness of the individuals performing them. They also change with the times. For example, when tree spiking became frowned upon by the public, many deep

---

[1]D. R. Jones, "Lost Legacies of Thoreau and Pinchot: A Review of Bob Pepperman Taylor's *Our Limits Transgressed: Environmental Political Thought in America.*" *Environmental Law* 23 (Spring, 1993):1032.

ecologists took to tree sitting as a way to protect the forests. Arne Naess, himself, has considerably revised his recommendations for environmental activism. The primary way most deep ecologists attempt to influence policy is through publicity events and nonviolent protest. They borrow heavily from the likes of Mahatma Gandhi and Martin Luther King, Jr. Some attempt to achieve revolution through reform while others actively promote revolution through revolution. The group Earth First! is the most recognizable group for its deep ecological leanings. "Members" form a loose association of local chapters that organize activism in their area. Deep ecologists tend to be very aware of local and national environmental politics and policies. They actively use the courts and lobby the legislatures in an attempt to gain greater influence. Earth First! in particular attempts to garner public support by promoting awareness through various publicity events. They are optimistic that the public will rally to their cause once they are educated about the vast environmental degradation.

Deep Ecology and the Congress

The relationship between deep ecologists and politicians is a very interesting one. Local and national politicians frequently are at the receiving end of the ire of deep ecologists. They are frequently criticized in the *Earth First! Journal* and other deep ecological literature. Despite the conflict, deep ecologists have been increasingly willing to coordinate with politicians and play the political game. These radical environmentalists thus work both within and outside of the "system." They lobby legislators while sabotaging development. This mix of tactics is both helpful and harmful to deep ecological activism. It helps advance the cause by utilizing every available option. When working within the system fails, they can simultaneously attempt to thwart development through alternative means. However, working outside of the system can bring bad publicity to groups such as Earth First! and make politicians wary of being associated with any radical environmentalists. This is where mainstream environmental organizations capitalize on the "radical" nature of deep ecologists. They are able to better gain access to the government officials and increase their bargaining position by asking them, "Would you rather deal with the deep ecologists or with us?" Though large, mainstream environmental organizations are frequently at odds with deep ecological groups such as Earth First!, it is just this tension that helps further the environmental cause.

The deep ecological call for government intervention is an interesting paradox. Deep ecology promotes grass-roots change by empowering private citizens to make environmentally ethical land use decisions. Yet groups such as Earth First! frequently ask the federal government for greater involvement in the protection of wilderness areas. This apparent paradox is explained in the difference between idealistic end–oriented deep ecology and realistic means–oriented deep ecology. Though many agree that the overall goal of deep ecology is to change the dominant social paradigm and dissolve the need for government intervention, the short-term reality is the need for greater government involvement in environmental protection. This need for government involvement is not a choice many deep ecologists willingly accept, for not only has the federal government been largely unsympathetic to deep ecological concerns, but there are also charges of government infiltration and conspiracy to actively destroy the movement.

The primary concern of this book has not, however, been just to study the history or tactics of deep ecology. Rather, this book attempted to provide a window into the world of American politics. It has detailed the rules of the "game" and looked at the why and how of environmental legislation. One of the rules that has long held back environmental legislation deals with the short-term nature of politics and the long-term characteristic of environmental protection. The political disregard for future generations was espoused in 1876 by Senator Timothy Howe, who noted, "I am . . . ready to labor by the side of the Senator from Massachusetts for the welfare of the Government today and of the generation now existing; but, when he calls upon us to embark very heavily in the protection of generations yet unborn, I am very much inclined to reply to that they have never done anything for me, and I do not want to sacrifice too much."[2] Senator Henry Teller, in 1909, echoed Howe's sentiments:

I do not think the sacrifice of trees for useful purposes can be set against the advance of our civilization. I would rather have an American home, with an American family, than to have a forest as big as all out of doors. I believe that the natural wealth of this country belongs to the people who go and subdue it. I do not believe that there is either a moral or any other claim upon me to postpone the use of what nature has given me, so that the next generation or generations yet unborn may have an opportunity to get what I myself ought to get.[3]

Though this attitude still dominates American politics, the influx of environmentalism has led some politicians to consider the long-term benefits to wilderness preservation. Congressional Representative Morris Udall explained in 1964 that the Wilderness Act "is a bill which we can take pride in telling our grandchildren about. . . . We are running out of land. What this bill will do is to set aside some of the choice, scenic areas of America to preserve them for generations to come."[4] Though Udall's primary motivation for environmental protection rests on human-centered objectives, it does signal a change in the rules of politics, a change fueled not just by deep ecologists, but by all environmentalists.

The increased concern for the long term is evident in the study of major environmental legislation. The Clean Air Act illustrates a commitment to improved environmental quality that does not rely on quick fixes and immediate results. The act, however, is very human centered, illustrating almost no deep ecological influence whatsoever.

---

　　　[2]Timothy Howe (4 Congressional Record 1085 [1876]), quoted in Edwin McCullough, "Through the Eye of a Needle: The Earth's Hard Passage back to Health," *Journal of Environmental Law and Litigation* 10 (1995): 389-390.

　　　[3]Henry Teller (44 Congressional Record 3226 [1909]), quoted in Edwin McCullough, "Through the Eye of a Needle: The Earth's Hard Passage back to Health," *Journal of Environmental Law and Litigation* 10 (1995): 391.

　　　[4]Morris Udall (110 Congressional Record 17,437 [1964]), quoted in Edwin McCullough, "Through the Eye of a Needle: The Earth's Hard Passage back to Health," *Journal of Environmental Law and Litigation* 10 (1995): 390.

It entrenched the economic growth mindset and the extrinsic worth of species. The next piece of environmental legislation examined in this book was the Wilderness Act. Though hailed by many environmentalists as a turning point in environmental protection, it still illustrated a predominantly shallow ecological influence. It borrowed heavily from the Pinchot school of conservationism and emphasized human ownership and stewardship of the land. The National Environmental Policy Act was another environmental statute that was primarily concerned with public health and welfare despite its name.

It was not until the Clean Water Act that a deep ecological influence first surfaced in a major piece of federal environmental legislation. The statement of intent of the act illustrated a significant change in tone from previously human-centered legislation. The Endangered Species Act took these principles one step further. It explicitly indicted economic growth and development. Though it still had some shallow ecological influence (that is, hardship exemption), the act incorporated many deep ecological principles. Unfortunately for the deep ecologists, the political climate of the 1980s and 1990s has turned much more shallow in its ecological outlook. This was illustrated in the review of congressional testimony.

The study found that the language of deep ecology is rarely used in congressional hearings. Terms such as "ecocentrism," "biocentrism," "anthropocentrism," "deep ecology," "shallow ecology," and "radical environmentalism" have yet to find their way into Congress. While many talk of environmental ethics and environmental consciousness, few use the term in a deep ecological sense.[5] The review of congressional testimony found that the various principles of deep ecology have gained differing amounts of acceptance. The belief in harmony with nature, instead of dominance over nature, has gained the most acceptance by those testifying before Congress. This is closely followed by a belief that "Earth supplies" are limited. There was a tendency for those testifying to support the shallow ecological perspective of high technology and centralization. Deep ecology has seen its influence most limited in the areas of intrinsic worth for species and "doing with enough." Most everyone described species worth in human terms and argued for greater economic growth. On the whole, most testimony before the U.S. Congress is shallow in its ecological outlook.[6]

---

[5]This does, however, indicate that environmentalism is gaining popularity, even though it is frequently of the shallow type.

[6]One major flaw in the research methods of this study concerns the lack of insight on the influence of political appointees on the political process. Frequently the appointed officials in the government bureaucracy can have an even greater bearing on the ecological outlook of environmental policy than Congress. For it is the executive agencies that frequently enforce and interpret congressional mandates. The direction of these agencies can differ drastically depending on the political appointee. For example, when Reagan appointed Anne Gorsuch to head the Environmental Protection Agency (EPA), any inroads made by deep ecologists to that point were severely curtailed. Gorsuch had very little background in environmental issues and quickly infuriated many environmentalists. Even after her oust, her legacy continued, for she had fired one out of five EPA employees and appointed numerous top-level officials before being cited for contempt of Congress. Further research should examine how political

Deep Ecology and the Courts

Deep ecologists frequently employ the courts in order to seek protection of wilderness areas left unprotected through either mismanagement or under-enforcement. Although there are signs of a deep ecological influence, the court continues to use an anthropocentric model when dealing with environmental issues. They have, however, begun to recognize the ecological principle of interconnnectiveness and the intrinsic worth of species. Some courts have shifted the burden on the polluter in order to further advance the goals of wilderness preservation. They have also used the public trust doctrine to incorporate a crude system of legal rights for nature into the law. Unfortunately for deep ecologists, the prospects for the legal rights of environmental objects are not very promising. However, deep ecology is gaining increased exposure in the field of legal scholarship. The debate over legal standing and the role of the legal system in promoting an environmental ethic is significant, for mere discussion can sometimes lay the foundation for greater influence.

Deep Ecology and the Media

The media is a reliable indicator of political trends. It serves as both the gatekeeper and sounding-board for ideas. In fact, some feel that the media is the driving force behind political decisions. Robert Nelson notes that "[t]he ultimate goal of many politicians seems to be the generation of favorable media attention rather than finding solutions to real problems. As Washington increasingly resembles Hollywood, its politicians become actors, the staff become script writers, and the federal departments and agencies become an administrative apparatus whose actual output is entertainment."[7] While this criticism may be a little severe, it does illustrate the influence of the media in guiding federal policy. This book's review of media reporting attempts to discern trends in bias toward deep ecology. A wide array of media sources were examined. They ranged from local newspapers to international news journals. The sample of over four hundred articles yielded various perspectives on deep ecology. Though the study found a ratio of 4:3 negative to positive articles on the subject, the results of the study went deeper. The study found a large increase in mentions of "deep ecology" in the news media over the last fifteen years. It also found that the major newspapers used by Washington politicians, the *New York Times* and the *Washington Post*, have gotten considerably more negative in their portrayal of deep ecology.

Another interesting discovery of the study was the finding that Northeast newspapers were the most negative in their reporting while Midwestern and Western newspapers were the most positive. Additionally, the study found that regional news sources were more open to deep ecological ideas than national news sources. These two findings

---

appointees and executive agencies guide environmental policy and to what degree they are influenced by the deep ecology movement.

[7]Robert H. Nelson, "'A New Era for the Western Public Lands': Government as Theater: Toward a New Paradigm for the Public Lands," *University of Colorado Law Review* 65 (Spring, 1994): 335.

seem to support the notion, advanced by the deep ecologists, that once people become aware of the problem, they are more sympathetic to the cause. The deep ecology movement, while international, concentrates primarily on grass-roots efforts, which would partly explain the difference between regional and national reporting. Additionally, the deep ecology movement is more active in the West and Midwest owing to its efforts to stop logging, and thus has gained greater exposure in those areas.

Overall, however, the study confirmed that the media is more often an opponent than a proponent of deep ecology. It also found that the relationship between deep ecology and the media is a two-way street. Deep ecologists depend on the media to spread their message but at the same time suffer from negative media reporting.

PROSPECTS FOR A DEEP ECOLOGY AND ENVIRONMENTAL POLICY

Deep ecology calls for sweeping changes in the present nature of industrial societies. This means that its goals cannot be realized without changes in policies.[8] These changes in policies have been explored throughout this book. But it is important to remember that a change in the law will not transform human behavior. Laws are fundamentally a reactive, not proactive, instrument of humans. They may codify and institutionalize societal values, but they have immense difficulties in establishing them. This can only happen through the transformation of individual priorities and values.[9] Notwithstanding the current conflict between deep ecologists and social ecologists, Murray Bookchin adeptly describes the situation: "We do not simply live in a world of problems but in a highly problematical world, an inherently anti-ecological society. This anti-ecological world will not be healed by acts of statesmanship or passage of piecemeal legislation. It is a world that is direly in need of far-reaching structural change."[10]

The implementation of policy is guided by the collective values of society. Thus, any new policy based on deep ecological values must take the necessary steps to educate the public on the ethical and moral issues. Absent ethical arguments for the preservation of biodiversity and endangered species, policy will continue to reinforce human-centered, utilitarian thought patterns.[11] Only when people feel differently about the land, the air, and the water will they change their actions. Most agree that this involves much more than passing laws. According to Stephen Jay Gould, "[w]e cannot win this battle to save species and environments without forging an emotional bond between

---

[8]Arne Naess and David Rothenberg, *Ecology, Community, and Lifestyle: Outline of an Ecosophy* (New York: Cambridge University Press, 1989): 153.

[9]Edwin R. McCullough, "Through the Eye of a Needle: The Earth's Hard Passage back to Health," *University of Oregon Journal of Environmental Law and Litigation* 10 (1995): 450.

[10]Murray Bookchin ("Death of a Small Planet: It's Growth That's Killing Us," *The Progressive* [August, 1989]: 21), quoted in Edwin R. McCullough, "Through the Eye of a Needle: The Earth's Hard Passage back to Health," p. 450.

[11]James Drozdowski, "Saving an Endangered Act: The Case for a Biodiversity Approach to ESA Conservation Efforts," *Case Western Reserve Law Review* 45 (1995): 561–562.

ourselves and nature as well—for we will not fight to save what we do not love (but only appreciate in some abstract sense)."[12] Deep ecologists who ask for immediate changes in the law should never forget that law can be no more than a mechanism by which society applies its philosophic views. Changes in the law must follow changes in the fundamental nature of society.[13]

Thus the prospects of deep ecological legislation are intrinsically tied with the outlook of the politicians and society (though many will claim that the two are one and the same). The vast majority of people do not hold deep ecological beliefs. This is evident not only in the laws and media reporting, but also in general polls of government officials and society. Though deep ecologists point to opinion polls that indicate most people want to preserve wildlife and natural objects, such polls never ask the question of why. A study conducted by Mark McBeth found that state development officials exhibited a decidedly shallow ecological perspective on environmental protection. It found that both politicians and the general public support environmental protection only when the human benefits outweigh the human costs.[14] These widely held beliefs make it difficult for active supporters of the deep ecology movement to influence environmental politics.

These supporters have run into depressing political struggles. Because politics are short-term and those of deep ecology are long-term, activists have difficulties in influencing politicians even when there is public support.[15] Thus while it may be "politically dangerous to be responsible for pollution that will clearly show itself within an election term . . . it is much less politically dangerous to arrange things so that it will be the next generation or the generation after that who will suffer the real effects."[16] Some political scientists have stated the most important goal of politicians is not good policy, but rather good politics so that they may be re-elected. This desire to appeal to a broad-based constituency and to avoid controversy means that few politicians will ever publicly support deep ecology even if they agree with it in their personal views. A study by Arne Naess in the mid-1980s supported this hypothesis. Naess polled 110 people who influence national environmental policy in Norway. Those who responded (approximately one of three) stated that they agreed with the principles of deep ecology but were unwilling to express these views publicly.[17]

---

[12]Stephen J. Gould, ("Unenchanted Evening," *Natural History* [September, 1991]: 14), quoted in Edwin R. McCullough, "Through the Eye of a Needle: The Earth's Hard Passage back to Health," p. 451.

[13]Eric T. Freyfogle, "The Railroad and the Holocaust," *University of Illinois Law Review* 1986 (1986): 301.

[14]Mark K. McBeth, " The Environment v. the Economy: Attitudes of State Rural Development Officials," *Spectrum: The Journal of State Government* 69, no. 1 (Winter, 1996): 17–25.

[15]Naess and Rothenberg, *Ecology, Community, and Lifestyle: Outline of an Ecosophy*, p. 33.

[16]Ibid., p. 139.

[17]McCullough, "Through the Eye of a Needle: The Earth's Hard Passage back to Health," p. 451.

What is true of Norway may be at least partly true in the United States. Everything from the wording of the Endangered Species Act to the opinions of some of our Supreme Court Justices indicates a suppressed agreement with deep ecology that occasionally bubbles up to the surface. Take, for instance, the words of Bruce Babbitt. In an interview in *Rolling Stone*, the Secretary of the Interior stated, "[w]hat a land ethic is about is discarding that concept of property and trying to find a different understanding of the natural landscape. We have a moral responsibility toward our surroundings."[18] David Graber of the National Park Service once declared that a free-flowing river has "more intrinsic value . . . than another human body, or a billion of them."[19] To help implement new changes in environmental law, Supreme Court Justice Stephen Breyer has proposed the creation of an environmental superagency that would centralize all environmental policy and thus be able to better deal with the issues of interconnectiveness and global linkages.[20] It is true that resourcism and preservationism dominate contemporary thoughts and actions. However, their triumph has not been complete. Deep ecology underlies some of the most important environmental laws such as the Endangered Species Act. It is an important example of holism because it acknowledges the essential role of every part of an ecosystem.[21]

Though deep ecology has gained at least a foothold in American environmental politics, many politicians are afraid of explicitly acknowledging its role. The prevailing perception of deep ecology is that its policy proposals are "anti-people." Its critics portray deep ecology as condemning the achievements of human civilization, which have led to what many regard as better living conditions for all people.[22] Furthermore, deep ecology is regarded as inhumane and callous to human suffering.[23] Deep ecologists attempt to point out that they oppose human-centeredness, not humans per se, but that has not prevented critics from ascertaining precisely the reverse. Many will never forget, nor allow deep ecologists to forget, radical statements such as when Dave Foreman suggested in 1987 to let starving Ethiopians die because their numbers had swollen to unsustainable levels. Although deep ecologists attempt to explain that they value all life, including human life, many are not ready to accept their explana-

---

[18]Bruce Babbitt ("Interview with Bruce Babbitt, Secretary of Interior," *Rolling Stone* [July 8–July 22, 1993]: 48), quoted in Edwin R. McCullough, "Through the Eye of a Needle: The Earth's Hard Passage back to Health," p. 450.

[19]David M. Graber, "Mother Nature as a Hothouse Flower," review of Bill McKibben's *The End of Nature*, *Los Angeles Times* 22 October 1989, Book Review: 9.

[20]Eric W. Orts, "Reflexive Environmental Law," *Northwestern University Law Review* 19 (1995): 1227.

[21]Max Oelschlaeger, *The Idea of Wilderness: From Prehistory to the Age of Ecology* (New Haven, CT: Yale University Press, 1991): 289.

[22]Ibid., p. 306.

[23]Daniel J. Kelves, "Symposium on Biomedical Technology and Health Care: Social and Conceptual Transformations: Article: Vital Essences and Human Wholeness: The Social Readings of Biological Information," *Southern California Law Review* 65 (November, 1991): 255.

tions.[24] Deep ecology runs into conflict on many fronts because it "touches every major contemporary, personal, economic, political, and philosophical problem."[25] The formidable forces opposed to deep ecology include: economic growth, development, property rights, habitual attitudes, consumerism, individual life-styles, and the beliefs in "fighting nature," "improving the land," "pushing back the jungle," and "conquering Mt. Everest."[26]

The deep ecology movement continues to struggle against its critics with hopes of one day transforming society and politics. Though deep ecologists have enjoyed success in developing an alternative political and social vision from their deep respect for nature, they have had only limited success in advancing their agenda.[27] Changes in policies are only stopgap measures for deep ecologists, for if they are successful in changing societal values, many regulations and laws will be unnecessary.[28] The influence on environmental politics documented in this book is not exhaustive, but does help to illustrate perhaps the greatest benefit of the ecophilosophy. By "'stirring up the blood' deep ecology is inherently healthy: hardening of the categories of existence the radical environmentalist helps society begin to grapple with its problems."[29] The problems of environmental degradation are real. How we address these problems in the coming years will provide valuable insight into who we are and what we value.

Can deep ecology reverse the engines of society? The findings from this book indicate that deep ecology has a long way to go, for most Americans feel that the mine is not near enough nor big enough to force them to alter their course. Deep ecology offers guidance that is difficult for most of us to follow. It asks each of us to substantially alter the manner in which we currently live. It calls for nothing short of a new dominant social paradigm. The example of environmental politics as a microcosm of the overall political process has contributed much to our understanding of the relationship between values, ethics, laws, and policy making. If the predictions of environmental disaster come true, the coming decades will offer an even better perspective of how the political process operates in America. Who knows, as awareness and education of environmental pollution increases, and people develop ethical attachments to natural objects, deep ecology may find its way into the hearts and minds of both the people and their politicians alike.

---

[24]Edwin Dobb, "Deep Ecology for the 21st Century," *Audubon* 97, no. 3 (May, 1995): 116.

[25]Naess and Rothenberg, *Ecology, Community, and Lifestyle: Outline of an Ecosophy*, p. 32.

[26]McCullough, "Through the Eye of a Needle: The Earth's Hard Passage back to Health," p. 451.

[27]Jones, "Book Review: Lost Legacies of Thoreau and Pinchot: A Review of Bob Pepperman Taylor's *Our Limits Transgressed: Environmental Political Thought in America*," p. 1027.

[28]Naess and Rothenberg, *Ecology, Community, and Lifestyle: Outline of an Ecosophy*, p. 159.

[29]Oelschlaeger, *The Idea of Wilderness: From Prehistory to the Age of Ecology*, p. 307.

Selected Bibliography

Adamson, David. *Defending the World: The Politics and Diplomacy of the Environment.* New York: I. B. Tauris & Co., 1990.

Aitchtey, Rodney. "The Ways of Deep Ecology." *Contemporary Review* 260, no. 1513 (February, 1992).

Babbitt, Bruce. "Testimony before the House Resources Committee regarding the Reintroduction of the Gray Wolf into Yellowstone National Park and Central Idaho." *Federal Document Clearing House Congressional Testimony* (January 26, 1995).

Bader, Mike. "Testimony on Behalf of the Alliance for the Wild Rockies, Hearing on H.R. 2638, the Northern Rockies Ecosystem Protection Act." *Federal Document Clearing House Congressional Testimony* (May 4, 1994).

Barbarash, David. "Activists Blockade Yukon Highway." *Earth First! Journal: The Radical Environmental Journal* (Brigid, 1995). Available from http://envirolink.org/orgs/ef/Brigid.html; INTERNET.

Bari, Judi. "The Bombing Story—Part 1: The Set-Up." *Earth First! Journal: The Radical Environmental Journal.* Available from gopher.ige.aoc.org:70/00/orgs/ef.journal/10; INTERNET.

Benford, Gregory. "The Designer Plague." *Reason* 25, no. 8 (January, 1994): 36.

Bishop, Katherine. "Militant Environmentalists Planning Summer Protests to Save Redwoods." *New York Times* 19 June 1990, sec. A, p. 18, col. 1.

Bock, Alan. "Are We at an Environmental Crossroads?" *Orange County Register* 21 April 1996, Editorial, sec. G, p. 1.

Bookchin, Murray. "Deep Ecology, Anarchosyndicalism and the Future of Anarchist Thought." 11 June 1992. Available from www.lglobal.com/TAO/Freedom/book2.html; INTERNET.

Brechin, Steven R., and Willett Kempton. "Global Environmentalism: A Challenge to the Postmaterialism Thesis?" *Social Science Quarterly* 72, no. 2 (June, 1994).

Brower, David. "Step Up the Battle on the Earth's Behalf." *San Francisco Chronicle* 18 August 1993, sec A, p. 15.

Brower, David. "David Brower on Zero Cut." *Earth First! Journal: The Radical Environmental Journal* (Mabon, 1995). Available from http://envirolink.org/orgs/ef/Mabon.html; INTERNET.

228   *Selected Bibliography*

Brown, Courtney. "Politics and the Environment: Nonlinear Instabilities Dominate." *American Political Science Review* 88, no. 2 (June, 1994): 294–301.

Browner, Carol, et al. "Testimony of Carol M. Browner, Administrator, U.S. Environmental Protection Agency, Richard Rominger, Deputy Secretary, U.S. Department of Agriculture, and David A. Kessler, Commissioner, Food and Drug Adminstration before Subcommittee on Department Operations and Nutrition, Committee on Agriculture, U.S. House of Representatives." *Federal Document Clearing House Congressional Testimony* (September 22, 1993).

Capra, Fritjof. "Biodiversity and Ecological Management: Ecologically Conscious Management." *Environmental Law* 22 (Winter, 1992): 535.

Carpenter, Betsy. "Redwood Radicals." *U.S. News & World Report* 109, no. 11 (September 17, 1990): 50.

Carson, Rachel. *Silent Spring*. Greenwich, CT: Fawcett Publications, 1962.

Cheek, Ronald G., et al. "Environmental Apocalypse Now: Environmental Protection Agency Policies as Threats to the Environment." *Industrial Management* 37, no. 3 (May, 1995): 6.

Choucri, Nazli. "Introduction: Theoretical, Empirical, and Policy Perspectives," in Nazli Choucri's *Global Accord: Environmental Challenges and International Responses*. Cambridge, MA: MIT Press, 1993.

Cobbs, John B. "Biblical Responsibility for the Ecological Crisis." *Second Opinion* 18, no. 2 (October, 1992): 10.

Crandall, Doug. "H.R. 1164, The National Parks, Forests and Public Lands, Subcommittee." *Federal Document Clearing House Congressional Testimony* (May 5, 1994).

Creedon, Jeremiah. "The Power of Global Thinking?" *Utne Reader*, no. 56 (March/April, 1995): 22.

Devall, Bill, and George Sessions. *Deep Ecology: Living as If Nature Mattered*. Salt Lake City, UT: Gibbs Smith Publisher, 1985.

Dobb, Edwin. "Deep Ecology for the 21st Century." *Audubon* 97, no. 3 (May, 1995): 116.

Dowie, Mark. "The Fourth Wave." *Mother Jones* 20, no. 2 (March/April, 1995).

Dowie, Mark. *Losing Ground: American Environmentalism at the Close of the Twentieth Century*. Cambridge, MA: MIT Press, 1995.

Dresser, Nathanael. "Cultivating Wilderness: The Place of Land in the Fiction of Ed Abbey and Wendell Berry." *Growth & Change* 26, no. 3 (Summer, 1995): 350–64.

Drozdowski, James. "Saving an Endangered Act: The Case for a Biodiversity Approach to ESA Conservation Efforts." *Case Western Reserve Law Review* 45 (1995): 553.

Drucker, Merrit P. "The Military Commander's Responsibility for the Environment." *Environmental Ethics* 11, no. 2 (Summer, 1989): 138.

Dryzek, John S. *Rational Ecology: Environment and Political Economy*. New York: Basil Blackwood, 1987.

Flevares, William M. "Ecosystems, Economics, and Ethics: Protecting Biological Diversity at Home and Abroad." *Southern California Law Review* 65 (May, 1992): 2039.

Foote, Jennifer. "Trying to Take Back the Planet." *Newsweek* (February 5, 1990): 24.

Foreman, Dave. "Dave Foreman on Zero Cut." *Earth First! Journal: The Radical Environmental Journal* (Mabon, 1995). Available from http://envirolink.org/orgs/ef/Mabon.html; INTERNET.

Foreman, David. "It's Time to Return to Our Wilderness Roots." *Environmental Action* 15, no. 5 (December–January, 1984). Available from www.envirolink.org/elib/enviroethics/deepsum.html; INTERNET.

Foster, John Bellamy. "Global Ecology and the Common Good." *Monthly Review* 46, no. 9 (February, 1995): 2–5.

French, Hillary F. "Partnership for the Planet: An Environmental Agenda for the United Nations." *World Watch Paper 126* (July 1995).

Freyfogle, Eric T. "The Railroad and the Holocaust." *University of Illinois Law Review* 1986 (1986): 301.

Gabriel, Trip. "If a Tree Falls in the Forest, They Hear It." *New York Times* 4 November 1990, sec. 6, p. 34, col. 1.

Gilliam, Harold. "The Greening of the Spirit." *San Francisco Chronicle* 22 December 1991, sec. Z1, p. 13.

Goltz, Thomas. "Earth First Meeting Reflects Gap Between Radicals, Mainstream." *Washington Post* 19 July 1990, sec. A, p. 3.

Gore, Albert. *Earth in the Balance: Ecology and the Human Spirit.* New York: Houghton Mifflin, 1992.

Gould, James Jay. Review of *Green Delusions: An Environmentalist Critique of Radical Environmentalism. The Progressive* 57, no. 3 (March, 1993): 39.

Greenwire. "Chile: Deputy Calls for Probe into Park, Deep Ecology." (April 27, 1995).

Grub, Michael, et al. *The "Earth Summit" Agreements: A Guide and Assessment.* London: Earthscan Publications, 1993.

Hackett, Steve. "Some Thoughts on a Deep Ecology Economy." (n.p., n.d.). Available from SH2@axe.humboldt.edu; INTERNET

Hague, Rod, et al. *Political Science: A Comparative Introduction.* New York: St. Martin's Press, 1992.

Hanson, Chad. "Mr. Hanson Goes to Washington." *Earth First! Journal: The Radical Environmental Journal* (Mabon, 1995). Available from http://envirolink.org/orgs/ef/Mabon.html; INTERNET.

Hardt, Scott W. "Federal Land Management in the Twenty-First Century: From Wise Use to Wise Stewardship." *The Harvard Environmental Law Review* 18 (Summer, 1994): 345.

Haugen, Tim. "The Wild Ranch Manifesto." *Earth First! Journal: The Radical Environmental Journal.* Available from gopher.ige.aoc.org:70/00/orgs/ef.journal/4; INTERNET.

Henning, Daniel H., and William R. Mangum. *Managing the Environmental Crisis.* Durham, NC: Duke University Press, 1989.

Hoch, David. "Stone and Douglas Revisited: Deep Ecology and the Case for Constructive Standing." *Journal of Environmental Law and Litigation* 3 (1988): 133–53.

Hoffman, Mark. "Normative International Theory: Approaches and Issues," in Groom and Light's *Contemporary International Relations: A Guide to Theory.* New York: Pinter Publishers, 1994.

Howard, Malcolm. "Communications: 'Green' Groups See Internet as Mixed Blessing." *Inter Press Service* (April 25, 1996).

Hubbard, Mark. "Zero-Cut: Ending Commercial Logging on Federal Lands." *Earth First! Journal: The Radical Environmental Journal* (Beltane, 1994). Available from gopher.ige.aoc.org:70/00/orgs/ef.journal/16; INTERNET.

Huffman, James L. "Book Review: Civilization in the Balance: Comments on Senator Al Gore's *Earth in the Balance." Environmental Law* 23 (Winter, 1993): 239.

Hurrell, Andrew. "The Global Environment," in Booth and Smith's *International Relations Today.* University Park: Pennsylvania State University Press, 1995.

Japenga, Ann. "Earth First! A Voice Vying for the Wilderness: Group Says Radical Tactics Will Continue Despite Arrests." *Los Angeles Times* 5 September 1985, part 5, p. 1, col. 3.

Jensen, Rita Henley. "Recycling the American Dream: Many People Talk About Simplifying Their Lives. These Lawyers Are Not Only Doing It, They Are Making It Part of Their Practices." *ABA Journal* 82 (April, 1996): 68.

Jones, D. R. "Lost Legacies of Thoreau and Pinchot: A Review of Bob Pepperman Taylor's *Our Limits Trangressed: Environmental Political Thought in America.*" *Environmental Law* 23 (Spring, 1993):1027–1032.

June, Robert B. "Citizen Suits: The Structure of Standing Requirements for Citizen Suits and the Scope of Congressional Power." *Environmental Law—Northwestern School of Law of Lewis & Clark College* 24 (Spring, 1994): 761.

Kamieniecki, Sheldon. "Political Mobilization, Agenda Building and International Environmental Policy." *Journal of International Affairs* 44, no. 2 (Winter, 1991).

Karp, James P. "Aldo Leopold's Land Ethic: Is an Ecological Conscience Evolving in Land Development Law?" *Environmental Law—Northwestern School of Law of Lewis & Clark* 19 (Summer, 1989): 737–55.

Kelves, Daniel J. "Symposium on Biomedical Technology and Health Care: Social and Conceptual Transformations: Article: Vital Essences and Human Wholeness: The Social Readings of Biological Information." *Southern California Law Review* 65 (November, 1991): 255.

Knauer, Josh. "Environmental Ethical Theory Applied in the Modern Environmental Movement." (1996). Available from www.envirolink.org/elib/enviroethics/essay.html; INTERNET.

Kuipers, Dean. "Eco Warriors; Environmental Activists." *Playboy* 40, no. 4 (April, 1993): 74.

Kupfer, David. "David Ross Brower; Environmentalist; Interview." *The Progressive* 58, no. 5 (May, 1994): 36.

Lal, Deepak. "Eco-fundamentalism." *International Affairs* 71, no. 3 (July, 1995): 526.

Lancaster, John. "The Green Guerrilla; 'Redneck' Eco-Activist Dave Foreman, Throwing a Monkey Wrench into the System." *Washington Post* 20 March 1991, sec. B, p. 1.

Lear, Norman. "A Call for Spiritual Renewal." *Washington Post* 30 May 1993, sec. C, p. 7.

Lee, Martha F. *Earth First!: Environmental Apocalypse.* Syracuse, NY: Syracuse University Press, 1995.

Leopold, Aldo. *A Sand County Almanac* (1949) Reprint, New York: Ballantine Books, 1966.

List, Peter C. *Radical Environmentalism: Philosophy and Tactics.* Belmont, CA: Wadsworth Publishing Company, 1993.

Logan, Robert A. *Environmental Issues for the '90s: A Handbook for Journalists.* Washington, DC: Environmental Reporting Forum, 1992.

Lopez, George A., et. al. "The Global Tide." *Bulletin of the Atomic Scientist* 51, no. 4 (July/ August, 1995).

Low, Patrick. *International Trade and the Environment.* Washington, DC: The World Bank, 1992.

Manes, Christopher. *Green Rage: Radical Environmentalism and the Unmaking of Civilization.* Boston, MA: Little, Brown and Company, 1990.

Mansbach, Richard W., and John A. Vasquez. *In Search of Theory: A New Paradigm for Global Politics.* New York: Columbia University Press, 1981.

Marsh, George P. *The Earth as Modified by Human Action: A Last Revision of "Man and Nature."* New York: Charles Scribner's Sons, 1898.

Martell, Luke. *Ecology and Society: An Introduction.* Amherst: UMASS Press, 1994.

McBeth, Mark K. "The Environment v. the Economy: Attitudes of State Rural Development Officials." *Spectrum: The Journal of State Government* 69, no. 1 (Winter, 1996): 17–25.

McCullough, Edwin. "Through the Eye of a Needle: The Earth's Hard Passage back to Health." *Journal of Environmental Law and Litigation* 10 (1995): 389.

Mensch, Elizabeth, and Alan Freeman. "The Politics of Virtue: Animals, Theology and Abortion." *Georgia Law Review* 25 (Spring, 1991): 923.

Meryers, Gary D. "Old-Growth Forests, the Owl, and Yew: Environmental Ethics Versus Traditional Dispute Resolution Under the Endangered Species Act and Other Public Lands and Resources Laws." *Boston College University Environmental Affairs Law Review* 18 (Summer, 1991): 662.

Muir, John. *Our National Parks* (1901) Reprint, New York: AMS Press, 1970.

Muir, John. *The Yosemite*. New York: The Century Company, 1912.

Naess, Arne. "The Shallow and the Deep, Long-Range Ecology Movements: A Summary." *Inquiry* 16 (Oslo, 1973): 95–100.

Naess, Arne. "Deep Ecology and Ultimate Premises." *The Ecologist* 18, nos. 4/5 (1988): 130.

Naess, Arne, and David Rothenberg. *Ecology, Community and Lifestyle: Outline of an Ecosophy*. New York: Cambridge University Press, 1989.

Naess, Arne, and George Sessions. "Deep Ecology's Basic Principles." Death Valley, California (April 1984). Available from www.envirolink.org/elib/enviroethics/deepeco.html; INTERNET.

Nash, Roderick Frazier. *American Environmentalism: Readings in Conservation History*. New York: McGraw-Hill, 1990.

Nelson, Robert H. "'A New Era for the Western Public Lands': Government as Theater: Toward a New Paradigm for the Public Lands." *University of Colorado Law Review* 65 (Spring, 1994): 335

Nolan, Cathal J. *The Longman Guide to World Affairs*. White Plains, NY: Longman Publishers, 1995.

Nolen, Kelly. "Residents at Risk: Wildlife and the Bureau of Land Management's Planning Process." *Environmental Law* 26 (Fall, 1996): 771.

Oeslchlaeger, Max. *The Idea of Wilderness: From Prehistory to the Age of Ecology*. New Haven, CT: Yale University Press, 1991.

Olson, James M. "Shifting the Burden of Proof: How the Common Law Can Safeguard Nature and Promote an Earth Ethic." *Environmental Law—Northwestern School of Law of Lewis & Clark College* 20 (Winter, 1990): 892, 909, 910, 913.

Ottenad, Mark. "Salvage: Timber Industry Welfare Is Ecological Disaster." *Earth First! Journal: The Radical Environmental Journal* (Beltane, 1995). Available from http://envirolink.org/orgs/ef/Beltane.html; INTERNET.

Pimm, Stuart L. "Testimony Before the Senate Environment/Drinking Water, Fisheries and Wildlife Subcommittee, Endangered Species Reauthorization." *Federal Document Clearing House Congressional Testimony* (July 13, 1995).

Rheem, Donald L. "Behind the 'Redwood Curtain.'" *Christian Science Monitor* 13 January 1987, p. 16.

Rice, Stanley E. "Standing on Shaky Ground: The Supreme Court Curbs Standing for Environmental Plaintiffs in *Lujan v. Defenders of Wildlife*." *Saint Louis University Law Review* 38 (Fall, 1993): 199.

Robbins, Jim. "Saboteurs for a Better Environment." *New York Times* 9 July 1989, sec. 4, p. 6, col. 1.

Rodgers, William H., Jr. "Symposium on NEPA at Twenty: The Past, Present and Future of the National Environmental Policy Act: Keynote: NEPA at Twenty: Mimicry and Recruitment in Environmental Law." *Environmental Law* 20 (Fall, 1990): 485.

Roselle, Mike. "The Man Without a Bioregion: The End of Humor." *Earth First! Journal: The Radical Environmental Journal* (Beltane, 1995). Available from http://envirolink.org/orgs/ef/Beltane.html; INTERNET.

Roselle, Mike. "A War of Words over Violent Analogies." *Earth First! Journal: The Radical Environmental Journal* (Litha, 1995). Available from http://envirolink.org/orgs/ef/Litha.html; INTERNET.

Roselle, Mike. "Conservation Biology Dons the Green Uniform." *Earth First! Journal: The Radical Environmental Journal* (Brigid, 1996). Available from http://envirolink.org/orgs/ef/Brigid96.html; INTERNET.

Sagoff, Mark. "Economic Theory and Environmental Law." *Michigan Law Review* 79 (1981): 1393, 1396–1397.

Sale, Kirkpatrick. "The Cutting Edge: Deep Ecology and Its Critics." *The Nation* 246, no. 19 (May 14, 1988): 670.

Sessions, George, and Bill Devall. "Deep Ecology," in *American Environmentalism: Readings in Conservation History*, ed. Roderick Nash. New York: McGraw-Hill, 1990.

Shadbecoff, Philip. "New Leaders and a New Era for Environmentalists." *New York Times* 29 November 1985, sec. D, p. 2d, col. 1.

Shue, Henry. "Ethics, the Environment and the Changing International Order." *International Affairs* 71, no. 3 (July, 1995).

Sipchen, Bob. "Gary Snyder's Path of the Deep Ecology Movement." *Los Angeles Times* 28 November 1986, part 5, p. 1.

Sipchen, Bob. Review of *Rules for the Ethical Exploitation of Nature: Environmental Ethics Duties to and Values in the Natural World. Los Angeles Times* 21 February 1988, Book Review, p. 6.

Sipchen, Bob. "The Muir Mystique: After 150 Years, the Naturalist Has Become Patron Saint to All Environmental Factions, but His Legacy Is Still in Dispute." *Los Angeles Times* 20 April 1988, p. 1, col. 2.

Sipchen, Bob. "Ecology's Family Feud: Murray Bookchin Turns Up Volume on a Noisy Debate." *Los Angeles Times* 27 March 1989, part 5, p. 1, col. 2.

St. Clair, Jeffrey. "Cashing Out: Corporate Environmentalism in the Age of Newt." *Earth First! Journal: The Radical Environmental Journal* (Eostar, 1995). Available from http://envirolink.org/orgs/ef/Eostar.html; INTERNET

Stanley, Phyllis M. *American Environmental Heroes*. Springfield, NJ: Enslow Publishers, Inc., 1996.

Stein, Mark A. "From Rhetoric to 'Ecotage': Environmental 'Fanatics' Try to Keep Things Wild." *Los Angeles Times* 29 November 1987, part 1, p. 1, col. 1.

Stone, Christopher D. *Should Trees Have Standing?: Toward Legal Rights for Natural Objects*. Los Altos, CA: William Kaufman, 1974.

Strickler, Karyn. "Environmental Politics Ain't for Sissies: Living Up to the Legend." *Earth First! Journal: The Radical Environmental Journal* (Samhain, 1995). Available from http://envirolink.org/orgs/ef/Samhain.html; INTERNET.

Suckling, Kieran. "Beyond Litigation: What's Left After the Trashing of Environmental Laws?" *Earth First! Journal: The Radical Environmental Journal* (Beltane, 1995). Available from http://envirolink.org/orgs/ef/Beltane.html; INTERNET.

Tarlock, A. Dan. "Earth and Other Ethics: The Institutional Issues." *Tennessee Law Review* 56 (Fall, 1988): 53.

Thoreau, Henry David. *Walden and Other Writings of Henry David Thoreau*, ed. Brooks Atkinson. New York: Random House, 1950.

Volokh, Alexander. Review of *The Green Crusade: Rethinking the Roots of Environmentalism. Reason* 26, no. 10 (March, 1995): 59.

Whaley Mander. "What Do You Mean You Won't Arrest Us?." *Earth First! Journal: The Radical Environmental Journal*. Available from gopher.ige.aoc.org:70/00/orgs/ef.journal/7; INTERNET.

White, Lynn, Jr. "The Historical Roots of Our Ecological Crisis." *Science* (March 10, 1967): 1206.

Wilson, James Q. *American Government: Institutions and Policies* (fifth edition). Lexington, MA: D. C. Heath and Company, 1992.

Worster, Donald. "The Rights of Nature; Has Deep Ecology Gone Too Far?" *Foreign Affairs* (November/December, 1995): 111.

Young, Oran R. "Negotiating an International Climate Regime: The Institutional Bargaining for Environmental Governance," in Nazli Choucri's *Global Accord: Environmental Challenges and International Responses*. Cambridge, MA: MIT Press, 1993.

Young, Oran R. *International Governance: Protecting the Environment in a Stateless Society*. Ithaca, NY: Cornell University Press, 1994.

Zhuangzi. *Zhuangzi Speaks: The Music of Nature*, adapted and ill. Tsai Chih Chung. Princeton, NJ: Princeton University Press, 1992.

Zimmerman, Michael E. *Contesting Earth's Future: Radical Ecology and Post Modernity*. Berkeley: University of California Press, 1994.

Index

About the Author

PHILLIP F. CRAMER is a John W. Wade Scholar at Vanderbilt Law School. He has held internships with the U.S. Department of State, where he served as the Country Desk Officer for Bahrain, and with the Students for an Energy Efficient Environment (SEEE), where he worked with the Environmental Protection Agency on the Greenlights program. He is currently working on a research project on environmentalism, international relations, and the American legal system.

ISBN 0-275-96051-X

9 780275 960513

90000>

EAN

HARDCOVER BAR CODE